Facing the Challenges of Whole-School Reform

New American Schools After A Decade

Mark Berends
Susan J. Bodilly
Sheila Nataraj Kirby

Prepared for
New American Schools

RAND
EDUCATION

The research described in this report was supported by New American Schools.

Library of Congress Cataloging-in-Publication Data

Berends, Mark, 1962-
    Facing the challenges of whole-school reform : New American Schools after a
decade / Mark Berends, Susan J. Bodilly, Sheila Kirby.
        p. cm.
    "MR-1498."
    Includes bibliographical references.
    ISBN 0-8330-3133-3
    1. New American Schools (Organization) 2. School improvement programs—
United States. I. Bodilly, Susan J. II. Kirby, Sheila Nataraj, 1946- III. Title.

LB2822.82 .B455 2002
371.2'00973—dc21

                                                                    200204810

Cover design by Stephen Bloodsworth

Published 2002 by RAND
1700 Main Street, P.O. Box 2138, Santa Monica, CA 90407-2138
1200 South Hayes Street, Arlington, VA 22202-5050
201 North Craig Street, Suite 102, Pittsburgh, PA 15213-1516
RAND URL: http://www.rand.org/
To order RAND documents or to obtain additional information, contact Distribution Services: Telephone: (310) 451-7002; Fax: (310) 451-6915; Email: order@rand.org

New American Schools, or NAS (known as New American Schools Development Corporation from 1991 to 1995), is a private nonprofit corporation that was created in conjunction with President Bush's America 2000 initiative. NAS was formed to fund efforts to develop and disseminate whole-school designs for elementary and secondary schools. Its original goal was to ensure that these designs, which presumably offer more-effective educational programs than "typical schools," were adopted in schools across the country so as to dramatically improve student performance. Since its inception, NAS has completed a development phase, a demonstration phase, and a scale-up phase.

During these phases (1992–2000) RAND provided analytic support to NAS. This book summarizes the findings from the RAND program of analysis. It is targeted toward educational policymakers interested in comprehensive school reform as well as others interested in improving the implementation of reform efforts in local governmental bureaucracies. This book should be of interest to anyone who wants to better understand the expanding area of whole-school school reform and its effects on teaching and learning within high-stakes accountability environments.

The RAND assessment of NAS schools has spanned several years. To date, RAND studies about New American Schools include:

Conflicting School Reforms: Effects of New American Schools in a High-Poverty District, by Mark Berends, JoAn Chun, Gina Schuyler, Sue Stockly, and R. J. Briggs, 2002 (MR-1483-EDU).

Implementation in a Longitudinal Sample of New American Schools: Four Years into Scale-Up, by Sheila Nataraj Kirby, Mark Berends, and Scott Naftel, 2001 (MR-1413-EDU).

The Relationship Between Implementation and Achievement: Case Studies of New American Schools, by JoAn Chun, Brian Gill, and Jodi Heilbrunn, 2001 (DRU-2562-EDU).

New American Schools' Concept of Break the Mold Designs: How Designs Evolved Over Time and Why, by Susan Bodilly, 2001 (MR-1288-NAS).

"Reforming Whole Schools: Challenges and Complexities," by Mark Berends, Susan Bodilly, and Sheila Nataraj Kirby. Forthcoming in *Bringing Equity Back,* edited by J. Petrovich and A. W. Wells.

Implementation and Performance in New American Schools: Three Years into Scale-Up, by Mark Berends, Sheila Nataraj Kirby, Scott Naftel, and Christopher McKelvey, 2001 (MR-1145-EDU).

"Teacher-Reported Effects of New American Schools' Designs: Exploring Relationships to Teacher Background and School Context," by Mark Berends in *Educational Evaluation and Policy Analysis,* 2000, 22(1), pp. 65–82.

"Necessary District Support for Comprehensive School Reform," by Susan J. Bodilly and Mark Berends. In *Hard Work for Good Schools: Facts Not Fads in Title I Reform,* edited by Gary Orfield and Elizabeth H. DeBray. Boston: Civil Rights Project, Harvard University, 1999, pp. 111–119 .

Assessing the Progress of New American Schools: A Status Report, by Mark Berends, 1999 (MR-1085-EDU).

Lessons from New American Schools' Scale-Up Phase: Prospects for Bringing Designs to Multiple Schools, by Susan J. Bodilly, 1998 (MR-1777-NAS).

New American Schools After Six Years, by Thomas K. Glennan, Jr., 1998 (MR-945-NASDC).

Funding Comprehensive School Reform, by Brent R. Keltner, 1998. (IP-175-EDU).

Reforming America's Schools: Observations on Implementing "Whole School Designs," by Susan J. Bodilly and Thomas K. Glennan, 1998 (RB-8016-EDU).

Lessons from New American Schools Development Corporation's Demonstration Phase, by Susan J. Bodilly, 1996 (MR-729-NASDC).

Reforming and Conforming: NASDC Principals Discuss School Accountability Systems, by Karen Mitchell, 1996 (MR-716-NASDC).

"Lessons Learned from RAND's Formative Assessment of NASDC's Phase 2 Demonstration Effort," by Susan J. Bodilly. In *Bold Plans for School Restructuring: The New American Schools Designs,* edited by Sam Stringfield, Steven Ross, and Lana Smith. Mahwah, NJ: Lawrence Erlbaum Associates, 1996, pp. 289–324.

Designing New American Schools: Baseline Observations on Nine Design Teams, by Susan J. Bodilly, Susanna Purnell, Kimberly Ramsey, and Christina Smith, 1995 (MR-598-NASDC).

CONTENTS

FIGURES

TABLES

New American Schools (NAS) was formed in 1991 to create and develop whole-school designs that would be adopted by schools throughout the country in order to improve student performance. It was established as a nonprofit and funded largely by private sector donations. NAS founders thought that in the past many reforms were "programmatic," focused on a particular set of individuals in a school or a particular subject or grade level. They believed that adoption of multiple and unconnected approaches to address each area of schooling resulted in a fragmented education program, a balkanized school organization, and low performance by students.

NAS's core premise was that all high-quality schools possess, de facto, a unifying design that allows all staff to function to the best of their abilities and that integrates research-based practices into a *coherent* and *mutually reinforcing* set of effective approaches to teaching and learning for the entire school. The best way to ensure that lower-performing schools adopted successful designs was to fund design teams to develop "break the mold" school designs that could be readily adopted by communities around the nation. After developing the design, teams would go on to implement their designs in schools throughout the country. This adoption would lead to NAS's primary goal of improving the performance of students.

This whole-school approach to educational improvement was a dramatically different way of initiating and disseminating large-scale educational improvements. It was a unique combination of (1) private sector involvement using a venture capitalist approach; (2) the choice of whole-schools designs as a vehicle for reform; and (3) the ambitious goal of scale-up across the country.

The NAS experimental approach required careful development and demonstration of designs prior to moving to scale-up; therefore it had a phased approach including:

- Competition and selection phases (1992);

- Development phase of one year (1992–1993);

- Demonstration phase of two years (1993–1995 including the 1993–1994 and 1994–1995 school years); and

- Scale-up phase of three years (1995–1998 from the school year starting in 1995 to the one ending in 1998).

This approach to educational improvement offered an unprecedented opportunity to study and understand a unique attempt at school reform from its beginnings to its completion. Any educational reform must have two components, a theory of learning and a theory of action. Following Fullan (2001, p. 187), a *theory of learning* focuses on the assumptions about how students learn, instructional strategies, and performance. A *theory of action* focuses on the local context such as the conditions under which a design or external model will work. The theory of learning in the NAS initiative was embodied in the individual designs. Design teams were to be responsible for their own development of a theory of learning and for its evaluation. This left open the issue of whether NAS's theory of action—at that point very unspecified—would be effective. To show important policy audiences that the NAS approach was efficacious, NAS would have to assess its theory of action as to whether it and the design teams could get schools to implement designs, and if and when schools did implement, whether this would lead to improved student performance.

RAND'S ANALYTIC TASKS AND PURPOSE OF THE STUDY

NAS approached RAND to assess and analyze its theory of action and to provide analytic support to its school reform efforts. This support took many forms, but primarily it was intended to document and analyze the conditions under which NAS made progress toward its goals of widespread use and implementation of its designs and improved student performance associated with that use. It included the following analytic tasks:

- Document the NAS efforts to assess its contributions to education reform;

- Describe the designs and analyze changes in them over time;

- Assess the level of implementation in design-based schools during the demonstration and scale-up phases;

- Identify factors that impede or encourage implementation in the demonstration and scale-up phases; and

- Measure whether the adoption of the designs resulted in the outcomes desired by NAS and its partnering districts in the scale-up phase.

These tasks were conducted over the first seven years of the NAS initiative from the demonstration phase through the scale-up phase, and the results are documented in a series of RAND reports, listed in the Preface.

The purposes of this book are to provide a retrospective look at the NAS initiative and the various RAND studies of that initiative; to draw together the findings from the diverse tasks undertaken on behalf of NAS; and to reflect on the lessons provided by this initiative for future school reform efforts. The document should be of interest to both policymakers and practitioners in K–12 education as it offers some important lessons learned about attempts to significantly improve student performance through the adoption of externally provided interventions.

A BRIEF HISTORY OF NAS FOCUSING ON ITS THEORY OF ACTION

To understand the RAND assessment of NAS, one must understand that NAS's theory of action and design teams' theories of learning were evolving through the entire period of the analysis. Therefore, the RAND analysis and analytic approaches had to remain quite flexible over this time. Here we summarize the important changes NAS made and how this affected NAS's theory of action.

Initially, its theory of action was quite simple and undeveloped: Designs would be developed, schools would adopt them in some unspecified manner, and this adoption would result in improved student outcomes. NAS helped create designs through a Request for Proposals process from October 1991 to July 1992 in which more than 600 teams applied. It chose 11 design teams for initial development. From July 1992 to July 1993, these teams worked to further develop their theories of learning. A year later it reduced the number of teams from 11 to nine in part due to funding difficulties. It removed two teams that had a district as the team lead, indicating its theory of action did not include locally based and led teams in part because of NAS's ambition for national scale-up.

The demonstration phase, 1993–1995, took place in 147 schools chosen by design teams as partners. RAND analysis of progress at that point indicated that an important component of the design team intervention was the assistance teams provided to schools to enable the schools to adopt designs. This became known as "design-based assistance." NAS's theory of change transformed to include this notion—that design teams did not just provide designs, but also had to provide design-based assistance for schools to successfully implement the designs. RAND analysis of progress in the demonstration schools also showed that school- and district-level factors had a strong relationship to implementation in schools. NAS then understood that to succeed, it would have to ensure a supportive environment for its designs. During this demonstration phase, NAS removed another two teams, both of which did not have national scale-up intentions and which appeared at the time to be closely associated with conditions specific to districts or states.

NAS outlined its scale-up strategy—a third iteration of its theory of action. Because of its experiences during the demonstration phase, NAS became more cognizant of the importance of gaining district-level support for teams and providing a supportive district structure, including resources, school autonomy, and professional development for the schools. Thus, it chose a concentration strategy—attempting to transform a few districts though the adoption of design-based assistance by a significant number of schools within those districts. Ten jurisdictions agreed to partner with NAS. These jurisdictions promised to get approximately 30 percent of their schools using designs within a three-year period and to provide a supportive environment for the schools' efforts. The 30 percent figure was admittedly somewhat arbitrary, but the theory of action was that if NAS could implement its designs in about one-third of a district's schools, there would be a critical core of schools that could be sustained over time. In addition, NAS insisted the design teams become more self-sufficient at this point. Design teams would charge the districts fees for the design-based assistance. NAS would work with districts to help a supportive environment evolve. NAS promised districts that by using its designs, the schools would be able to show dramatic test score improvements within that time period.

The seven teams entering scale-up included:

- Audrey Cohen College (AC) (currently renamed Purpose-Centered Education);

- Authentic Teaching, Learning, and Assessment for All Students (ATLAS or AT);

- Co-NECT Schools (CON);

- Expeditionary Learning Outward Bound (EL);

- Modern Red Schoolhouse (MRSH);

- National Alliance for Restructuring Education (NARE) (currently renamed America's Choice Design Network); and

- Roots & Wings (RW).

NAS partnered with the following jurisdictions: Cincinnati, Ohio; Dade County, Florida; Kentucky; Maryland; Memphis, Tennessee; Philadelphia, Pennsylvania; Pittsburgh, Pennsylvania; San Antonio, Texas; San Diego, California; and three districts in Washington state. About 185 schools partnered with designs in these jurisdictions, while as a whole, NAS design teams spread to over 550 schools by 1995.

By 1999, NAS design teams had over 1,000 partnering schools across the country. Since the scale-up phase, NAS has effectively and successfully been a proponent for the creation of a federal program to provide schools with funding to adopt designs. The Comprehensive School Reform Demonstration program was created in 1997 to provide schools with funding to implement designs similar to those created and developed by NAS, thus ensuring a market for NAS-like designs. This has allowed NAS designs to spread to over 4,000 schools by 2001.

CONCEPTUAL FRAMEWORK

The overarching concept underlying NAS is the development of an intervention by external change agents who provide assistance during the implementation process in order to improve schools and student outcomes. In this case, the level of implementation achieved by the schools and teams working together is one important outcome. The other is the changes in student performance associated with adoption and implementation. These two concepts form the dependent variables in all the RAND analyses of NAS.

Past research on external change agents as a reform mechanism in K–12 education has shown that as these externally developed interventions are implemented, they tend to go through significant changes over time as they adapt to local conditions and contexts or in the process of scaling up. Often they develop implementation assistance strategies to assist schools in understanding and implementing the intervention. Despite this, implementation tends to be variable across sites, and the outcomes—in terms of the desired change—also vary considerably.

The conceptual framework underpinning the RAND studies of NAS draws from previous research on implementation of school reforms and educational change. A critical assumption underlying the designs is that coherent, focused, and sustained implementation of key design components (including professional development, curriculum and instructional materials, content and performance standards, assessments, organization and governance, and parent and community involvement) will eventually change school and classroom learning environments and thereby students' academic outcomes. Implementation consists of the process of putting into practice the elements or set of activities defined by design teams as core components of their design.

However, throughout the history of educational reform efforts, a prominent theme has emerged that the process of planned educational change is much more complex than initially anticipated (Fullan, 2001; McLaughlin, 1990). This is largely because of the number of players involved and the number of factors that need to be aligned to support such fundamental change.

The factors that could be expected to affect both implementation and outcomes include the following, some of which were not readily controlled by NAS or its design teams:

- The design itself and its ability to offer coherent, comprehensive, and consistent education programs as well as assistance offered by the design teams to schools to ensure implementation;

- The efficacy of the selection and matching process between designs and schools to ensure teacher "buy-in" to the design;

- The capacity of the specific schools for undertaking the reform including the schools' other efforts at reform, educational leadership, and teaching capability;

- School-specific demographics, structure, and climate;

- District contexts including the existing infrastructure supports and incentives for design implementation and improved student performance; and

- Other factors such as state contexts of testing and accountability, community contexts, and NAS funding policies.

The relationship between the independent and dependent variables is shown in Figure S.1.

METHODS AND CAVEATS

At the request of NAS (the client), RAND undertook different analyses at different periods of time that together amounted to a program of analytic studies on NAS. This program of analyses is summarized in Table S.1. The table highlights the purpose of each study, the approach taken, the sample used, the data sources, the measures developed, the contribution to the overall assessment, and the publications produced. (More information on methodology is provided in each chapter and in the Appendix as well as the accompanying RAND reports.)

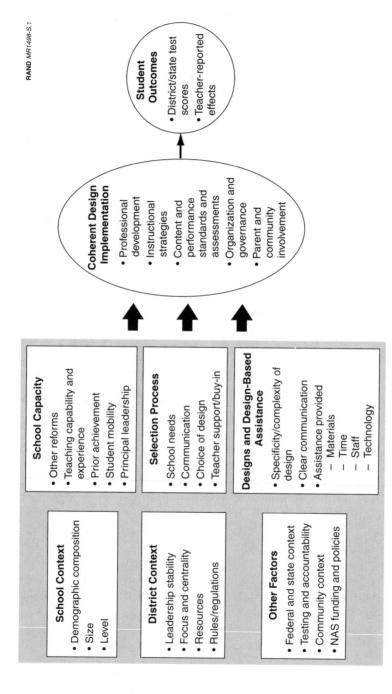

RAND *MR1498-S.1*

Figure S.1—A Conceptual Framework for Analyzing Implementation Progress and Performance in NAS Schools

These analyses can be thought of as "action-based research" during the developmental phase of an intervention. The RAND research on NAS was consistent with such an approach in that the program of studies:

- Allowed for a systemic view of the initiative from the teachers and students implementing the reforms to the district administrators trying to support them to design teams and NAS decisionmakers attempting to improve the reforms;

- Provided early information from front-line implementers on how to improve the effort; and

- Included a variety of methods, measures, and analytic techniques that were adapted to a changing environment to provide information that was relevant to NAS's evolving theory of action.

The research and analysis was undertaken on behalf of a client involved in an experiment to engineer strong designs for schools. The use of the term experimental does not mean a controlled environment with random assignment of designs to districts or schools. It refers to NAS's successive attempts to develop strong products called whole-school designs that would produce the outcomes NAS desired. This included successive efforts to learn what might have gone wrong in previous attempts, make adjustments, and try again. Therefore, the analyses reported here were adapted to the complex realities of the unfolding situation.

Each of the pieces of the RAND program of studies provides an important building block toward a full understanding of the NAS initiative. Together, they provide a cogent, consistent, and comprehensive examination of the NAS initiative and offer useful and timely information to decisionmakers considering or engaging in whole-school reform.

FINDINGS

We summarize the specific findings of the different analyses here. We group these findings into three broad areas. The first concerns designs and their development and refers in the conceptual frame-

Table S.1

Phases of NAS and RAND's Program of Studies

Phase/Time	Purpose	Approach	Sample	Data Sources	Measures	Contribution	RAND Publications
Demonstration July 1993– July 1995	Compare & contrast designs; track progress & indicate issues	Longitudinal comparative case studies of design teams using qualitative analysis	9 teams, 32 schools, at least 2 for each team; National Alliance sites included schools at all grade levels within a district	Document review; interviews with design leads; survey of principals; nested interviews for each site from district to teachers two years in a row; site observations	No measures; Identify elements of design & levels of complexity of designs by coverage of elements & needed interactions to attain implementation	Identified notions of: process vs. product teams; design specificity; design-based assistance; implementation issues; lack of district support	Bodilly et al., 1995; Bodilly, 1996; Mitchell, 1996

Table S.1—continued

Phase/Time	Purpose	Approach	Sample	Data Sources	Measures	Contribution	RAND Publications
Scale-up July 1995– July 1997	Measure & analyze progress toward implementation	Longitudinal comparative case studies of design teams using qualitative analysis	7 teams 40 schools, at least 4 schools each, including elementary & secondary as possible; random selection	Document review; interviews with design leads; survey of principals; nested interviews for each site from district to teachers 2 years in a row; site observations; resources analysis	Implementation index based on progress toward design-specific elements	Showed contrast in progress by design & by district support; raised quality assurance issues; indicated types & quantity of resources required	Bodilly, 1998; Keltner, 1998; Bodilly & Berends, 1999

Table S.1—continued

Phase/Time	Purpose	Approach	Sample	Data Sources	Measures	Contribution	RAND Publications
Scale-up March 1997–June 1999	Measure & analyze progress toward implemen-tation & improved performance	Quantitative analysis of longitudinal sample of schools	7 teams; target sample of 184 schools in 7 districts actively implementing designs; complete longitudinal response from 71 schools from 1997–1999	Survey of all principals; survey of teachers; collection of quantitative outcome data	Two indices of implementation based on teachers' reports; a core index that included five common elements across all designs; a design team–specific index that included elements unique to specific designs; school level measures of performance based on district-wide mandated tests	Identified factors affect-ing implemen-tation & performance including principal leadership, resources, teacher support for design teams, design team capacity & district policies	Berends, 1999, 2000; Berends & Kirby et al., 2001; Kirby, Berends, & Naftel, 2001

Table S.1—continued

Phase/Time	Purpose	Approach	Sample	Data Sources	Measures	Contribution	RAND Publications
Scale-up April 1998– September 1999	Analyze factors leading to classroom implementation & effects on student achievement	Quantitative & qualitative analyses of NAS & non-NAS elementary classrooms within a high-poverty district	All 64 elementary schools in San Antonio district, 279 classrooms, 3,823 students; RAND sample of 23 schools; 63 classrooms; 861 students with wide array of data	Survey teachers; classroom observations; interview teachers, instructional guides, school & district staff; collect teacher logs & samples of student work; administer Stanford-9 open-ended reading test to 4th graders; district longitudinal data on student demographics & test scores, teacher & school characteristics	Student level achievement on RAND-administered test and state-mandated tests; classroom instruction practices consistent with designs	Identified complexity of reform progress & role of district in high-stakes environment & high-poverty, low-performing schools	Berends et al., 2002

Table S.1—continued

Phase/Time	Purpose	Approach	Sample	Data Sources	Measures	Contribution	RAND Publications
Scale-up March 1999– June 1999	Analyze factors leading to schools with high implementation, but low performance outcomes	Case studies of schools indicated by teams as highly implementing	7 matched pairs of elementary schools; matched by district, demographics & purported levels of implementation	Level of implementation from designs; nested interviews for each site from district to teachers	Consistency between observed level of implementation and that reported by design teams	Inability to obtain target sample precluded strong analysis; pointed to concerns over design team knowledge of site conditions & implementation issues; indicated multiple factors affecting performance other than design	Chun, Gill, & Heilbrunn, 2001

Table S.1—continued

Phase/Time	Purpose	Approach	Sample	Data Sources	Measures	Contribution	RAND Publications
Ongoing research October 1992– October 1998	Track & analyze changes to designs & design teams & NAS	Longitudinal case study analysis of designs starting with 11 & declining to 7; longitudinal analysis of NAS development	NAS and designs over period	Document review; interviews with design teams; review by teams & NAS; interviews with NAS staff; observations at NAS conferences, meetings, and briefings	Analyzed reasons for changes including: planned development, gradual adaptation to meet needs of sites, adaptation to conflicting policies	Showed significant changes in teams over time; points to importance of district, teacher, & student factors as causative in evolution of designs	Glennan, 1998; Bodilly, 2001

work chart (Figure S.1) to the box labeled "Designs and Design-Based Assistance." The second concerns the ability of NAS and the design teams to implement the designs in schools. It first covers the level of implementation observed (i.e., the measure of the dependent variable), and then discusses the factors related to implementation (i.e., independent variables). Finally, we address student outcomes as an additional set of dependent variables as well as the related factors.

Overview of Changes to Designs Over Time

These findings are based on a continual tracking of the designs and teams throughout the analytic effort (Bodilly, 2001). Our purpose was to understand what intervention the schools attempted to adopt. It is based on a longitudinal case study analysis of each team. The analysis is based on a document review, interviews with teams, and reviews by NAS and the teams of the findings. The original design proposals were used as a baseline and changes to teams and designs were assessed against those original proposals. Interviews helped us understand why the changes were made.

Consistent with the literature on external change agents, the designs adapted over time. While some of the design development was beneficial for enabling schools to improve, other developments appeared less likely to help schools. For example, the growth in the assistance packages, the further development of curricular units, and the development of protocols for school choice of design all appeared on the surface to be positive adaptations. The development of basic skills curriculum could also be considered positive when well-integrated with the principles of the design and not simply a quick add-on to meet district demands.

Other changes, while understandable, remained more problematic. Adaptation to district and school policies led some designs to accept unaligned and incoherent mixes of standards, assessments, curriculum, instruction, and professional development. This also allowed for considerable local adaptation to the point where one might question the unifying nature of a design.

These changes to some designs over the demonstration and scale-up phases meant that a major component of NAS's theory of action—a coherent, unifying design—was often missing or was constantly in the process of being revised. It cannot be emphasized enough that during the entire time of the RAND studies, designs were still in a state of development. Consistent with the literature, implementation assistance—what NAS termed "design-based assistance"—became an important part of the intervention as time went on.

Overview of Implementation Findings

RAND studied the implementation of designs in both the demonstration and scale-up phases. The purpose was to measure the level of implementation in schools and to determine the conditions under which implementation prospered (Bodilly, 1998; Keltner, 1998; Bodilly and Berends, 1999; Berends, 2000; Berends and Kirby et al., 2001; Kirby, Berends, and Naftel, 2001; Berends et al., 2002; see Table S.1 for a brief descriptions of these studies).

The demonstration schools showed some promise, but RAND identified many barriers to implementation (Bodilly et al., 1995; Bodilly, 1996; Mitchell, 1996). During scale-up, NAS and the design teams partnered with schools and districts that were characterized by a host of problems related to poverty, achievement, and school and district climate characteristics (Berends, 1999). Achieving high levels of implementation within these schools across all teachers proved challenging. The case study analyses found that two years into implementation approximately half of the sample sites were implementing at a level consistent with NAS and design team expectations. The other half were below this level. All sites reported many barriers to further implementation.

The longitudinal sample of teachers supported the findings of the case studies showing lack of strong implementation and lack of increasing progress toward implementation:

- For the entire sample of schools we surveyed, implementation in the scale-up schools increased modestly from 1997 to 1999. The between-school variance in the level of implementation decreased somewhat over time, but the within-school variance increased. There was much greater variance in implementation *within* schools than between schools, suggesting that designs had failed to become "schoolwide."

- There were large differences in implementation by jurisdiction, by design, and across schools.

- For schools newly adopting designs, implementation increased and deepened over the first four years after schools adopted designs, although at decreasing rates each year.

As expected, many factors influenced the level of implementation and the different analyses identified similar conditions leading to higher levels of implementation. The following summarized the key factors related to implementation as portrayed in our conceptual framework (Figure S.1) across all the RAND studies summarized in Table S.1.

Designs and Design-Based Assistance. Implementation varied by design. In the longitudinal survey sample, schools with CON, NARE, and RW designs clearly reported higher implementation. Reported high levels of implementation in all the studies were related to clear communication and strong assistance by design teams. These in turn brought about stronger teacher support for the designs in their schools. We remind the reader that in many cases designs were changing significantly over time and were still in the process of development during this entire period. Teachers reported poor communication of the design to the school staff at many sites because of the changing nature of the designs. Finally, in our last case study analyses of a small sample of schools we found that several designs did not have strong information about their schools nor had they adequately measured implementation for their schools. Taken together the evidence shows that several designs need to make significant improvements to ensure implementation of their designs in schools.

Selection Process. Our case study (Bodilly, 1998) revealed that those schools that felt they had a well-informed choice process reported higher levels of implementation than those that reported being forced to accept a design or not understanding the nature of the design. In the longitudinal survey sample, teacher support and buy-in were related to higher levels of implementation. Our case study work also revealed that principals played an important role in ensuring a sound selection process and the buy-in of teachers.

School Capacity. School capacity was important in supporting implementation. Principal leadership was an important contributor to implementation across all the studies. The survey analyses indicated teacher views of principal leadership was the most important indicator of the implementation level achieved. The teacher survey also indicated that teacher perceptions of students and their readiness to learn were all significantly related to level of implementation. The different case studies indicated that many other reforms were taking place in the schools while the NAS reform was under way. In many instances this caused teacher overload, and reduced the capacity of teachers to implement the designs.

School Context. The teacher surveys revealed that implementation was higher in high-poverty schools as well as schools serving high numbers of minority students. However, in schools that served significant numbers of *both* poor and minority students, implementation levels were significantly lower. Across our implementation studies, we found implementation was higher in elementary schools than in secondary schools and in smaller schools versus larger ones.

District Context. There were large differences in implementation between jurisdictions across all our studies. In general, implementation was higher in those districts that were more supportive of the NAS designs and characterized as having stable district leadership that backed the reform and made the reform central to its improvement efforts; a lack of crises such as budget crises or redistricting; a coherent program of reform; resources dedicated to the effort; significant school-level autonomy; and a trusting relationship between school, district and union staff. The several case study analyses highlighted significant barriers to implementation embedded in district and union policies.

The San Antonio classroom study gave particular insight into how district-level behaviors affected schools and their willingness to undertake and implement designs (Berends et al., 2002). Teachers' views of consistent and effective district leadership proved to be positively associated with teacher efforts toward implementation. Adoption of multiple reforms easily overwhelmed teachers and their efforts at this particular reform. Most importantly, the high-stakes state testing regime, which inadvertently encouraged a specific focus on basic skills, resulted in district adoption of specific curricular programs in addition to the designs. In fact, these curricular programs conflicted with the designs and resulted in lower levels of implementation.

Exit interviews with principals of schools that had dropped the NAS designs and related RAND research highlighted the importance of adequate resources in funding. Lack of funding was the single most important reason cited by most of the schools in the decision to drop a design. The costs of implementing the designs were far greater than the costs paid in fees to design teams. In fact, these fees made up less than one-third the cost to schools of implementing designs. Significant costs were borne by teachers in terms of teacher time and effort in implementing these designs.

Overview of Student Outcome Findings

We tracked school outcomes for those schools included in the scale-up phase, see Table S.1. Our analysis of performance trends across the set of schools three years into scale-up focused on whether NAS schools made gains—any gains—in test scores relative to their respective jurisdictions. While these school-level measures allowed us to compare performance in NAS schools with that of the district as a whole, they are subject to important limitations. For example, these aggregated measures may fail to capture changes in the tails of the distribution, or miss some significant achievement effects that may be captured if student-level data were available and comparable across jurisdictions. We found that:

- Among the four jurisdictions with 10 or more implementing NAS schools, Memphis and Kentucky schools appeared to be the most successful in terms of improvement in mathematics, while Cincinnati and Washington state did better in reading.

- In total, of the 163 schools for which we had data allowing comparisons in performance relative to the district or state, 81 schools (50 percent) made gains relative to the district in mathematics, and 76 schools (47 percent) made gains in reading.

Because of the wide variation in implementation and environments that occurred within schools and among jurisdictions, it may have been too early to expect robust performance results across the NAS sites. Better and longer-term performance data are needed in order to make conclusive judgments about designs and their effects on school performance.

However, our implementation analysis showed that the overall level of implementation increased modestly over time, and there was continuing within-school variation in implementation. If the NAS approach to school improvement is correct, then weak implementation will lead to weak impacts on student performance. Our findings suggest that we cannot expect stronger performance results unless implementation significantly deepens.

The detailed classroom study of San Antonio allowed us to examine whether variation in instructional conditions was related to student achievement, controlling for other student, teacher, classroom, and school characteristics. We found that:

- Strong principal leadership as reported by teachers had significant positive effects on students' state test scores in reading and mathematics.

- Instructional conditions promoted by reforms such as NAS—including teacher-reported collaboration, quality of professional development, and reform-like instructional practices—were not related to student achievement net of other student and classroom conditions.

- In general, early implementation of NAS designs in a high-poverty district within a high-stakes accountability system did not result in significant effects on student achievement.

Other analyses of schoolwide reforms have found similar results.

CONCLUSIONS

In the end the RAND analysis illuminated three important areas. First, it provided evidence that an external agent such as NAS could deliberately create and promote design teams. Second, it indicated that some of the theory of action behind the NAS efforts was underdeveloped, and our various analyses pointed to important conditions for implementation and improved student outcomes. Third, it pointed to important lessons about how to carry out future efforts at reform. We expand briefly here.

The Contribution of New American Schools

NAS did accomplish several of the goals it had set for itself and in the process made several important contributions to educational reform that need to be kept in mind. These included:

- NAS funding and leadership led to the deliberate development of several functioning design teams.

- NAS showed that initially dependent external change agents could be moved toward self-sufficiency over time.

- NAS explicitly sought scale-up of the reform initiative.

- NAS actions as a change agent have significantly influenced policy in its areas of interest.

- NAS explicitly made analysis and good consumer education a part of its efforts.

Our review of the NAS experiences indicated that this deliberate effort did succeed in some important ways, and the approach of providing venture capital with specific goals could be used as a policy instrument in the future when innovative approaches and new actors are desired. NAS itself evolved from a venture capitalist organization to a provider of district- and design-based services.

NAS's Theory of Action

RAND findings provide mixed evidence to support NAS's theories of change.

The initial hypothesis, that by adopting a whole-school design a school could improve its performance, was largely unproven. We found specific positive examples of school implementation and improvement under certain conditions; however, negative examples were found under more common conditions. Our general findings showed difficulties in implementation and lack of strong improvements in school performance in a significant percent of the schools in our samples.

The hypothesis that designs alone were not helpful to schools and that schools needed assistance in implementation was proven correct. Teachers and school administrators clearly reported higher levels of implementation associated with strong assistance from design teams. Just as importantly and consistent with the implementation literature, conditions at the schools and within the districts and the manner of selection also proved important to implementation and outcomes.

The scale-up hypothesis that a district that converted 30 percent of its schools using whole-school approaches would become high performing and not revert to unproductive practices was disproved. Districts, such as Memphis, reverted back to their former status quickly with changes in administrations.

The scale-up hypothesis that a district needs to provide a supportive environment was dramatically proven. Without a supportive environment the designs did not flourish. Barriers to implementation reported by school staff focused on unsupportive district practices. They also pointed to the challenges inherent in adopting multiple reforms, high-stakes testing regimes and designs simultaneously.

In general then, we conclude that NAS's initial theory of action was largely underdeveloped and unspecified in terms of ensuring a successful scale-up experience. The causal chain of events leading to strong implementation and outcomes has proven to be far more complex than that originally considered by NAS and one that remained largely outside of its control and influence. This finding is in keeping with the literature on implementation indicating the complexity of the change process.

Implications for Future Efforts

Based on our experience with NAS, we offer the following implications for future attempts at scaling up of school reforms.

Externally developed education reform interventions cannot be "break the mold" and still be marketable and implementable in current district and school contexts. NAS attempted to have both "break the mold" designs and designs that would appeal and be implemented nationally. The evidence of our evolution analysis and the implementation analyses all point to the fact that schools did not have a ready place for these designs. Schools were not by and large fertile ground for "break the mold" ideas, often because of a lack of capacity or local, state, or district regulations. Rather, the designs had to change to be suitable to school conditions or simply not be implemented. In order for the design to be well implemented, the district and school contexts have to change to allow for "break the mold" school-level ideas to flourish.

External interventions need to address systemic issues that can hinder implementation. The relatively weak implementation of the designs during scale-up was associated with several systemic factors: lack of teacher capacity to undertake the designs especially in terms of time and subject area expertise; lack of principal leadership; and an incoherent district infrastructure that did not match the needs of design implementation. This implies the design concept and NAS's initiative did not focus on important dimensions of school improvement when attempting to increase schools' effectiveness.

A rush to scale up when interventions are not completely developed weakens results. NAS designs and teams were not ready to scale up when NAS called for this move in 1995. Many of the problems associated with the scale-up phase are attributable to pushing toward full-scale production before all the kinks in the product were worked out. However, these problems are likely to persist partly because developers are under financial pressures to scale up their interventions before they are thoroughly evaluated and partly because districts and schools are under severe political pressure to adopt external solutions—whether proven or not—as a means of addressing the lackluster performance of their students.

A key component of successful implementation is consistent, clear, and frequent communication and assistance between design developers and schools, particularly teachers. A reasonable inference from our research is that a strong, trusting relationship between a school and an external agent is a prerequisite for strong implementation of complex interventions that require significant changes in behavior. If funders and developers expect teachers to change behavior significantly, then they need to invest considerable time and effort to build trusting relationships with teachers.

Monitoring site progress, self-evaluation, and reflection are necessary if external developers are to be successful and to improve their offerings over time. In part, this is a resource issue—the push to scale up can leave developers with few resources for evaluation and cycles of self-improvement. In part, it is a priority issue—developers want to spend money on development of the ideas they are committed to, oftentimes whether or not they are effective, and may not see evaluation as either important or even necessary. But, unless systems for tracking progress in schools and understanding school-level concerns are created and used for improving the external intervention, the effort cannot succeed over the long term. This capacity must be deliberately built into the development effort and continuously maintained.

The typical outcome measures used in public accountability systems provide a very limited measure of student and school performance. Years of evaluations indicate that the best way to measure whether an intervention is having an effect is to measure variables most closely associated with the interventions. This truism would lead evaluations away from using district and state test score data toward a richer set of assessments and indicators for whole-school reform. In the developmental phases of an intervention, however, the assessment instruments needed to adequately measure progress do not exist. The assessment measures that do exist—district-mandated tests—do not adequately measure the impact of innovative approaches. This tension will be a constant hindrance to understanding the impact of innovative approaches unless alternative indicators and assessments are developed in ways that are well aligned with the reforms' goals. The high-stakes testing regimes currently in vogue and the overwhelming emphasis given to test scores on state- or district-mandated tests as *the* measure of improvement do not bode well for many innovative reform efforts.

ACKNOWLEDGMENTS

A program of studies of this depth and breadth is not accomplished without significant contributions from, cooperation with, and collaboration among many people. Space limitations do not allow us to list all the many individuals who have contributed over time to this effort.

We would like to thank New American Schools for its continuing support over the years and its willingness to use the information we provided to try to improve its efforts at reform.

The analytic program was supported by NAS with funding from several different donors over the years: the MacArthur, Knight, Pew, and Ford foundations, and an anonymous donor. Funding for this book was provided under a contract with NAS and supported by the Ford Foundation and the Atlantic Philanthropic Service Company. We thank them all for their support and continued interest in our work.

Obviously, this work would not be possible without the cooperation of all the districts, school staff, and students involved with NAS. They were cordial and supportive of our work and have been avid consumers as well.

Scholars and analysts outside of RAND played a major role in improving our work and we owe them a debt of gratitude for their sound advice. Members of the Research Advisory Panel sponsored by the Annenberg Foundation provided critical guidance to the research. They include Barbara Cervone, Paul Hill, Janice Petrovich, Andrew Porter, Karen Sheingold, and Carol Weiss. In addition, several scholars provided assistance in development of instruments

xlii   Facing the Challenges of Whole-School Reform

including Tom Corcoran, Adam Gamoran, and Fred Newmann. Finally, the work was reviewed at different times by insightful outside critics who offered their best advice: Tom Corcoran, Bob Croninger, Amanda Datnow, Milbrey McLaughlin, Andrew Porter, and Carol Weiss. In addition, several colleagues within RAND also provided critical reviews that improved the analyses immensely.

This book and other RAND documents were written under the aegis of RAND Education. Different staff members were involved over the years. The authors of different reports are listed in the Preface; in addition, each chapter lists the authors who contributed to the individual reports on which the chapter was based. We have tried to be faithful to the original reports while trying to set them in the context of the larger set of studies. We give special thanks to Thomas Glennan whose leadership and insight was essential to this effort.

For this particular report, we are especially grateful to Tora Bikson of RAND and Milbrey McLaughlin of Stanford whose insightful reviews vastly improved this final report of RAND's research on NAS. In the end, any remaining errors are our own.

ACRONYMS

ATLAS or AT	Authentic Teaching, Learning and Assessment for All Students
AC	Audrey Cohen College of Education or Purpose-Centered Education: the Audrey Cohen College System of Education
CLC	Community Learning Centers
CON	Co-NECT
CPN	Cumulative Percent of Norm
CSR	Comprehensive school reform
CSRD	Comprehensive School Reform Demonstration
CTBS	Comprehensive Test of Basic Skills
EL	Expeditionary Learning Outward Bound
EQI	Education Quality Institute
FIE	Fund for the Improvement of Education
LAEP	Los Angeles Educational Partnership
LALC	Los Angeles Learning Centers
MRSH	Modern Red Schoolhouse
NARE	National Alliance for Restructuring Education

NAS	New American Schools
NASDC	New American Schools Development Corporation
NR	Non-restructured
RFP	Request for Proposals
RW	Roots & Wings
SD	Standard deviation
SFA	Success for All
TAAS	Texas Assessment of Academic Skills
TCAP	Tennessee Comprehensive Assessment Program
TVAAS	Tennessee Value-Added Assessment System
ULC	Urban Learning Centers (formerly Los Angeles Learning Centers)

Chapter One

INTRODUCTION

Mark Berends, Susan Bodily, Sheila Nataraj Kirby

Spurred by the piecemeal approach to school reform that had produced little change in the nation's test scores, New American Schools (NAS) launched its efforts for whole-school reform in 1991. This initiative was based on the premise that high-quality schools are established with external providers (design teams) providing assistance to schools for implementing designs.

> A Design Team is an organization that provides high-quality, focused, ongoing professional development for teachers and administrators organized around a meaningful and compelling vision of what students should know and be able to do. The vision, or design, offers schools a focus for their improvement efforts, along with guidance in identifying what students need to know and be able to do and how to get there. (NASDC, 1997, p. 6.)

The mission of NAS was to help schools and districts significantly raise the achievement of large numbers of students with whole-school designs and the assistance design teams provide during the implementation process. To make this goal a reality, NAS initially organized its work into several phases: a competition phase to solicit proposals and select designs; a development phase of one year to develop the ideas in the proposals in concrete ways; a demonstration phase of two years to pilot the designs in real school settings; and a scale-up phase in which the designs would be widely diffused in partnering jurisdictions across the nation.

Over the last ten years, RAND has been providing analytic support to and monitoring the NAS initiative. During this time period, RAND documented the NAS efforts in order to assess its contributions to education reform; described the designs and analyzed changes in them over time; assessed the level of implementation in design-based schools during the demonstration and scale-up phases; identified factors that impeded or encouraged implementation in the demonstration and scale-up phases; and measured whether the adoption of the designs resulted in the outcomes desired by the partner districts in the scale-up phase. The results of these efforts are contained in a series of reports, listed in the Preface.

The purposes of this study are to provide a retrospective look at the NAS initiative and the RAND analyses of that initiative; to draw together the findings from RAND research conducted over the course of a decade; and to reflect on lessons learned from the unfolding and maturing of NAS. The book helps highlight the significant contributions made by NAS to the reform debate and to actual reform in schools. It also highlights the complexities and challenges of trying to reform schools through whole-school designs and provides a timely warning to the policymakers and practitioners looking to significantly raise student performance through the adoption of externally provided interventions.

This introduction sets the context for the remainder of the report. It provides a brief overview of NAS, its intentions, and RAND's analytic role in understanding and assessing NAS's progress toward its goals. More detail about NAS is provided in Chapter Two, while Chapter Three examines the evolution of the designs. In this chapter, we also outline the conceptual framework that guided the RAND work, along with brief descriptions of the individual research analyses done by RAND, the methodologies used, and the limitations of our approach. Because the work represented here took place over many years and had many distinct tasks, a separate appendix is included that covers in detail methodologies for each task.

AN OVERVIEW OF NAS

In July 1991, in conjunction with President Bush's America 2000 initiative, the New American Schools Development Corporation (NASDC) was established as a nonprofit corporation funded by the private sector to create and support design teams capable of helping existing elementary and secondary schools transform themselves into high-performing organizations by using "whole-school designs."

Its core premise, taken from the effective schools literature, was that all high-quality schools possess a de facto unifying design that allows all staff to function to the best of their abilities and that provides a consistent and coherent education instructional program to all students.[1] NAS posited that designs could be created for schools that would, if adopted, help schools improve their students' performance. The best way to create "break the mold" school designs was to invest in talented teams of innovators. Then, NAS thought, schools across the country would adopt the designs. It referred to this adoption by schools nationally as "scale-up," indicating large numbers of schools adopting NAS designs was an important goal.

The NAS effort was, and still is, a dramatically different way of initiating and disseminating large-scale educational improvement. From the outset, NAS's vision was of a large scale-up effort to transform thousands of schools, not just a handful. Not only did the emphasis on eventual scale-up set it apart, but so too did the involvement of the private sector and the choice of school designs as the vehicle for reform. This scale of private sector involvement was unique in K–12 education as was the venture capital notion of deliberate development of designs. Prior to this, the private sector contributions to educational reform were often relatively small amounts of funding or materials to individual schools in "partnership" programs to help promote specific activities such as reading or science. To a large extent, this is true of many private sector reform efforts even today.

In short, the NAS initiative could be viewed as an innovative approach to school reform as an experiment. Given its unique approach based in business principles, the announcement of its creation caused some commentary. Opinions were divided about the value of a private sector reform initiative, as the following quotations demonstrate:

---

[1]See Purkey and Smith (1983).

It is wrong-headed to suggest that the greatest problem in education is not knowing what to do and that we must wait for privately-
funded design teams to come up with ideas. (Timpane, 1991,
pp. 19–20.)

I cannot comprehend why the Secretary and the President consider
a private research effort to be the centerpiece for system changes
for the most important function of government—education.
(Ambach, 1991, p. 39.)

Schools are highly constrained by various laws, regulations, non-
government policies (e.g., SAT and the Carnegie units), and organizational rigidity.   The New American Schools Development
Corporation is needed to break loose from these impediments.
(Kirst, 1991, p. 38.)

To make its goal of improving student achievement a reality, NAS
initially organized its work into several phases (see Figure 1.1):[2]

- A competition phase to solicit proposals and select designs;

- A development phase of one year to develop the ideas in the proposals in concrete ways;

- A demonstration phase of two years to pilot the designs in real
  school settings; and

- A scale-up phase in which the designs would be widely diffused
  in some as yet unspecified fashion.

NAS selected 11 teams with unique associated designs in its competition phase. After a year of further development, NAS funded nine of
the 11 teams to demonstrate and implement whole-school designs in
real schools during the school years 1993–94 and 1994–95. During
this time, the number of NAS schools grew to 147. From 1995 to

---

[2]A more detailed description of the history of the NAS initiative and the design teams
appears in Bodilly (1998), Glennan (1998), and Stringfield et al. (1996). See also
Desimone (2000), Herman et al. (1999), Ball et al. (1998), Stringfield and Datnow
(1998), Datnow and Stringfield (1997), Ross et al. (1997, 1998). For descriptions of NAS
and the design teams on the Web, see http://www.newamericanschools.org, which
has links to each design team's website.

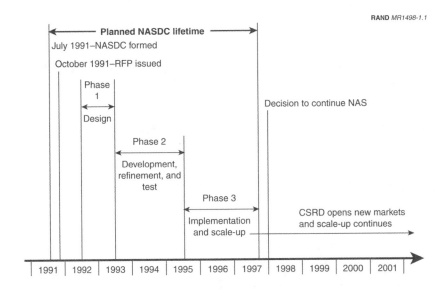

RAND *MR1498-1.1*

Figure 1.1—Original Schedule for New American Schools Program, 1991

1998, NAS led a scale-up phase in ten jurisdictions across the country. More details of this initiative are contained in the following chapter, so we do not cover them here. Table 1.1 summarizes the growth pattern of NAS for the reader.

After the scale-up phase, the NAS Board decided not to go out of business, but rather to transition NAS into a new organization. It currently has ten primary design teams working for the improvement of whole-school reform efforts and their successful adoption nationwide. It has brought more designs under its network; reportedly, its designs are now associated with over 4,000 design-based schools.

RAND'S PURPOSE AND ANALYTIC TASKS

The NAS effort offered an unprecedented opportunity to study and understand a dramatic attempt at school reform—one based in an experimental approach of research and development, demonstration, and scale-up. Analyzing the initiative could potentially provide

Table 1.1

Phases of NAS

Phase	Time	Purpose	Design Teams	Number of schools	Jurisdictions
Competition	Oct. 1991–July 1992	Develop and field RFP; choose teams to develop designs	More than 600 applicants		
I. Development	July 1992–July 1993	Allow teams one year to further develop designs for implementation	11 teams[a]	Handful; most not working in schools in this time period	National Alliance team partners with jurisdictions
II. Demonstration	July 1993–July 1995	To implement designs in schools to show what can be done and to work out implementation issues	9 teams[a]	147 schools	Only National Alliance districts
III. Scale-up	July 1995–July 1998	To spread designs within districts to create districts where good schools are the norm	7 teams[a]	Begin with about 550 schools nationwide and end with over 1,000; 184 schools in partnering jurisdictions	Cincinnati; Dade; Kentucky; Maryland; Memphis; Philadelphia; Pittsburgh; San Antonio; San Diego; 3 districts in Washington state
IV. Planned Phase-out	July 1998	Original plan called for NASDC to go out of business; Board and design teams support continuation of NAS			
At present	July 1998–2001	To promote comprehensive school reform and to provide venture capital for new teams	10 teams[a]	4,000 by 2001	National

[a]Teams are listed in Chapter Two.

significant policy lessons for those involved in educational reform. NAS asked RAND to provide such a broad ranging and long-term analysis of its ambitious school reform initiative. This early involvement of an outside, third party to provide analytic support was another uncommon approach, but one in keeping with NAS's business approach of gathering information to improve quality over time.

As Fullan (2001) points out, any educational reform must have two components, a theory of learning and a theory of action. NAS had no formal, explicit theory of learning; rather NAS intended each design team to create its own specific theory of learning and imbue it with life through the design and materials supporting the design. Each of these designs was to be "research based" or use proven educational principles. Each design team was responsible for the development, and evaluation of its own theory of learning. RAND was not to address these issues per se.

NAS's initial theory of action was quite simple. After design teams developed designs, they would interact with schools, in some unspecified way. Schools would adopt the designs and, by adoption, improve student performance. It was that simple.

RAND's mission was to concentrate on the theory of action—to analyze whether and how teams were making progress toward NAS goals of school adoption and eventual student performance improvements. From 1991 to 1999, RAND provided analytic support primarily intended to document NAS's progress toward its goals. RAND's research tasks were broadly defined:

- Document the NAS efforts to assess its contributions to education reform;

- Describe the designs and analyze changes in them over time;

- Assess the level of implementation in design-based schools during the demonstration and scale-up phases;

- Identify the factors that impede or encourage implementation in the demonstration and scale-up phases; and

- Measure whether the adoption of the designs results in the outcomes desired by the partner districts in the scale-up phase.

CONCEPTUAL FRAMEWORK FOR UNDERSTANDING IMPLEMENTATION AND PERFORMANCE IN NAS SCHOOLS

The conceptual framework that guided RAND research on implementation and performance had as its theoretical underpinnings the literature on external change agents. These are groups outside of the hierarchy of the school systems that attempt to bring about meaningful change in schools. This is the model that NAS adopted.

External Change Agents and School Improvement

Attempting to fundamentally change the behaviors and tasks of an existing organization is one of the most difficult reforms to accomplish. This is especially true when multiple levels of government are involved; when significantly different behaviors are called for; when the tasks and behaviors are those of a large and diverse group; and when these actors have varying incentives to change (Mazmanian and Sabatier, 1989).

These conditions all apply to the NAS initiative. Implementation of a design created by an external agent (the design teams) in a school involves federal, state, and local governments, the design teams, and multiple other actors. Being "break the mold," design adoption could be expected to require significantly different sets of behaviors on the part of students, teachers, principals, and administrators. Those groups respond to and are driven by many varying incentives, rules, and regulations inherent in the infrastructure of schools and schooling (Gitlin and Margonis, 1995; Cuban, 1984; Huberman and Miles, 1984).

Many previous studies of implementation of school reform have highlighted that local capacity and will are ultimately the two factors that determine successful implementation:

> Policy makers can't mandate what matters most: local capacity and will . . . . Environmental stability, competing centers of authority, contending priorities or pressures and other aspects of the social-political milieu can influence implementor willingness profoundly. . . . Change is ultimately a problem of the smallest unit. (McLaughlin, 1987, pp. 172–173.)

What is often true, however, is that attempts at implementation lead to "mutual adaptation" with local educational agencies, school staff and intermediaries changing behaviors in significant ways (Berman and McLaughlin, 1975). As McLaughlin put it "Local variability is the rule; uniformity is the exception" (1990, p. 13). The original users of the term "mutual adaptation" meant to invoke a benign or positive process of movement toward mutually agreed-upon goals with the intervention changing for the better in some sense so as to support those goals.

Others have found that adaptation does not always lead to enhancement of the original policy, or necessarily promote the desired performance outcomes. These less-benign effects have been categorized in different ways as unanticipated consequences, policy disappearance, policy erosion, policy dilution, policy drift, or simply poor or slowed implementation (Cuban, 1984; Pressman and Wildavsky, 1973; Daft, 1995; Mazmanian and Sabatier, 1989; Weatherley and Lipsky, 1977; Yin, 1979).

It is often the case that these less-desirable outcomes occur because policymakers do not put in place needed support mechanisms or change the supporting infrastructure to help the external agent implement the intervention. McDonnell and Grubb (1991) make clear that successful implementation of any educational mandate, whether by an external agent or by the school itself, requires support of the implementers, capacity on their part to follow the mandate, and some enforcement or incentives to support compliance. The building of capacity requires the infusion of resources in terms of time, funding, and information—either social or intellectual. These resources are often referred to as "slack" or "slack resources" without which reform cannot be successfully undertaken. Capacity cannot be mandated, but must be built with slack resources.

The education literature does point to important supports that if provided, often lead to implementation closer to that expected by policymakers (fidelity). These conditions include (McLaughlin, 1990):

- Active participation and support of district leadership, including the removal of conflicting priorities and initiatives;

- Funding to get the initiative under way and indicate its importance;

- Understanding by stakeholders and implementers of the intervention and its intended effects gained through clear communication;

- Specific attention and assistance for implementation, such as:

    — Concrete and specific teacher training including classroom assistance by local staff;

    — Teacher observations of similar projects in like settings;

    — Stakeholder acceptance of the initiative and participation in project decisions and regular project meetings focused on practical issues; and

    — Local development of project material.

Implementation is a progressive activity, with full implementation sometimes only evident after several stages of activity (Mazmanian and Sabatier, 1989; Yin, 1979). This phenomenon occurs in part because of the developmental nature of some interventions, but it can also be due to the cycles of political support and interest that come and go depending on the values of leaders in office, competing policy issues, and the funding picture.

Finally, consistent with the development of needed implementation strategies, sometimes the actual intervention becomes less important in producing the wanted effect than the implementation assistance offered for the intervention. In short, the intervention might never be implemented, but outcomes might improve because of important assistance offered by the developers or change agents (Bikson and Eveland, 1992, 1998; Bikson et al., 1997; Eveland and Bikson, 1989).

Rather than a simple theory of change, this literature points to a very complex process that might or might not lead to implementation and improved student outcomes because of the multiple factors and actors that are involved. It also indicates that mutual adaptation between the designs and the schools might be very beneficial if it leads to the ultimate goals of the initiative—improved student performance. It could be harmful if it only results in extreme local adaptation with little increase in internal coherence evident in the schools. In short, the goal is to gain improved outcomes, not to faithfully implement the model. But, if the model is not implemented and the goals are met, one must look elsewhere for the cause of improvement.

RAND's Conceptual Framework

The framework portrayed in Figure 1.2 is an attempt to capture the complex system of variables that is at the heart of educational change. This framework is explicated in greater detail in Berends and Kirby et al. (2001); Kirby, Berends, and Naftel (2001); and Berends et al. (2002). Here, we highlight some of the relationships that are important from a policy perspective.

The right side of the figure represents NAS's theory of action and the designs' theory of action. NAS's core premise is that *coherent, focused, and sustained* implementation of key design components by school-level personnel (including professional development, curriculum and instructional materials, content and performance standards, assessments, organization and governance, and parent and community involvement) will eventually change *school and classroom learning environments and thereby students' academic outcomes.* Implementation consists of the process of putting into practice the elements or set of activities defined by design teams as core components of their design. However, both implementation and outcomes are themselves affected by a number of interrelated factors, many of which are not readily controlled by NAS or its design teams. These factors are shown in the boxes in the left side of the figure and further discussed below:

- *The design itself and its ability to offer coherent, comprehensive, and consistent education programs and assistance to ensure implementation.*

  — To accomplish the goal of improving performance, each design team has embedded in it a "theory of action" that establishes a link between elements of the design and student performance. Designs range from relatively specific

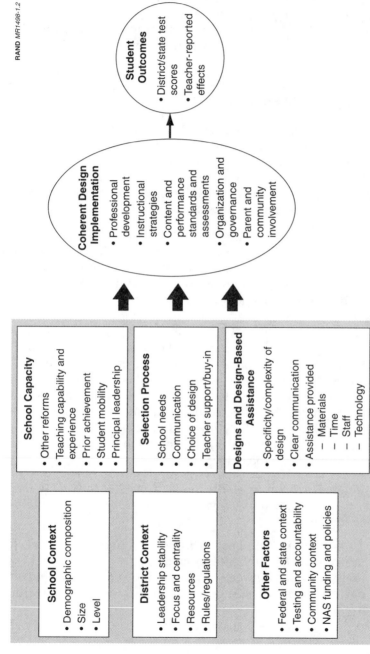

RAND *MR1498-1.2*

School Context
• Demographic composition
• Size
• Level

District Context
• Leadership stability
• Focus and centrality
• Resources
• Rules/regulations

Other Factors
• Federal and state context
• Testing and accountability
• Community context
• NAS funding and policies

School Capacity
• Other reforms
• Teaching capability and experience
• Prior achievement
• Student mobility
• Principal leadership

Selection Process
• School needs
• Communication
• Choice of design
• Teacher support/buy-in

Designs and Design-Based Assistance
• Specificity/complexity of design
• Clear communication
• Assistance provided
  – Materials
  – Time
  – Staff
  – Technology

Coherent Design Implementation
• Professional development
• Instructional strategies
• Content and performance standards and assessments
• Organization and governance
• Parent and community involvement

Student Outcomes
• District/state test scores
• Teacher-reported effects

Figure 1.2—A Conceptual Framework for Analyzing Implementation Progress and Performance in NAS Schools

descriptions of how schools should be organized and what materials and professional development should be relied on to less specific visions and processes for school restructuring. Implementation is likely to be related to the inherent features of the designs themselves, the ability of the design teams to clearly communicate the design components, and the type of assistance they provide during implementation. For example, a highly specified design such as Roots & Wings (RW) provides an abundance of print materials, assessments, professional development, and specified organizational changes. In contrast, some of the other NAS designs are more process oriented. For instance, Expeditionary Learning Outward Bound (EL) is less structured than RW and is based on design principles that reflect the design's origins in the Outward Bound program. Teachers play a critical role in developing the expeditions, which involves a great deal of effort and imagination.

— Clear communication by designs to schools is critical for not only the selection of the design, but also the implementation of it. Fullan (2001) emphasizes that clarity of the change is an important factor affecting implementation; the more complex the reform, the greater the need for clarity. Communication to schools both in the selection and implementation process can take several different forms, including design fairs, print materials, use of computer software and the Internet, workshops, retreats, school visits, and site-based facilitators.

— The unique aspect of design-based assistance is the commitment of the designs to provide ongoing assistance to provide a variety of services to further implementation and the transformation of the whole school—its organization, curriculum, instruction, and professional development of staff. For implementation of any program, resources are critical (Keltner, 1998; McLaughlin, 1990). It is a common finding that when resources decrease or disappear, the implementation is likely to diminish (Glennan, 1998; Montjoy and O'Toole, 1979). If teachers receive the funds, the professional development from design teams for design implementation, the materials to support implementation, and the time to plan and develop the program, it is likely that implementation will deepen over time.

- *The efficacy of the selection and matching process between designs and schools to ensure teacher "buy-in" to the design.* How schools go about selecting a design has implications for the implementation that follows (Bodilly, 1998; Ross et al., 1997). For example, if a school were forced to adopt a design without careful assessment of its needs, it is not surprising that teachers would resist engaging in the activities of the design. Yet, some schools are often targets for forced restructuring efforts, particularly those that exhibit chronic poor performance. Thus, a critical aim of the NAS designs before implementation even begins is to obtain the buy-in of teachers for the planned restructuring activities. Most of the designs require between 75–80 percent of the teachers voting in favor of the designs. The rationale is that if the vast majority of the staff vote to adopt the design, they will commit to making the changes necessary during the implementation process.

- *The capacity of the specific schools for undertaking the reform including the schools' past and current efforts at reform, educational leadership, and teaching capability.*

  — Schools that are committed to change and have made previous efforts at reform are likely to be more successful at implementing the whole-school reform design. However, if too many reforms are being attempted (for example, state- or district-mandated curricular changes), the capacity of the school to implement the design may be seriously undermined as the school's staff and time is spread too thin.

  — Teachers are the "street-level bureaucrats" at the core of educational change (Weatherley and Lipsky, 1977) and as Fullan succinctly stated, educational change depends on "what teachers do and think—it's as simple and as complex as that" (Fullan, 2001, p. 115). Researchers have also pointed to the importance of working relationships among teachers in implementation of change: collegiality, open communication, trust, support, learning on the job, and morale are closely interrelated (Fullan, 2001; Rosenholtz, 1989).

— The capacity of the school to improve student performance is adversely affected by low prior achievement of its students and high student mobility. Several studies have shown that changes in schooling activities are related to mobility patterns between schools, and preexisting levels of students' academic achievement, attitudes, and engagement in school (Berends et al., 1999; Koretz, 1996; Meyer, 1996).

— Research has consistently shown that the principal strongly influences the likelihood of change (Fullan, 2001; Berman and McLaughlin, 1975). For example, in their study of innovations in the teaching of science in 60 elementary schools, Hall et al. (1980) concluded that "the single most important hypothesis emanating from these data is that *the degree of implementation of the innovation is different in different schools because of the actions and concerns of principals*" (p. 26, emphasis in original). However, there is general consensus that direct principal influence is by itself not a powerful influence on change; rather principals "facilitate" the process of change. For example, leadership of the principal may translate into the ability to obtain sufficient resources for the school and support teachers in their efforts to implement change.

• *School-specific demographics, structure, and climate.* Characteristics of schools are also likely to influence the adoption of schoolwide designs and their effects on student learning: for example, the school's "structural" characteristics such as the minority and socioeconomic composition of the school, school size, and school level (elementary, middle, and high school).

— Schools that face challenges in terms of poverty may encounter difficulties with restructuring efforts such as whole-school designs because high-poverty schools may lack the necessary resources to provide a quality education (Lippman et al., 1996), because students may have lower levels of engagement, effort, and aspirations (Hoffer, 1992; Ralph, 1990; Fordham and Ogbu, 1986), and because teachers may not have the kinds of support they need to foster collaborative relationships necessary for school improvement efforts (Hoffer, 1992; Berends and King, 1994). While policymakers focus on the "lever" at the school level to manipulate to improve learning opportunities and performance, several studies have shown the importance of student background in the learning process (see Coleman et al., 1966; Jencks et al., 1972; Gamoran, 1987, 1992; Bryk, Lee, and Holland, 1993).

— Other school structural factors (size and level) may inhibit schoolwide implementation of schoolwide reforms. For example, larger schools and secondary schools are more complex organizations and are likely to resist organizational change (Perrow, 1986; Lee, Bryk, and Smith, 1993; Lee and Smith, 1995, 1997).

- *District contexts including the existing infrastructure supports and incentives for design implementation and improved student performance.* District-level politics, policies, and practices may promote or derail schoolwide reform efforts such as the NAS designs.

  — The district can facilitate and foster change by providing resources for the school and for professional staff development, and showing active support for schools implementing designs.

  — Moreover, while crucial, central office political support and attention can be buttressed by significant changes in regulatory and financial practices. Schools attempting reforms to address their particular problems can be supported through increased site-level control over their curriculum and instruction, their budgets, their positions and staffing, and most essentially their mission.

  — Comprehensive school reform requires the rethinking and adoption at the school level of new curriculum and instructional approaches and the accompanying professional development. District flexibility in allowing schools to pursue this rethinking is a critical aspect for design-based schools.

- *Other factors.* Those who have studied implementation of educational programs have pointed to other factors that affect implementation such as the federal and/or state policy environment, testing and accountability reforms, and the larger community context (e.g., Elmore and Rothman, 1999; Berends et al., 1999; Grissmer and Flanagan, 1998; Fullan, 2001).

— In particular, the new standards and accountability regimes being adopted by almost every state are likely to fuel expectations of immediate improvements in student outcomes; designs may well be abandoned or at least marginalized if they fail to meet these unrealistic expectations.

— In the case of NAS, these other factors would also include NAS funding and policies, which critically influenced the strategy for development and scale-up.

— The support of the larger community and parents is likely to affect implementation as well (Fullan, 2001). Parent and community demand for reform, their readiness for it, and their ongoing support of it have important ramifications for implementation (Berends and King, 1994; see also Jennings, 1996, 1998).

However, at the beginning of the research, much was unknown. The NAS initiative was, and in some ways remains, a developmental effort without strong controls over the environment. One part of the RAND research was to measure implementation and outcomes; just as importantly, the other part was to understand the factors that affected those outcomes and the interrelationships among these factors themselves.

RAND'S PROGRAM OF STUDIES OF NEW AMERICAN SCHOOLS

This section provides a brief overview to the entire set of RAND studies conducted over the first nine years of the NAS initiative. This program of studies is summarized in Table 1.2. As NAS matured over time, the focus of the RAND studies also shifted from issues of development and early implementation of designs in demonstration schools to scale-up issues, implementation in a larger set of schools, and student outcomes.

Development and Demonstration Phase

During the earliest period, the program of study concerned primarily understanding the differences and similarities among designs and the implications for implementation of designs in real schools

Table 1.2

Phases of NAS and RAND's Program of Studies

Phase/Time	Purpose	Approach	Sample	Data Sources	Measures	Contribution	RAND Publications
Demonstration July 1993–July 1995	Compare & contrast designs; track progress & indicate issues	Longitudinal comparative case studies of design teams using qualitative analysis	9 teams, 32 schools, at least 2 for each team; National Alliance sites included schools at all grade levels within a district	Document review; interviews with design leads; survey of principals; nested interviews for each site from district to teachers two years in a row; site observations	No measures; Identify elements of design & levels of complexity of designs by coverage of elements & needed interactions to attain implementation	Identified notions of: process vs. product teams; design specificity; design-based assistance; implementation issues; lack of district support	Bodilly et al., 1995; Bodilly, 1996; Mitchell, 1996

Table 1.2—continued

Phase/Time	Purpose	Approach	Sample	Data Sources	Measures	Contribution	RAND Publications
Scale-up July 1995–July 1997	Measure & analyze progress toward implementation	Longitudinal comparative case studies of design teams using qualitative analysis	7 teams 40 schools, at least 4 schools each, including elementary & secondary as possible; random selection	Document review; interviews with design leads; survey of principals; nested interviews for each site from district to teachers 2 years in a row; site observations; resources analysis	Implementation index based on progress toward design-specific elements	Showed contrast in progress by design & by district support; raised quality assurance issues; indicated types & quantity of resources required	Bodilly, 1998; Keltner, 1998; Bodilly & Berends, 1999

Table 1.2—continued

Phase/Time	Purpose	Approach	Sample	Data Sources	Measures	Contribution	RAND Publications
Scale-up March 1997– June 1999	Measure & analyze progress toward implementation & improved performance	Quantitative analysis of longitudinal sample of schools	7 teams; target sample of 184 schools in 7 districts actively implementing designs; complete longitudinal response from 71 schools from 1997–1999	Survey of all principals; survey of teachers; collection of quantitative outcome data	Two indices of implementation based on teachers' reports; a core index that included five common elements across all designs; a design team–specific index that included elements unique to specific designs; school level measures of performance based on district-wide mandated tests	Identified factors affecting implementation & performance including principal leadership, resources, teacher support for design teams, design team capacity & district policies	Berends, 1999, 2000; Berends & Kirby et al., 2001; Kirby, Berends, & Naftel, 2001

Table 1.2—continued

Phase/Time	Purpose	Approach	Sample	Data Sources	Measures	Contribution	RAND Publications
Scale-up April 1998– September 1999	Analyze factors leading to classroom implementation & effects on student achievement	Quantitative & qualitative analyses of NAS & non-NAS elementary classrooms within a high-poverty district	All 64 elementary schools in San Antonio district, 279 classrooms, 3,823 students; RAND sample of 23 schools; 63 classrooms; 861 students with wide array of data	Survey teachers; classroom observations; interview teachers, instructional guides, school & district staff; collect teacher logs & samples of student work; administer Stanford-9 open-ended reading test to 4th graders; district longitudinal data on student demographics & test scores, teacher & school characteristics	Student level achievement on RAND-administered test and state-mandated tests; classroom instruction practices consistent with designs	Identified complexity of reform progress & role of district in high-stakes environment & high-poverty, low-performing schools	Berends et al., 2002

Table 1.2—continued

Phase/Time	Purpose	Approach	Sample	Data Sources	Measures	Contribution	RAND Publications
Scale-up March 1999–June 1999	Analyze factors leading to high implementation, but low performance outcomes	Case studies of schools indicated by teams as highly implementing	7 matched pairs of elementary schools; matched by district, demographics & purported levels of implementation	Level of implementation from designs; nested interviews for each site from district to teachers	Consistency between observed level of implementation and that reported by design teams	Inability to obtain target sample precluded strong analysis; pointed to concerns over design team knowledge of site conditions & implementation issues; indicated multiple factors affecting performance other than design	Chun, Gill, & Heilbrunn, 2001

Table 1.2—continued

Phase/Time	Purpose	Approach	Sample	Data Sources	Measures	Contribution	RAND Publications
Ongoing research October 1992– October 1998	Track & analyze changes to designs & design teams & NAS	Longitudinal case study analysis of designs starting with 11 & declining to 7; longitudinal analysis of NAS development	NAS and designs over period	Document review; interviews with design teams; review by teams & NAS; interviews with NAS staff; observations at NAS conferences, meetings, and briefings	Analyzed reasons for changes including: planned development, gradual adaptation to meet needs of sites, adaptation to conflicting policies	Showed significant changes in teams over time; points to importance of district, teacher, & student factors as causative in evolution of designs	Glennan, 1998; Bodilly, 2001

(Bodilly et al., 1995). This research was based on a review of the relevant literature, content analysis of design documents, and extended interviews with designers.

From 1993 to 1995 the research focused on whether and under what conditions the design teams could implement their designs in demonstration sites. It also provided considerable feedback to both NAS and the design teams as to issues and challenges that were arising in the demonstration sites (Bodilly, 1996; Mitchell, 1996). This research was based on literature review, content analysis of the design documents, interviews with design teams, interviews with district and school staff who were involved in implementing the design in 32 different schools, and a survey of principals.

Scale-Up Phase

In 1995, RAND began an assessment of the scale-up of NAS designs to many schools. While NAS intended partnerships with ten jurisdictions, by the 1995–1996 school year, partnerships where schools were actually beginning to implement designs were only evident in the following jurisdictions: Cincinnati, Ohio; Dade County, Florida; Kentucky; Memphis, Tennessee; Philadelphia, Pennsylvania; Pittsburgh, Pennsylvania; San Antonio, Texas; and three districts in Washington state.[3] The RAND assessment of the scale-up phase was confined to these jurisdictions. This longitudinal assessment of the scale-up phase covered years 1995 to 2000 and addressed three major questions:

- What was the level of implementation in NAS schools?

- What impeded or facilitated that implementation?

- Did the adoption of NAS designs result in any changes to student and school outcomes?

Over this time period, RAND's program of studies included a longitudinal study that examined implementation and performance

---

[3]At the time we decided on the longitudinal sample of schools, Maryland and San Diego were not far enough along in their implementation to warrant inclusion in RAND's planned data collection efforts. Since then, several of the design teams report that they are implementing in Maryland and San Diego.

changes across the entire group of schools implementing designs in the partner jurisdictions; case studies of schools; and a classroom study of implementation and performance in a specific district.

Longitudinal Study of Implementation and Performance (Berends and Kirby et al., 2001; Kirby, Berends, and Naftel, 2001). At the beginning of scale-up, there were 184 schools that were implementing the NAS designs in the eight partnering jurisdictions. We collected a variety of data to monitor the progress in implementation and performance in the NAS sites: (a) teacher surveys administered to all the teachers in the NAS schools; (b) principal phone interviews; and (c) data provided by districts on school performance indicators (e.g., mandated test scores, attendance rates, promotion and drop out rates, and school demographic characteristics). The final sample of schools analyzed, about 70–100 schools, was smaller than the original 184 due to nonresponse, panel attrition, and schools dropping the designs. Survey data were collected in 1997, 1998, and 1999 and provide information two, three, and four years after the scale-up. In addition, in 1999, schools that had dropped their previously adopted design in either 1998 or 1999 were surveyed regarding the reasons for the decision. About 30 schools responded.

Implementation Case Studies (Bodily, 1998; Keltner, 1998; Bodily and Berends, 1999). The sample for the case studies consisted of 40 schools in seven districts. The schools were fairly representative of NAS schools in general and included urban and rural schools and districts; elementary, middle, and high schools; and schools that were well-resourced as well as schools that were not. The research encompassed site visits to each of these schools; a review of archival data (such as documents produced by design teams, schools, and districts; plans for transformation; and news releases); structured interviews with district and school staff; school data on enrollment, demographics, and test scores; and classroom observations and observations of special events if they had application to the design.

Classroom Study in San Antonio (Berends et al., 2002). The in-depth classroom study in San Antonio addressed the following questions: (1) Do the NAS designs extend beyond changes in school organization and governance and permeate classrooms? (2) Do NAS teachers and students interact with each other and subject materials in ways that reflect the innovative curricular and instructional approaches of the design teams? and (3) What factors at the district, school, and classroom level are related to implementation of designs, changes in classroom instruction, and student achievement? The schools in this study were those involved in the early stages of the district's partnership with NAS including: Co-NECT (CON), Expeditionary Learning Outward Bound (EL), Modern Red Schoolhouse (MRSH), and Success for All/Roots & Wings (RW).[4] We gathered a variety of data about NAS and non-NAS schools and classrooms, including: principal and teacher surveys conducted at the end of the 1997–1998 and 1998–1999 school years; interviews with district staff, design team leaders, local facilitators, principals, and teachers; classroom observations; illustrative examples of student work; student, teacher, and school data provided by the district on individual test scores and student and teacher demographic characteristics; and achievement data from a supplementary test administered to students (Stanford-9 open-ended reading).

Further Case Studies (Chun, Gill, and Heilbrunn, 2001). The scale-up studies indicated that sites did not make as much progress in student achievement as NAS had hoped, and that progress did not appear to be closely related to implementation. As a result, with the help of the four design teams that agreed to participate (ATLAS, CON, MRSH, and RW), RAND selected a sample of matched pairs of elementary schools, one of which had shown increases in student performance and the other of which had not. Both were at similar levels of implementation (as judged by the designs). The research included site visits and interviews with principals, teachers, and district officials. Data were collected from the design teams about the schools as well as from the districts and the schools themselves.

---

[4]While Success for All (SFA) has been around for the past couple of decades, NAS provided funding to the Success for All Foundation to develop and implement RW, which not only includes the reading program of SFA, but also builds in other curricular programs such as MathWings and WorldLab. San Antonio schools were only implementing the SFA component of RW during the time of this study. Because the Success for All Foundation considers all SFA schools as potential RW schools and because NAS provided funding for RW, we refer to this design as "RW."

Ongoing Research

Over the entire period, RAND has tracked the changes to the designs and changes in NAS as an organization. Changes in designs were documented in an analysis of the evolution of the design teams (Bodilly, 2001). The purpose of this study was to document changes to the designs over their life (1992–1998) and the reasons for those changes to better understand the likely contribution of these designs to improving student outcomes. The study used historical analysis of the design documents, interviews with design teams, and notes from site visits conducted over a period of time to establish changes that had occurred. We used the original proposals submitted in response to NAS's Request for Proposals (RFP) as the baseline for making comparisons. Similarly, Glennan (1998) described the changes NAS had undergone over the early time period.

CAVEATS AND LIMITATIONS

The research and analysis reported here was undertaken on behalf of a client involved in an experiment to engineer strong designs for schools. The use of the term experimental does not mean a controlled environmental research design with careful measures. It refers to the NAS's successive attempts to develop and engineer a strong product called a whole-school design that would produce the outcomes NAS desired. This included successive efforts to learn what might have gone wrong in previous attempts and to try again. NAS was interested in promoting real teams working in real schools in real districts attempting to create designs in real time. At no time did the NAS agenda or those of schools and districts allow for an experimental research design with options for random selection or assignment of students, teachers, schools, or districts, although this approach was often suggested.[5] Nor did the strategies NAS adopted allow for pure control sites within a longitudinal framework.

---

[5]The Annenberg Foundation paid for RAND and NAS to have an Advisory Board to help construct the analyses to be done. This board and RAND often suggested alternative means for analyzing the issues facing NAS including the development of a unique set of student assessments geared toward the performance goals of the teams, experimental designs, and strong control groups. While considered, NAS never funded these efforts for practical reasons: it did not have the financial wherewithal to

Therefore, the analyses reported here were adapted to the complex realities of the unfolding situation. They can be thought of as "action-based research" during the developmental phase of an intervention. The RAND research on NAS has the usual characteristics of such an approach:

- It allowed for a systemic view of the initiative from the teachers and students implementing the reforms to the district administrators trying to support them to design teams and NAS decisionmakers attempting to improve the reforms.

- It provided early information from front-line implementors on how to improve the effort.

- Because of crude measures and the inability to control the environment, it did not produce fine distinctions among the influences of different independent variables, nor fine grained measures of outcomes. It did provide information on the effects of influences, but could not measure their magnitude.

Each of the pieces of the RAND program of analysis provides an important building block toward a full understanding of the NAS initiative. Deficiencies in methodology, documented in the individual reports themselves, are more than compensated for by the in-depth understanding of all the different components of the initiative that the approach provided, by the ability to draw out the general relationships between the many parts of the system being constructed, and by the illuminating insights into real practice in real situations. Taken together, the set of RAND studies provides a cogent, consistent, and broad examination of the NAS initiative and offers useful and timely information to decisionmakers considering whole-school reform.

ORGANIZATION OF THIS STUDY

The rest of this book is divided into sections dealing with each major research phase and study. Chapter Two relies on RAND research from the development, demonstration and scale-up phases to de-

---

do so and it would have caused political problems to challenge the districts on this issue.

scribe the development of NAS, largely taken from Glennan (1998). It focuses on NAS as a whole and its evolution. Chapter Three focuses on changes to designs over the same period of time. It provides a synopsis of the findings concerning evolution of the designs based on Bodily (2001). Chapter Four discusses the findings from the scale-up phase on implementation and the factors related to it. It relies both on our quantitative studies (Berends, 2000; Berends and Kirby et al., 2001; Kirby, Berends, and Naftel, 2001) as well as the qualitative data from our case studies (Bodily, 1998; Chun, Gill, and Heilbrunn, 2001). Chapter Five discusses the findings concerning implementation and performance in a high-poverty urban school district, focusing on classroom instruction (Berends et al., 2002). Chapter Six describes in more detail the progress that NAS designs made in terms of raising students' academic achievement during the scale-up phase with results from school- and student-level analyses (Berends and Kirby et al., 2001; Berends et al., 2002; Chun, Gill, and Heilbrunn, 2001). Chapter Seven discusses the policy implications from RAND's studies on New American Schools for policymakers and practitioners at the federal, state, and local levels. The Appendix covers the methodologies used in the individual tasks and should be referred to by readers interested in more details than presented here.

The chapters list the contributors to the individual reports on which each chapter is based.

Afterword

This study concludes with an afterword by New American Schools. This afterword provides an update on NAS's new strategy and an overview as to where NAS stands today. This afterword represents NAS's point of view. It did not go through the rigorous peer review process that all RAND publications undergo.

Chapter Two

THE DEVELOPMENT OF NEW AMERICAN SCHOOLS
Thomas Glennan, Susan Bodilly

This chapter covers the evolution of NAS, both planned and un-planned. It offers more precise statements of NAS's goals and theories of action over time. It also provides details into decisions NAS made and why. Perhaps most importantly the chapter covers where NAS is now headed.

The information presented here was pulled from previous reports by RAND, especially Glennan (1998). The original work itself is based on the following data sources: document reviews; attendance and observations at NAS and design team meetings from 1991 through 2001; interviews over this same period with NAS, design team leads, district leaders, and NAS consultants about NAS's decisions and progress.

This chapter is organized around important decisions and actions associated with each phase of NAS activities as outlined in the introduction Figure 1.1 and Table 1.1. It covers the following:

- The NAS whole-school design concept;

- Activities during the RFP phase;

- NAS's decision to reduce the number of teams at the end of the development phase;

- Activities during the demonstration phase and NAS's decision to further reduce the number of teams;

- NAS's development of a scale-up strategy given what had been learned;

- The selection process wherein NAS chose 11 teams for funding;

- The selection of scale-up partners;

- Scale-up activities and experiences; and

- The current status of NAS.

NAS'S WHOLE-SCHOOL DESIGN CONCEPT

NAS was established in 1991 as a nonprofit funded by the private sector to create and support design teams. Some concepts of a design were already clear at that point. Its core premise was that all high-quality schools possess a de facto unifying design that allows staff to function to the best of their abilities and that provides a consistent and coherent education instructional program to all students. NAS thought the best way to ensure that lower-performing schools would adopt successful designs was to create design teams to develop "break the mold" designs that could be readily adopted by communities around the nation. A design "articulates a school's vision, mission, goals; guides the instructional program; shapes the selection and socialization of staff; and establishes common expectations for performance and accountability among students, teachers, and parents" (Glennan, 1998, p. 11).

It is important to make clear here that NAS was different in many respects from other types of reforms in that initially it did not want design teams to target specific populations, grades, or schools with peculiar characteristics. The designs were to cover grades K–12 for all schools and students.[1]

The design would be comprehensive, covering all aspects of the school and all students within the school. The design would provide coherence to the usually fragmented set of programs schools offered. Much of this would be done by carefully aligning high standards for all students with matched assessments, curriculum, and instruction. Some aspects of existing schools would disappear; others would gain precedence. But, whatever the mix, it would provide a coherent

---

[1]Early debates about the choice of developers or teams indicated concern for one particular design based on these grounds (RW) intended to develop a design for high-poverty, elementary schools only. Despite these misgivings, the design was accepted.

vision for administrators, teachers, staff, parents and students to follow on a path toward constant organizational improvement. These notions are contrasted with those of past programmatic approaches in Table 2.1.

Other of NAS's guiding principles were derived from its involvement with the private sector:

- The design developers (known in NAS as design teams), while needing some initial investment funds, would transition within three to five years to self-sufficiency based on fees for services provided.

- Schools adopting designs might need some initial investment funds, but sustaining design implementation would not incur additional costs over the normal operating budget.

- These efforts were expected to have immediate impacts. The private sector sponsors wanted results in the form of many schools adopting designs and showing improved student performance within a five-year period. At the end of five years, NAS was to go out of business.

NAS, with some understanding of the ambitiousness of its goals, planned a phased approach to its mission to see whole-school reform take root across the country. These phases, shown in Figure 1.1 and in Table 1.1 in Chapter One included an RFP and selection period, a development phase, a demonstration phase, and a scale-up phase.

REQUEST FOR PROPOSALS

The founders of NAS sought to both develop designs and support their spread throughout the country to schools seeking the means for significant improvement. NAS held a competition through an RFP process that brought in nearly 700 proposals from existing teams in

Table 2.1

Comparison of Whole-School Design-Based Assistance with Traditional Means of School Reform

Elements of Reform	School-Level Reform Using Design-Based Assistance	School-Level Reform Under More-Traditional Conditions
1. Development of a school vision	Starting point is choice of design; evolves through implementation. High standards for all required.	Not required. Reform typically centers on component of school program.
2. Focus of reform effort	The entire school. Seeks to create team with shared responsibility for high outcomes.	Usually subject matter or grades—sometimes governance, e.g., site-based management.
3. Duration of reform effort	Intense initial effort lasting 2–3 years, but reform is continuing process.	No set time.
4. Sources of technical assistance	Initial assistance largely from design team. Long-term assistance from sources deemed most effective by school.	No set pattern. Frequently provided by school district or local teachers college. Training sometimes provided by program vendors.
5. Source of curricular materials	Varies. Some design teams provide detailed materials; others provide frameworks for curriculum development; others use commercially available materials.	No set pattern. Frequently provided by school district or local teachers college. Training sometimes provided by program vendors.
6. Strategy for sequencing assistance	Strategy for sequencing actions is explicit. Design teams have different approaches.	None.
7. Conception of professional development	Professional development is integral to design. Implementation of design results in professional development. Network of like schools is key source of expertise.	Tends to be responsibility of individual staff member. Often dependent on district staff development policies.

Table 2.1—continued

Elements of Reform	School-Level Reform Using Design-Based Assistance	School-Level Reform Under More-Traditional Conditions
8. Organization of staff	Integral to design. Some transitional roles defined. School revises organization and staffing structure to meet its needs.	Tends to be function of district rules. Divided along disciplinary or programmatic lines.
9. Measurement of progress of reform	Benchmarks established by design team or by school with design team guidance.	Not usually explicit.

universities, to districts attempting reforms, to newly formed teams from private for-profit groups. NAS imposed several conditions on the designs and their associated teams:

- In creating designs, teams should not be limited by the constraints facing "real" schools in real districts, but rather let their imaginations develop truly innovative and provocative ideas.

- Designs had to enable all students to meet high standards. Designs geared toward a particular subgroup were not acceptable.

- The design should be adaptable to local circumstances. As stated in the proposal, "This is not a request to establish 'model' schools. The designs must be adaptable so that they can be used by many communities to create their own new schools" (NASDC, 1991, p. 21).

- While it was accepted that the designs would require funds to implement in a real school, the long-term costs of operating a design-based school should not be greater than those for operating an average school.

- Teams had to commit to a scale-up phase starting in 1995 where they would promote their design in schools across the country. A specific criterion for judging designs was "potential for widespread application and the quality of plans for fostering such application" (NASDC, 1991, p. 35).

Table 2.2 shows the general principles that NAS held at the beginning of this effort.

Table 2.2

Original NAS Principles and Concepts

Principle	Description
Private Funding	Initially, the effort was privately funded and supported—it was not a local or federal government policy or mandate. Ideally, schools and districts would enter into a relationship with a design team on a voluntary and well-informed basis.
Whole School	Designs were to be for "whole schools." This notion had two parts. First, the designs would be coherent, thoughtful sets of school-level policies and practices. The adoption and adept use of coherent, inter-related, and mutually reinforcing practices would be the antithesis of the fragmented programs and idiosyncratic teacher practices often found in schools. In addition, designs were to be for all students. They were not special programs targeted on specific populations to be added to the school's repertoire.
Adaptive Approach	NAS designs were not supposed to be perspective molds for model schools to ensure uniformity of practice. Designs were to adapt to local conditions and were to enable local communities to create their own high-performance schools.
Design Teams	Teams were deliberately created organizations of experts. NAS intended that teams would develop coherent designs and then work with schools in further ground-level product development to perfect those designs. Later, they would promote the use of their designs in schools across the nation. Nearly 700 potential teams responded to the RFP. The 11 initially chosen were mostly private nonprofit organizations connected to universities or research organizations. The exceptions were one for-profit firm, two districts, and one nonprofit without a research or university connection.
Multiple Designs	There was no one best school design, but many, depending on the needs of individual schools. Multiple teams would be supported, allowing schools a choice of designs.
Reasonable Costs	While it was understood that transforming schools might require investment funding, the operating costs of the schools after trans-formation were to be equivalent to those for the "typical" school in that community. In other words, "break the mold" designs were to be no more costly in daily operation than other schools, making them affordable to all districts.

Table 2.2—continued

Principle	Description
Market Driven	NAS would not be a self-perpetuating organization. From the beginning, it planned to "go out of business" after accomplishing its purpose. One consequence of this was that design teams had to become financially self-sufficient over time, creating their own client base to support their work. Thus, teams over the five-year time line to which NAS originally committed (1992–1997) would need to transform themselves from visionaries, to product developers, and finally to entrepreneurial organizations.

NAS DESIGN TEAM SELECTIONS

While NAS received nearly 700 proposals, only about 30 were responsive to the RFP. Those reviewing the proposals thought that most simply did not offer new approaches or pay attention to the NAS concept of design. The impression left was that most proposals were recycled requests for funding of existing programmatic approaches.

The 30 responsive proposals were considered carefully and potential awardees were asked to present their proposals to NAS in more detail. Eventually NAS selected 11 proposals for funding. These proposals and the associated teams are briefly described below. These descriptions date back to the time of the proposals. As the design teams have changed along with their designs, these paragraphs do not adequately or accurately describe design teams and designs today. The point of this chapter and the next is to examine some of the reasons behind the extensive changes that took place.

Authentic Teaching, Learning and Assessment for All Students: Newton, Massachusetts. ATLAS (or AT) was proposed by a team headed jointly by Ted Sizer, Howard Gardner, James Comer, and Janet Whitla. The design assumed that high-performing schools were not possible in the current bureaucratic structure. The design aimed to change the culture of the school to promote high institutional and individual performance through: (1) helping students acquire valuable habits of heart, mind, and work; (2) helping students develop deep understanding; (3) using only activities that are developmentally appropriate; and (4) creating a community of learners. The design required the establishment of a semiautonomous feeder pattern of high school, middle school, and elementary schools and significant development of a committee structure within schools and across schools. It did not prescribe standards or curriculum.

Audrey Cohen College: New York, New York. AC (now called Purpose-Centered Education: the Audrey Cohen College System of Education) was proposed by the College for Human Services in New York City led by Audrey Cohen. It emphasized adoption of a developmentally appropriate, transdisciplinary curriculum based on semester-long units focused on particular purposes for learning—not subject area. For example, kindergarten was dedicated to "We build a family-school partnership" and "We care for living things." Embedded in each purpose were content areas and essential skills. Semester-long purposes were to be generated by the design team along with significant guidance for curriculum development. But, teachers developed their own curriculum. Each purpose culminates in a constructive action taken by the class to serve the community. These purposes and actions become the guiding principles for the organization of the school.

Bensenville New American Schools Project: Bensenville, Illinois. The Bensenville project was proposed by the Bensenville School district in Illinois by a team that included union members, government leaders, business owners, parents, and others. It called for a complete rethinking of the classroom so that the entire community would serve as a campus. The instruction would be hands-on and project based, taking place at sites throughout the community. A Lifelong Learning Center would provide assessments of all community members' health and learning needs.

Co-NECT: Cambridge, Massachusetts. CON was proposed by the private for-profit firm Bolt, Berenek, and Newman with support from other partners such as Boston College. It focused on creating a school environment through the ubiquitous use of technology that would motivate children through interdisciplinary projects that extended outside the classroom walls. The design called for autonomy of the school and planning and budgeting by houses or grade levels within the school.

Community Learning Centers: Minneapolis, Minnesota. CLC was proposed by a coalition of education groups led by Public Schools Incentives, a private not-for-profit educational group. This design covered children from birth to 21. It was based on full school autonomy similar to that provided to charter schools using a contractual vehicle to maintain autonomy and accountability. It emphasized project-based learning, authentic assessments, and a student-led curriculum. It called for school-level provision of health and social services in community learning centers.

Expeditionary Learning Outward Bound: Cambridge, Massachusetts. EL was proposed by Outward Bound, a private nonprofit organization and led by Greg Farrell. It wanted to take the ideas espoused by Outward Bound and apply them to schools. These ideas included an interdisciplinary field-based curriculum, personalized instruction, and more-authentic assessments. Children would be in groups of no more than 25 students per teacher with the same teacher for three years. Schools would have no more than 350 students. Teachers would be required to develop their own curriculum. This curriculum would be largely in the form of long-term interdisciplinary projects known as expeditions with significant student choice as to topic and work. The projects would lead to authentic student products upon which their learning could be judged.

Los Angeles Learning Centers (LALC), now Urban Learning Centers: Los Angeles, California. ULC was proposed by a coalition of the Los Angeles Unified School District, the Los Angeles Educational Partnership (LAEP), the University of California–Los Angeles, the University of Southern California, and others. It was to be led by LAEP. The design called for the creation of preK–12 schools that provided for student educational, health, and social services needs. Each child would have mentors: community members, other school children, and teachers. Teaching would be thematic and project based with teachers developing curriculum. The design would develop and use its own standards. Students would be in small groups.

Modern Red Schoolhouse: Indianapolis, Indiana. MRSH was proposed by the Hudson Institute, a private not-for-profit organization. The design team would create a set of unique standards to be adopted by all its schools. Schools would adopt Core Knowledge curriculum in the elementary grades and use Advance Placement–type curriculum in the higher grades. The curriculum would be a mix of styles, with a significant increase in interdisciplinary units developed by teachers. Students would be in multiage, multiyear groups and have Individual Education Compacts that articulated personalized education programs. Student records, lessons, and assessments would be managed by a schoolwide computer system and teachers would use this to help manage personalized instruction as well as share curriculum units. The school would require complete autonomy from district control and parental choice of school.

National Alliance for Restructuring Education: Rochester, New York. NARE (now America's Choice) was proposed by the National Center for Education and the Economy and led by Mark Tucker. The design team promised to create New Standards for schools that included important workplace skills and that were matched to a set of assessments against which student progress toward the standards could be measured. The schools would have increased autonomy under districts and states that fundamentally restructured their education system along lines proposed in the Total Quality Management literature. But, students would be expected to meet the New Standards as assessed in the design team–developed system. Teachers would develop curriculum and instructional packages after learning about the New Standards and being exposed to best practices. Health and social service resources would be provided at each campus.

Odyssey Project: Gaston County, North Carolina. The design was proposed by the school district of Gaston County. The design team leader was the head of research and development for the district and all team members were employed by the school system with one exception. The design addressed needs of children ages 3–18 by including extensive interventions in preK years. The early interventions might include: prenatal monitoring and education for the mother; monitoring and diagnosis of preschool children to enable early interventions, parenting training, and nursery school and kindergarten. It proposed year-round schooling, use of Paideia instructional strategies, a high-technology environment, multigrade grouping, school-level provision of social services and health care, and required community service. Curriculum and instruction would be "outcomes based" and geared toward developing the multiple intelligences of all students.

Roots and Wings: Baltimore, Maryland. RW was proposed by the Johns Hopkins Center for Research on Effective Schooling for Disadvantaged Students, St. Mary's public schools, and the Department of Education for the State of Maryland. It covered only elementary grades. The roots part of the design would ensure that all children got coordinated, relentless attention to core academic areas from birth and onward. The design started in schools with the existing Success for All reading program and then incorporated two new components: one for math and the other for social studies and science. The overall design would develop all curriculum and detailed instructional practices for everyday use. The team would train teachers in its use. Schools would provide extended day care, health and family services, tutoring, site-based management, and parental choice.

DEVELOPMENT PHASE AND THE DECISION TO REDUCE THE NUMBER OF TEAMS

In 1992, the 11 teams were awarded contracts for a year of further specification and development of concepts. NAS indicated that specification and development was to have three important parts.

First, in that year, teams were to work their original 50-page proposals into the full range of ideas and materials needed by schools and districts to understand and implement the designs. NAS expected that the outcome of this phase would be a full and rich set of materials for each design describing for laymen and practitioners what they needed to do to set the design in motion in their schools or providing them with the actual materials to be used as in the case of a team-developed curriculum. The teams were to move past rhetoric and provide the substantive materials for implementation.

Second, teams had provided very little in the way of implementation strategies in their original proposals. NAS indicated this time was to be used by teams to develop their implementation approaches and to outline plans for Phase 3 as indicated above. For example, teams were to specify how schools would choose to align with a design; training regimes for teachers and principals; how schools would afford the design; and plans for the acquisition of needed materials and technology in schools.

Finally, NAS expected the teams to articulate how each intended to promote the goal of national diffusion of the designs and to indicate their ability to do so. NAS carefully warned teams that traditional means of presentation to research groups at national conferences was not what it had in mind.

Note that at this point in time, NAS has given relatively little thought to its theory of action; it had focused primarily on ensuring that design teams developed their own theories of learning. The upper third of Figure 2.1 shows NAS's theory of action at this point. Simply put, designs would be developed, schools would adopt them in some unspecified manner, and this would result in improved student outcomes.

By the end of the development year, NAS was experiencing funding difficulties (Glennan, 1998). It was uncertain as to whether it would have significant funding to proceed through its full initiative as originally planned. It began to look for ways to reduce its funding commitment. The most obvious were to reduce the number of teams or to reduce the average amount given to teams. It was fairly clear by the time of the decision to proceed to the demonstration phase, that NAS intended to cut teams. The question was: What would be the basis for that decision?

To help in this regard, NAS set out on fact-finding missions to understand the extent to which teams had made progress in the three areas indicated above. At this time NAS was a comparatively small organization, with only a handful of staff. It therefore had to rely on external help. It sent teams of NAS staff, RAND staff, and members of the NAS Educational Advisory Committee to visit design teams and assess them according to criteria developed by NAS.[2] Notes from these missions were assembled and reviewed internally by NAS. Design teams were also provided with opportunities to display, discuss, and present their progress verbally to NAS in extensive meetings. With these data, NAS moved to make its decisions.

---

[2]NAS created a group of educational advisors to act in a consultative capacity when called upon. These included policy experts, principals, teachers, and university professors.

RAND *MR1498-2.1*

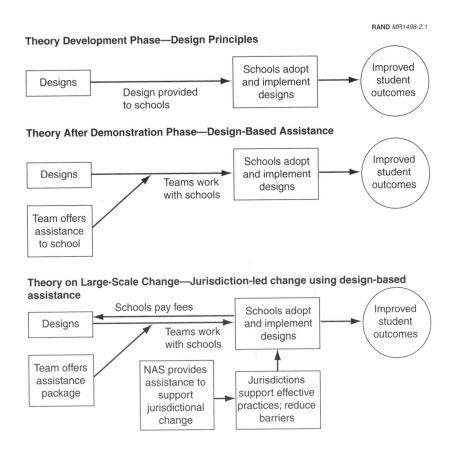

Figure 2.1—New American Schools' Evolving Theory of Action

In general, the review showed that most teams were well behind in their development. Some had struggled to develop a complete set of standards and assessment. Many had not completed this, nor had they gotten to the development of curriculum. Others who had adopted an existing set of standards struggled to develop the matched curriculum. RAND review indicated at the time a need for significant further development by all the teams (Bodily, 1996; Glennan, 1998).

Two teams, Odyssey in North Carolina and Bensenville New American Schools Project in Illinois, could be characterized as having "district based" or invented designs and "district led" teams. The proposals came from and were led by district personnel and focused on how those districts would reform themselves. Both proposals included ideas about "break the mold" schools, but they were centered in and peculiar to those districts' needs. Other design teams could be characterized as external providers (not part of the governmental structure of local education) or had a significant group of external providers leading the design.[3]

During the development year both of these district-led teams became embroiled in local political battles that centered on the designs (Mirel, 1994; Mickleson and Wadsworth, 1996). In both cases the district initiatives had led to reactions by forces against some of the constructs of the designs or against the manner in which the district had tried to accomplish change.[4] For example, some teachers and parents accused the central office in Gaston, North Carolina, of not allowing them to participate in the creation of the design and not allowing opportunities to hear their views about some of the constructs of the designs. NAS's fact-finding indicated that in both cases the districts had not effectively led the initiatives so as to build stakeholder support of the design. In both cases it was clear that the design could not go forward given the level of political antagonism evident from important constituencies. NAS's review of materials developed indicated that district staff time was being taken up in these political battles and not in the further specification and development of the design parameters.

NAS's reading of the proposals for development and diffusion for these two teams concluded that the district-led teams did not understand NAS's intentions concerning national scale-up or simply

---

[3]LALC was also "district based," but with a difference. The district was one of several partners to the effort. The teachers' union, a major not-for-profit reform group, and two universities were also co-partners. The not-for-profit evolved into the lead of the team. In this way the design was not tied exclusively to the dictates of the central office, rather it was an attempt of several actors to combine forces for reform.

[4]In one case, the unions became set against the design. In another, conservative religious groups were actively set against implementation of the design in their community.

did not choose to follow those intentions. The scale-up proposals focused on presentations at conferences and mailing of materials about the district-led efforts. They did not deal with how the design team would support implementation in other districts. In contrast, other teams talked of moving to schools throughout the country and of a strong implementation support system.

In June 1993, NAS dropped the two district-led teams and proceeded with nine teams that were not connected exclusively to specific districts or led exclusively by district personnel. NAS would no longer have teams whose ability to develop the design would rest so heavily on the team's ability to navigate the dangerous waters of local politics in a single district. In short, the lesson learned was that district-led designs were politically untenable and unscaleable.

The impact on the portfolio was straightforward. NAS would not support design teams led by a central office, nor would it support designs that were not transferable to schools or districts around the country. NAS would support only design teams that were external to the local governance structure. Only those teams that were serious about scale-up outside a "home" district or locality were acceptable.

THE DEMONSTRATION PHASE AND FURTHER REDUCTION IN THE TEAMS

The demonstration phase (from July 1993 to July 1995) was to be used by design teams to demonstrate that their concepts could be implemented in real schools and to work with schools to adapt the designs as needed for scale-up. In addition, the design teams were to submit business plans for expansion and scale-up at the end of this period by which NAS would judge their readiness to proceed. Clearly, all needed to do further development work in this phase as well.

A considerable grant from the Annenberg Foundation relieved some of NAS's budget constraints. But, NAS had a very business oriented board that had wanted to bring more business-like practices to schools. It emphasized the ability of teams to show performance and financial independence. In keeping with its business oriented philosophy, the board made clear to the NAS staff that it was not interested, and never had been, in promoting a group of financially dependent organizations. It insisted that the scale-up phase would include a move to fee-for-service by the teams. Thus, the NAS staff was encouraged to use its best judgments to delete teams that could not show an ability to deliver on the promises of the design, that had a limited potential market within the United States, or that could not show an ability to become financially independent from NAS.

NAS again set up a fact-finding team. The fact-finding team included NAS staff and members of the NAS Educational Advisory Committee. In addition, RAND reports on progress were used to assess each team's situation. At this time, RAND reported that the teams showed a great deal of variation in approach, stability, and ability to scale up (Bodilly, 1996). Four teams appeared to be able to implement their designs, while four others were having more difficulty. In addition, NAS staff's review of the business plans submitted by the teams indicated that several teams were not taking the switch to fee-for-service seriously. Several also did not address the issue of scale-up in a manner deemed acceptable by NAS.

CLC was identified as facing serious implementation challenges and also appeared to be reluctant to expand in a manner that NAS deemed acceptable. CLC had always been closely aligned with the charter school movement in Minnesota. It wished to expand, at least for the time being, only within the confines of Minnesota under the charter school laws of that state. From NAS's point of view the charter school focus limited the market of CLC, as did the state-based focus.

LALC (now ULC) was identified as being relatively behind in its development. At this point in time LALC was experiencing a leadership turnover and had not completed its design work. It was in a situation similar to the two district-based designs dropped earlier. It had strong ties to the central office and union, which were partners to the effort. It was very focused on solving the educational problems in the Los Angeles school district. And, its design development had suffered from the difficulties involved in building a collaborative effort among partners driven by local political concerns. It could not commit to a scale-up strategy outside of Los Angeles for several years, until it completed its design work. Later, it planned to remain within the Southern California area or near western states. By committing to this limited geographical area the LALC design team argued it could potentially reach a significant percentage of the school-age population of the United States and serve its target population of urban schools.

In July 1995, NAS removed CLC from its portfolio. It provided funding to LALC to complete its development, but did not invite it to be part of the NAS scale-up strategy. It offered to reconsider later whether LALC was ready to join the NAS scale-up initiative. Neither team would be part of the scale-up movement into partner jurisdictions in fall 1995. De facto, this removed the last of the district-associated teams from the portfolio (LALC) as well as one associated with the laws of a particular state (CLC).

As a final footnote to this progression, LALC continued its own development, eventually transforming itself into ULC. It further developed its materials through strong stable leadership and began to expand to districts within the Los Angeles basin. It continued to attend NAS conferences and meetings. It matured to the point that in 1997, NAS decided the team was ready for full participation in scale-up. It is now considered a fully participating NAS team. However, LALC/ULC did not take part in NAS's district scale-up strategy and did not expand outside of its original jurisdictions until very recently.

LESSONS AND THE STRATEGY FOR SCALE-UP

At the same time as NAS was considering its scale-up strategy, NAS leadership turned over for the third time. John Anderson, formerly of IBM and the Business Roundtable, became president of NAS. His thinking seriously guided the scale-up strategy. Anderson, through his own experiences and from growing evidence from the RAND work in the demonstration phase, was convinced that design teams had to become independent of NAS and that districts and states had to provide a supportive environment for the design concept to thrive.

The RAND work on the demonstration phase indicated that demonstration sites were having difficulties implementing the designs (Bodilly, 1996). One of the strongest lessons learned from the RAND work during the demonstration phase was that designs, by themselves, could not transform schools. Schools needed significant amounts of professional development, technical assistance, and materials geared to the design to implement. RAND found that sites that had received significant assistance from design teams progressed further in implementation. It coined the term "design-based assistance" (Bodilly, 1996) to capture this phenomenon.

Discussions at NAS led to the adoption of this notion as an important part of the package that design teams would offer during scale-up. Design-based assistance became a key component of the NAS initiative and distinguishes it from the more traditional approaches to school reform. Such design-based assistance includes:

- Giving schools a choice of designs with which to partner;

- Specified designs that clarify both the end outcomes for the school and also intermediate implementation steps;

- Assistance by the teams to the school in the form of professional development, training, materials, conferences, networks, and curriculum and instructional packages; and

- Payment by the school to the teams for these services.

Thus NAS emphasized the role of the external agent in enabling whole-school transformation, but also richened that role substantially. That enrichment would be supported by fees-for-services. This change in the theory of action is contained in the middle section of Figure 2.1.

Experiences in the demonstration phase also pointed to the need for a more supportive district infrastructure to aid implementation. NAS began to understand that school transformation could not occur unless there was strong district support. The concept of a supportive environment as developed by NAS included: school-level autonomy on budget, staffing and curriculum and instruction; high standards that matched those of the designs and matched assessments; significant sources of professional development funding and technology; systemic support for community services at the school level; and public engagement in educational reform (Bodilly, 1998; NASDC, 1997). These concepts had considerable overlap with the NARE district-level strategy.[5] Indeed, NARE and its advocates had heavily influenced Anderson and NAS in their thinking.

Another lesson learned by NAS, or beginning to be learned, was the extent of investment funding a school might need in order to implement a design. This varied among teams from $40,000 to $150,000 per year for three years (Keltner, 1998). Going into the scale-up period, the exact amounts were not known, but it was obvious that schools or districts would need access to significant discretionary funds to adopt designs using a fee-for-service basis.

Given the above, NAS decided on a strategy of scale-up in a limited number of districts with which it could work closely to support its designs and scale-up strategy.[6] It imposed four ideas on design teams.

- Teams would have to work in districts NAS chose and that were presumably supportive of the design concept (offered a supportive environment as defined above).

- NAS would oversee the process of choosing those districts and guiding the initial school selection process.

- Multiple designs would work within a single district.

- The teams would charge fees for design-based assistance. Not only would schools "buy" the design, more importantly, they would buy the services of the teams to help them implement the designs (design-based assistance).

This final addition to the theory of action for NAS is shown in Figure 2.1 in the bottom section. Here the emphasis is on how NAS would promote scale-up of the design-based assistance concept.

---

[5]While NAS rejected the district-led teams, it did not reject the need for a strongly supportive district environment. The NARE team was not district led. It was like the other remaining teams, an organization external to the school systems in which it worked. However, unlike the other teams, it had developed state and district concepts for a supportive environment.

[6]Design teams were also free to partner with schools outside of the NAS-selected districts.

SELECTION OF SCALE-UP PARTNERS

In a closed RFP process, NAS sent letters to 20 or so districts asking if they were interested in partnering with NAS in the scale-up phase. If so, the district was to apply in the form of a brief proposal for a partnership. NAS offered $250,000 per year for two years to each jurisdiction chosen. In each proposal submitted by jurisdictions, each claimed to have a history of significant restructuring and pledged to create an even more supportive environment for school transformation.

It should come as no surprise that the districts that responded to NAS's request for partners generally had one of two things in common. They were in states that had adopted or were moving to adopt standards and accountability systems that required districts to show improvement on students' assessments or were otherwise branded as low-performing districts within their states. Or, they tended to serve students from poverty backgrounds and had significant numbers of schools designated for schoolwide programs under Title I.

Title I is the largest federal education program, providing more than $10 billion annually to support school intervention and strategies for improving the learning opportunities of students at risk of education failure.

A critical change embedded in the reauthorization of Title I played a crucial role in providing impetus and support for the whole-school reform movement and NAS in particular. The 1994 reauthorization expanded the opportunities for schools to use Title I money for schoolwide programs to integrate services, strategies, and resources for comprehensively reforming the entire institutional program to meet the educational needs of all students in the school (the 1994 Improving America's Schools Act, see U.S. Department of Education, 1993; American Association of School Administrators, 1995; Borman et al., 1996; Wong and Meyer, 1998). Schoolwide programs, available for funding since 1988, allow high-poverty schools to use Title I money, combined with other federal, state, and local funds, to improve their entire educational program. The 1988 changes allowed this schoolwide designation for schools serving populations of students with 75 percent or more eligible for free or reduced-price lunch. The 1994 language expanded the schoolwide category to schools serving 50 percent or more of the students eligible for free/reduced-price lunch.

This gave a very specific set of schools the impetus and the discretionary funding needed to adopt design-based assistance: low-performing schools with significantly high levels of students from poverty backgrounds.

NAS chose ten jurisdictions to work with based on the proposals submitted: Cincinnati, Dade County, Kentucky, Maryland, Memphis, Philadelphia, Pittsburgh, San Antonio, San Diego, and a collection of five districts in Washington state. These partners really came from two different pools: NAS and NARE.

NARE, during its conception, development, and demonstration phases, had already entered into agreements with several different jurisdictions. It believed that individual schools could not implement and sustain design concepts by themselves. NARE thought that schools needed a network of other schools and districts working together to sustain changes. Given this district-level approach, NARE developed partnerships with several districts and states including Arkansas; Vermont; New York; Rochester, New York; White Plains, New York; San Diego, California; Pittsburgh, Pennsylvania; Kentucky; and Washington state. These partnerships predated the NAS jurisdiction strategy and in fact were the philosophical basis for that strategy. These NARE jurisdictions already had multiple schools implementing the NARE design in 1995. NAS worked with several of these original NARE jurisdictions, in concert with NARE, to make them NAS's partners as well. These included San Diego, Pittsburgh, Kentucky, and Washington state.

NAS meanwhile, representing the seven teams, entered into negotiations with six jurisdictions (that had not been NARE districts) during this time frame: Cincinnati, Dade, Maryland, Memphis, Philadelphia, and San Antonio.

NAS soon found that it had partnered with primarily urban districts with very challenged student populations and schools that had histories of being low performers. The Kentucky and Washington state schools are the exceptions. Several of the states involved had moved or were moving toward high-stakes testing regimes. This encouraged low-performing schools to search for the means to improve their test scores. It was exactly the combination of low performance and high poverty that allowed and impelled most of these districts to partner with NAS. They had performance problems, they had federal resources to devote to fixing it, and they had strong incentives to address their performance shortfalls. NAS appeared to be a solution that fit this market need.

SCALE-UP EXPERIENCES, 1995–1998

NAS worked with these jurisdictions for three years. As discussed by Glennan (1998), NAS's choice of districts was less than ideal, in part because the demographic and performance characteristics of the schools would be a challenge for the designs—some of which had not been developed in these environments.

More importantly, these districts, despite their rhetoric, had not in large part adopted the reform strategy outlined by NAS as supportive of whole-school designs. To remedy this situation, NAS promised the teams it would work with the districts to build a supportive environment. It proposed to aid, in some unspecified ways, partnering districts to provide more coherent and cohesive support for design-based schools (Glennan, 1998).[7]

This new strategy and role combined with the portfolio reduction to produce the following strategy of complex interactions necessary for success:

- Design teams would provide design and assistance to schools;

- NAS would market the designs in a set of districts that had stated they were willing to work with NAS and design teams toward a supportive environment, but were primarily motivated by a need to increase student test scores in low performing schools quickly;

- Districts would work to become more supportive of designs and design-based assistance; and

---

[7]As the years have gone by, NAS has aided districts in different ways. In particular, it has published a series of "How to" papers by various NAS staff and consultants offering guidance.

- Jointly, teams, NAS, and districts would develop a new system of education supportive of designs and improved student performance.

A major issue that immediately arose concerned how to measure progress in NAS schools. The districts were held accountable by state-mandated tests—usually standardized, multiple-choice exams. However, several design teams had spent considerable effort in searching out or developing more-authentic assessment systems and had developed standards and curriculum in a matched set with their authentic assessments.

In negotiations with NAS, the districts were demanding. The districts wanted the schools to be held to the standards in the districts and to be held accountable to the mandated state tests. Furthermore, districts stated that significant improvement would need to be made within three years or the districts would not continue with the designs. NAS promised, on behalf of the teams, that the schools adopting designs would use the state-mandated standards and assessments and produce dramatic results within three years.

Much of the rest of this book examines the lessons learned from this scale-up experience in more detail. NAS and the design teams struggled to implement their designs in these districts. In general, the teams quickly had to adopt their designs for the students and teachers in these districts (see Chapter Three) and struggle with fully implementing them when districts provided neither sufficient funding nor other supports needed by the teams or schools (see Chapter Four). The remaining chapters will explain the difficulties involved, the lack of strong implementation, and the need to revise the designs to deal with the populations of teachers and students being served. In the end about half of the NAS-related schools implementing designs did not show strong progress on state-level assessments in large part because designs were never implemented well enough to enable the schools to show progress (see Chapter Four).

The bottom line is that by 1999, most of the districts involved were no longer actively partnering with NAS, many schools had dropped the designs, and indications were that the design teams working in these districts had not been able to produce the results desired by the districts and schools. Despite this lackluster record, NAS persevered, took the lessons on the need for a supportive environment to heart, and made further strides in developing new concepts for education reform.

COMPREHENSIVE SCHOOL REFORM AND THE NEW NAS

NAS had started with a mission to go out of business after the scale-up phase. This decision had been postponed and reconsidered. In 1998, the NAS board decided to grant NAS further life by reconstituting it with a new board. In October 1998, a new board of directors and new CEO of the board were instated at NAS. The old NAS whose purpose was to develop designs was dismissed. A new NAS was created to promote design-based assistance and whole-school reform nationwide.

One of the major coups in this regard is the outcome of advocacy on the part of NAS, and other backers of the design approach, to establish further sources of funding for designs and design teams. NAS presented its views and lessons learned to staff of the U.S. Department of Education and Congress in 1997, when they deliberated language that would provide a source of funding for schools attempting whole-school reform. NAS was successful in getting some of its views incorporated into the federal program.

Budget authorization language in November 1997 furthered the implementation of comprehensive, whole-school reforms by establishing the Comprehensive School Reform Demonstration (CSRD) program, also known as the Obey-Porter legislation. The conference report acknowledged eight NAS designs, along with about ten others, as comprehensive school designs that were illustrative of the concept being promoted. These appropriations committed $145 million to be used to help schools develop comprehensive school reform based on reliable research and effective practices. The majority (83 percent in fiscal year [FY] 98 and 77 percent in FY99) of the funds are committed to Title I schools. Part of the money ($25 million in FY98 and FY99) was available to all public schools, including those ineligible for Title I, as part of the Fund for the Improvement of Education (FIE) program. Approximately 1,800 schools will receive at least $50,000 per year for three years under the CSRD program, beginning in FY98. There was an increase of $75 million for FY00 ($50 million in Title I/Section 1502 funds and $25 million in FIE funds) over the $145 million appropriated for FY98 and FY99, which will allow 1,000 additional schools to undertake comprehensive reform (see Kirby et al., in review; http://www.ed.gov/offices/OESE/compreform). In FY02 the appropriations had grown to $130 million.

This congressional language and the supporting documents clearly recognize several NAS contributions in the realm of school reform. The language of "comprehensive school reform" recognizes the NAS idea of whole-school reform based in a design. The financial package promotes the idea of an external agent supported by fee-for-service as an essential pathway to school improvement. The language embedded in supporting Department of Education documents echoes the notion of a supportive district environment. The ideas and concepts developed by NAS and others have found widespread acceptance through this program, and are having a growing impact in the field.

NAS now uses CSRD funding and the schoolwide provisions of Title I to support growth. Currently NAS encourages implementation of comprehensive school approaches in 4,000 schools through the implementation of designs with assistance from NAS teams. In addition, it has added several teams to its portfolio: Accelerated Schools Project, the Leonard Bernstein Center for Learning, and Turning Points. ULC, formerly LALC, is once again a full partner.

The New NAS

The CSRD program has in some ways lessened the need for NAS. Design teams no longer need the protection of NAS to grow. However, NAS now has announced four new goals (for more information see http://www.newamericanschools.org). The following paragraphs represent NAS's current program of activities.

Goal 1: Encourage the development of quality approaches, products, and services. NAS now attempts to promote quality products in several ways.

- In 1999, NAS convened a blue ribbon panel of educational and business leaders from across the geographic and political spectrum to develop a set of national guidelines of quality. Today these guidelines are available to help educators, parents, and others make decisions about an array of educational programs.

- In early 2001, NAS announced the creation of the New American Schools Development Network to identify and develop innovative educational products and services. The network is intended to help these education entrepreneurs to move beyond a few pockets of excellence and access the expertise and the resources they need to touch the lives of more and more students.

- The Education Entrepreneurs Fund, the financing affiliate of New American Schools, supports the NAS Development Network by making strategic investments in education providers producing quality products and services that can be delivered to large numbers of schools and students. The fund fills the capital gap in social investment by making loans to and investments in high-quality social enterprises that are often hard-pressed to access capital through traditional financial channels.

Goal 2: Create and support environments conducive to continuous school improvement. NAS now offers an array of consulting services through the New American Schools Services Network that is supposed to provide "end to end" assistance for states, districts, and schools working on comprehensive school improvement strategies. The NAS Services Network delivers its services through two client-focused divisions and three service area divisions: State and District Services; Charter and Contract School Services; Accountability and Evaluation Services; Special Education Services; and School Funding Services.

Goal 3: Share the latest research, best practices, and networking with schools. NAS has made plans to establish its own in-house, research arm called the Center for Evidence-Based Education and to continue its outreach efforts to share best practices and network with schools. It proposes to conduct applied research on the use of school improvement strategies in schools and at the state and district level. The center also intends to support the development of effective leaders for quality reform and promote the use of proven approaches to school improvement nationally.

Goal 4: Inform the national agenda through research and results. Since its inception, NAS has advocated for policies at all levels of government that support and enhance quality improvement strategies under way in schools. Its intent is to continue this tradition, using the best research and proven results to influence and shape decisionmaking by the public and private sectors as they seek solutions to help students reach their greatest potential.

SUMMARY

This brief overview of NAS's history parallels the findings from the literature cited earlier on external change agents. The design teams changed over time as NAS learned from its experiences, but NAS made forward progress in developing the teams and enabling them to function in a marketplace it helped grow through advocating federal funding. The most pivotal points in the evolution were:

- The early decisions to eliminate four designs that were not interested in NAS's goal of national scale-up or design teams as external assistance providers. This reemphasized NAS's view that schools and districts are likely to need outside help in reforming and that NAS teams would offer that type of assistance using a school-level focus. It also sent a signal that NAS meant business and was willing to make tough decisions such as paring down its portfolio to meet its goals.

- The recognition of design-based assistance as an essential concept in meshing NAS's theory of learning to its theory of action. NAS learned and then supported the concept that designs by themselves are not enough. Schools need significant assistance to implement designs and teams should provide this assistance.

- The development of the scale-up strategy. This development recognized the importance of district-level reform and a preexisting supportive environment.

- The press for funding sources for teams based on fee-for-service. NAS thought schools and districts would be willing to pay for effective, externally developed design-based assistance and design teams could operate and implement their designs in a competitive, fee-for-service market. This market-based approach proved to be unique and important in shaping the federal government's approach to reforms.

- The advocacy for a CSRD program. This activity moved NAS away from advocating solely for its design teams, and began its current program of advocating for whole-school reform more generally.

- NAS's consistent press for maintaining the quality of design services. NAS has held to this throughout in a unique manner, which is different from other education intervention developers. The notion that design teams should be held accountable for providing high-quality services and helping to improve student performance has led to increased performance over time.

Overall, NAS has had an influence on the education reform movement well out of proportion to its size. To this day, it remains a small organization with a handful of staff committed to the idea of whole-school reform. Nevertheless, NAS has contributed several important concepts to the reform debate by developing and promoting the growth of several design teams and their designs. It has also helped to spawn an educational reform movement embedded in the federal government's CSRD program.

Chapter Three

CHANGES IN NAS DESIGNS
Susan Bodilly

In contrast to the previous chapter, this chapter deals with the evolution of the individual designs themselves. Unlike the other research tasks with specific views of events in particular phases, this task covered a longer time period, from 1992 to 1998. It takes a case study approach using the designs as the unit of analysis to understand the changes to designs over time and why they occurred. Original designs submitted in 1992 are the starting place for the historical comparison. Newer documents, submitted to NAS and RAND, were used to mark the changes in designs at pertinent intervals. NAS in 1998 requested that design teams submit final design documents. These are used as the final point of comparison for the evolution.

This research relied on the accumulated data from previous studies, especially the interviews with design teams, document reviews, and implementation analyses. These data sources were reviewed comparing designs as they were first proposed to the latter documents describing the designs. Notes from yearly interviews with design teams were reviewed to understand the design teams' perspectives on why the changes were occurring. In addition, notes from our implementation analysis and site visits were reviewed for insights offered on actions taken by districts and schools in response to the teams. The initial draft was submitted to design teams for comment, an essential step in the process. Their insights and corrections were added to the analysis of design evolution.

In this analysis, we paid special attention to the concepts of comprehensiveness and coherence. The theory of learning embedded in the designs was premised on the need for comprehensive and coherent school designs that could provide a unifying vision to the schools. Over time, we looked for any signs that the designs had become more or less comprehensive and coherent. Internal inconsistencies or the promotion of extreme local adaptation would be indications that that a design was becoming less unifying in its vision.

This chapter first provides a rationale for why generally the designs could be expected to change over time taken from the implementation literature. It then reviews the findings from the analysis, looking at elements and their changes over time and then probable causes for the changes. Finally it draws out implications.

GENERAL VIEW OF WHY EDUCATION INTERVENTIONS CHANGE OVER TIME

The original design team proposals forcefully expressed ideals for the quality of teaching in the nation's schools and provided some specifics about how to meet those ideals. They blended progressive educational practices with more-traditional ones, and even a few conservative ones, into new combinations intended to produce constantly improving schools. They incorporated intentions by teams: to develop unique standards and assessments; to create curriculum and instructional strategies to support those standards; to develop better ways to group students to promote learning; to demand significant school-level autonomy; to require parental choice of schools; and to provide health services at the schools. They represented a heady brew of some of the most innovative ideas by some of the most well-known educators and some of the most practical tried and true methods. In themselves, they are of interest as historical documents of what passed for innovation at the time.

They are more interesting because by the end of the scale-up phase, the designs had changed dramatically from these original plans. Some of these ideals remained in the design team documents; many did not. This phenomenon has been seen before in education and in other attempts at organizational improvement where innovations change slowly over time, often in unexpected ways.

This result presented an opportunity to explore why the education system lends itself to this phenomenon of retraction, mutual adjustment, or wandering innovation. RAND analyzed the evolution of designs to understand what changes had taken place and why. In part this was necessary to be able to understand implementation and ultimately whether the designs had effects in schools. Just as important, we believed that these changes and the reasons behind them might offer important lessons to groups attempting education reform.

In judging the effects of these types of adaptations, past policy analysts looked for strict adherence to the original policy or policy fidelity (Goggin et al., 1990)—in this case strict development of the design as originally outlined. For the purposes of this chapter we propose a different scheme that accords with the original ideas of the RFP.

The comprehensive design was to align the standards, assessments, curriculum, instruction, professional development, and governance components of a school and supporting policies into a complementary whole that worked to produce a coherent and effective educational experience for students to enable improved student performance on multiple dimensions. The operative words are *coherent* and *complementary*, characteristics that could lead to a *comprehensive* whole. The designs after several years might change, but they should still be coherent. If, as they adapted or as they were implemented, the designs become incoherent with internally inconsistent components, then the concept of a design itself is brought into question.

The literature on external change agents provides insights into what expectations were reasonable for NAS as it proceeded; however, NAS was not necessarily aware of these. Starting in 1991 with the creation of design proposals, one might have reasonably expected the following:

- The number and emphasis of the teams could be expected to change given their dependence on NAS. As with other efforts of this kind, the livelihood and political fortunes of the parent organization or major funding source would affect the practices of the funding recipients. The development and funding picture of NAS would have an effect on the teams themselves and their ability to meet their vision.

- The designs and their theories of learning including their notions of standards, assessment, curriculum, and instruction (Fullan, 1999) could be expected to have significant further planned development over time. NAS chose a developmental approach and expected teams to carefully plan further development needs such as more fully articulated curriculum packages aligned to more fully developed standards, etc.

- Significant changes to designs and design teams could be expected because of unplanned mutual adaptation during the demonstration and scale-up phases as teams interacted with local districts and schools. Language in the RFP implied that NAS expected the design teams to learn from their experiences in real schools during the first several years and further improve their designs to ensure the final outcomes desired—significant student performance increases. This benign view of mutual adaptation emphasizes that the end product of change would still result in comprehensive and coherent designs leading to improved performance, but that the implementing site's fidelity to the specifics of the design would vary from locale to locale.

- It could also be expected that adaptation to local district politics and prerogatives, poor communication by design teams about their designs, shifts in funding, leadership turnover, and competing priorities would lead, in some instances, to incoherence and fragmentation as teams and schools struggled to make progress. Alternatively, schools might lack the capacity to undertake design-based reforms. School staff might not have the time or capability to comply with the design requirements and without further support might fail in their implementation. This equally plausible scenario was not recognized in the RFP.

- While the RFP asked for implementation strategies, few teams focused on these in the proposal stage (Bodilly, 1996, 1998). The literature indicates that these would have to be developed for the teams to be successful in implementing across many schools. Thus, it could be expected that teams would create more fully developed implementation strategies over time, especially ones that might address issues of teacher capacity or lack of funding. In addition, these implementation strategies might become more powerful interventions than the original designs, under certain conditions.

We now turn to the review of the changes made to designs. We then summarize the types of changes that took place and why. We end by summarizing the implications for other types of reform efforts.

FINDINGS

Our review of design changes and why they occurred bore out the expectations outlined above and reinforced the earlier literature on external change agents. Indeed, during the NAS initiative from 1991 to 1998, the NAS portfolio of designs changed, the designs themselves changed, and strategies for implementation that were not in the original proposals developed. We found that these changes were driven by: planned development of the teams; adaptations to teacher and student needs in the scale-up districts; adaptations to the generally non-supportive policy environment in the scale-up districts; and learning from the teams.

Some of these adaptations and developments appear to have positively affected the concept of a design, making the designs more adaptable to local circumstances, implementation more easily achieved, and the design elements more internally aligned with one another. Other changes appear more problematic as they seem to lend themselves to maintaining or increasing the incoherence in schools rather than unifying schools behind a single vision.

Intervening Experiences

Several experiences or contextual factors proved crucial to the adaptations made to the designs from 1992 to 1998. We cover a few examples here to help the reader understand the interactions that took place that helped shape the designs from their original ideas to where they stood as of 1998.

Standards, Assessment, and Accountability Development. When NAS began, few states and districts had adopted standards and assessments. Therefore, each design team had taken pains to discuss what standards it would use as the basis for its design, how it would develop them, and how it would develop assessment systems to match. Each argued how it would carefully match curriculum and instruction to these standards. Teams began the development of their standards or meshed together existing sets from the few professional societies standards that existed.

By 1998, NAS was riding a wave of state-mandated standards, curriculum, assessments, and accountability. In particular, the NAS district partners had state or district standards that they had taken pains to develop and begin to implement. Given high student mobility rates in several districts and high-stakes accountability mechanisms in place, these districts insisted that design teams meet the state or district standards and use those assessments. By 1998, regardless of what their original stance on development of their own standards had been and of what progress they had made toward that development, all teams agreed to use existing standards and assessments in the partner districts and changed the language of their designs to indicate that the design standards and assessments would be accommodated to the districts in which the teams worked.

Curriculum and Instruction. The teams took varying stances on curriculum and instruction in their proposals, but one theme was clear: Curriculum and instruction were to be aligned with standards into a coherent whole. Most favored at least some significant amount of time in the school day or year dedicated to project-based learning, expeditions, or interdisciplinary exploration. Several teams required that teachers develop this curriculum using the design team standards. In addition, some had significant parts of the curriculum written into prescribed units or topics to be covered. Adoption of this curriculum required the use of specific textbooks or design team–supplied materials. Pedagogy favored the use of block schedules, flexible space, nonstandard reading and resource materials, and up-to-date technology. In short, the design teams, even those with prescriptive materials, favored a very rich and stimulating approach with significant need for teacher time and flexibility. With the exception of the RW design, none had developed or provided basic skills acquisition programs.

The districts in which the teams worked immediately challenged these design tenets. First, several districts, given their student populations, were focused on basic skills acquisition. They demanded design teams provide more curriculum and instruction geared toward basic skills acquisition. In some districts, all schools were forced to adopt districtwide textbooks and basic skills acquisition programs. This was reinforced by the growing need among these schools to perform well on state assessments that tested basic reading and math skills. Second, teacher time for curriculum development was highly constrained in all districts.

During the development and demonstration phases, design teams continued in the development of curriculum and instructional practices as promised. When they began working in the scale-up school districts, however, this progress slowed considerably. In the face of these demands and teacher needs, the teams oftentimes made concessions in their design documents for adopting existing district-mandated basic skills curriculum. Alternatively, they quickly adopted existing basic skills packages as part of their designs.

In addition, given the lack of time for teachers to individually develop curriculum, the teams began to develop more curriculum units or to move away from notions of teacher-developed curriculum toward teachers sharing existing units. This cut down on the total amount of teacher time in any given school needed to implement the design. It did, however, move away from some teams' original notions that teachers needed this curriculum development experience to become better teachers. Oftentimes in actual implementation, the design curriculum and instructional strategies were confined to social studies and science periods after the teachers had delivered the district-mandated math and language arts curriculum.

Other Elements of the Designs. Similar patterns occurred for other elements of the designs, including student placement and grouping, professional development, governance, and supporting services. For example, even during the demonstration phase it became clear that districts would not give schools the autonomy (including budgetary and staffing control) required by several designs. It also became clear that the local context in many areas would not allow schools to develop the health and other support services at school sites that some designs had described. Teachers often did not understand the reasons behind certain student placement practices and refused to implement them. Design teams began to drop these notions from design documents or at least removed strong statements concerning them. With a few exceptions, the designs were changed to drop many of these elements or to take more-accommodating stances.

Assistance and Support to Schools. While many of the elements of the designs became clouded in response to working in the scale-up districts, at least one area blossomed—the development of implementation strategies and supports. Here the scale-up experiences pushed the teams to provide more services and more assistance. Working with demanding schools with low capacity for change, design teams concentrated individual team efforts on the development of assistance packages and implementation supports—better articulated descriptions of the designs, a process for selecting designs, specific fee information and assistance choices, professional development options, training supports, curricular materials, visits and networking with other design-based schools, newsletters, and websites. In particular, NAS design teams found the introduction of the intervention into the school was crucial to the eventual success of the effort. The teams attempted to improve this process and the materials supporting it to encourage informed choice on the part of teachers. However, district context and resources still heavily influenced the process in each locale.

Quality Assurance. The teams made strides in quality assurance through the significant development of what came to be known as "benchmarks." This came about at least in part as an adaptation to the demands by districts and the clients for accountability. Schools had reported in earlier phases that they did not understand what was expected of them. In particular, they wanted to know what type of changes were expected and when. Later in the scale-up phase, districts asked the same questions. They wanted to know how to gauge the progress of schools in terms of implementation. The designs began to develop such information about milestones in implementation—commonly referred to among NAS associates as benchmarks or "implementation checklists."

Benchmarks or checklists began to perform several functions. First, they offered the opportunity of better communication of expectations between design teams, schools, and districts as to what needed to be accomplished and when. Second, they could be used by evaluators, such as the University of Memphis in the case of the Memphis City School system, to measure implementation. Third, they could be used by design teams to measure and understand the progress of schools and to help improve their assistance to ensure strong implementation. Thus, it was through client demand that an important quality assurance mechanism came about.

Yet, districts have also inadvertently limited the furtherance of quality assurance. By insisting on one accountability measure—performance on mandated tests—districts have influenced teams' development of assessment components. Teams had little incentive to develop unique tests or assessments geared to their more complex performance expectations. They had every incentive to accept the tests, but still advocate for curriculum and instruction that teaches more complex or interdisciplinary approaches than those measured by the mandated tests.

SUMMARY AND POLICY IMPLICATIONS

Our analysis found that designs changed over this time period in several ways: planned development; response to the needs of students and teachers in the schools served; adaptation to conflicting policies, rules, and regulations; and complete reconceptualization of the design. We found the following:

All designs continued in their planned development. During early phases, design teams developed their own standards or adapted others. Throughout the initiative, schools and teams developed significant amounts of curriculum that could then be shared among new schools. Teams improved processes for the professional development of teachers.

Interactions with students and teachers in the scale-up districts led to unplanned adaptations. The experiences of going to scale-up in large, poor, urban districts led to the adoption or development of basic literacy and numeracy programs and the development of processes to train teachers to develop rubrics for assessing student work against state or district standards. Lack of teacher time and capability led all teams to further develop their assistance packages and to develop curricular and other materials more suited to this group of teachers and students.

Interactions with existing policy environments resulted in further unplanned adaptations. Designs adapted significantly to the pressures posed by states, districts, schools, and unions to meet the existing regulatory, organizational, and cultural environment. The reality of working in the scale-up districts drove design teams to gradually lengthen implementation schedules, drop elements of their design, or move from required activities to principles to be worked toward. In particular, designs now generally accept state or district standards, assessments, and mandated basic skills curriculum. They also work within the level of autonomy that is normal within the district. The exception is the NARE design, which did not have a gradual adaptation to districts. Rather, it held to its design until it formally reconceptualized the entire design and dropped the old design.

Adaptation has led to the probability of significant local variation among schools using the same design and potential incoherence in design-based schools. The accommodating stance taken by most designs in their newer versions of design documents allows significant variation in sites associated with a single team. Teams allow mandated standards, assessments, curriculum, and other professional development to substitute for their own. This raises the probability of the incoherence of the schools' programs. Allowing a large range of implementation around elements of design instead of strong adherence to design principles increases the probability that implementing schools will still have fragmentation and incoherence as individual parts of the design adapt to already existing fragmented structures.

Consistent with expectations set up in the literature review, the designs did adapt over time. While some of the development in the designs that took place has been positive from the point of view of enabling schools to improve, other developments appear less likely to help schools. For example, the growth in the assistance packages, the further development of curricular units, and the development of protocols for school choice of design all appear to be positive adaptations. The development of basic skills curriculum also is positive if it is well meshed with principles of the design and not simply a quick add-on to meet district demands. Other changes, while understandable, remain more problematic. This includes the less-than-thoughtful mix of standards, curriculum, instruction, and assessment now permitted by the design documents. While the standards movement as a whole might raise the achievement bar nationally, individual schools implementing designs in the above fashion will continue to have an unintegrated mix of standards, curriculum, and assessments.

In part, this discussion is undertaken at this point to help readers understand what occurred in implementation in the scale-up phase and why implementation and performance results might not be as dramatic as expected. A major element—a coherent design—was often missing or was constantly in the process of being revised. It should also point to the fact that the design itself was not the only intervention, but as time went on, the implementation assistance, what NAS termed "design-based assistance," became an important part of the intervention. Consistent with the literature, improved student outcomes could be less a function of the designs' adoption, especially given the weakened nature of many of them, and more a function of strong assistance given to the schools in strategic planning and implementation.

Chapter Four

IMPLEMENTATION OF NAS DESIGNS DURING THE SCALE-UP PHASE

Sheila Nataraj Kirby, Mark Berends, Scott Naftel,
Christopher McKelvey, Susan Bodilly, JoAn Chun,
Brian Gill, Jodi Heilbrunn

This chapter examines implementation of designs during the scale-up phase. First, we provide an overview of the schools in which scale-up occurred in order to set the context for understanding implementation and performance. The second section describes the research questions and provides a brief summary of the methods used by the various studies of implementation during the scale-up phase. These methods are described in considerable detail in the Appendix. This section also lists some caveats on the findings of the longitudinal analysis. The third section presents our findings on the levels of implementation achieved by the scale-up schools. The final section describes some of the important factors that affected implementation and some of the reasons why some schools eventually dropped designs.

AN OVERVIEW OF NAS SCHOOLS

Understanding the progress of NAS sites, particularly in terms of implementation and their performance on achievement tests (discussed in the next chapter), requires an understanding of where the schools were before implementing a design. Most of the schools receiving design team assistance could be considered socially and academically disadvantaged in terms of poverty, racial-ethnic composition, climate, and student test scores. The NAS sites in our sample were below "average" when comparing a number of school characteristics with national norms (Berends, 1999). For example, as Table 4.1 shows, the NAS schools in Cincinnati, Dade, Memphis, Pittsburgh, and San Antonio were serving mostly poor student populations—over two-thirds of the students were eligible for free/reduced-price lunch at these NAS sites. Philadelphia used a more stringent measure of poverty (percentage of students receiving benefits under the Aid to Families with Dependent Children program); hence the somewhat lower poverty rate in these schools. Design teams in Kentucky and Washington state were assisting schools that were more affluent than the national average. If these latter schools were excluded from the sample, the school poverty composition of the NAS sample increases to 68 percent.

The NAS design teams in Cincinnati, Dade, Memphis, and San Antonio were assisting schools that had a vast majority of minority students. By contrast, the NAS schools in the states of Kentucky and Washington are mostly non-Hispanic white schools. If the Kentucky and Washington schools were removed from the sample, over 80 percent of the students in NAS schools would be minority.

When examining implementation and performance of the NAS schools, it is important to consider the particular challenges that NAS design teams face when implementing their design. For the 104 schools that constitute the sample for our implementation analyses (see the Appendix for the derivation of the sample), Table 4.2 shows selected school characteristics by design team. MRSH and RW tend

Table 4.1

Comparison of School Composition: NAS Schools Versus Jurisdiction Schools, 1994–1995

	Percent Free/ Reduced-Price Lunch		Percent Minority	
	NAS Average	Jurisdiction Average	NAS Average	Jurisdiction Average
Cincinnati	74.9	58.0[a]	71.3	69.0
Dade	83.6	59.3	95.3	87.0
Kentucky	50.4	40.3	23.2	11.1
Memphis	80.2	66.0	89.6	86.0
Philadelphia	68.1	42.0[a]	56.4	80.0
San Antonio	99.2	91.1	95.0	95.0
Washington state	8.5	10.3[a]	13.2	16.3

[a]Data obtained from Common Core of Data for students on free lunch only.

to be in the poorest schools, while AC and RW tend to be in the schools with the highest percentage of minority students.

High student mobility is likely to have an adverse effect on implementation as well as school performance. As is evident from Table 4.2, highly mobile student populations characterize many of the schools that design teams are assisting. For example, nearly one in five students in RW and CON schools is likely to move during the academic school year.[1]

The distribution of the 104 schools across levels reveals that 64 percent are elementary schools, 14 percent are middle schools, and 14 percent are high schools. Eight percent are mixed levels.

In terms of school climate, NAS principals reported greater problems with absenteeism and school readiness when compared with the nation's principals (for details see Berends, 1999). School readiness included principal reports about problems such as students coming to school unprepared to learn, poor nutrition, poor student health, student apathy, and lack of academic challenge.

Table 4.2

Selected School Characteristics, by Design Team

	Free/Reduced-Price Lunch	Minority	Mobility	English Language Learners	Number
	Percent				
AC	79.6	95.8	7.8	2.8	5
AT	47.2	50.3	14.9	4.4	17
CON	71.9	80.6	19.3	1.2	12
EL	82.9	80.8	17.8	4.9	16
MRSH	88.1	84.3	13.4	3.9	7
NARE	40.3	19.5	10.3	2.0	32
RW	88.2	88.9	20.0	0.1	15
NAS Average	63.9	59.0	14.5	2.6	104

_____

[1]Mobility rates are based on the following question in the principal survey: "On average, what percentage of your total student body enrolled at the beginning of the school year are still enrolled at the end of the school year?" Percentages in Table 3.5 are calculated as 100 minus this reported percentage.

In general, our data indicated that the majority of NAS sites were located in low-performing, urban school districts. Not surprisingly, within these districts and with few exceptions, the NAS design teams began assisting schools that were scoring at or below the district average on the district- or state-mandated tests.

STUDIES OF IMPLEMENTATION: RESEARCH QUESTIONS, METHODOLOGY, AND LIMITATIONS

In 1995, RAND began an evaluation of the scale-up of NAS designs to many schools. The longitudinal evaluation of the scale-up phase covers years 1995 to 2000 and addresses five major questions:

- What was the level of implementation of NAS designs across this set of early-implementing NAS schools two to five years after scale-up? Has implementation increased over time? Does implementation differ by jurisdiction and design team?

- Has implementation deepened over time across schools, as measured by the change in the within-school and between-school variance of reported implementation levels between schools?

- What are the factors—in terms of teacher, school, design team, and district characteristics—that help explain the variation in implementation across schools and jurisdictions?

- Among schools that dropped the NAS designs and for which we have data, what factors contributed to this decision?

- Does the adoption of NAS designs result in any changes to student and school outcomes?

Our findings with respect to questions 1–4 are addressed in this chapter. Question 5 is the focus of Chapter Six.

As we showed in Chapter One, RAND's program of implementation studies has included:

- 1996–1997: Case studies in 40 schools two years into scale-up to analyze implementation and the role that districts play in impeding or enabling comprehensive school reform (Bodilly, 1998);

- 1995–1999: A longitudinal analysis of between 70 and 100 NAS schools that began implementing early on in the scale-up phase, for which data on implementation and performance were gathered from principals, teachers, and districts (Berends and Kirby et al., 2001; Kirby, Berends, and Naftel, 2001); data collected from these schools cover the period two to four years after scale-up;[2] and

- 1999: A case study analysis of what factors contributed to performance differences in high-implementing NAS sites five years after scale-up, using a matched set of schools (matched on the basis of design, district, grade span, years of implementation, and implementation level, as measured by our surveys but validated by the design teams). One school was high performing and the other was not.

The methodology for each of these studies is discussed in some detail in the Appendix.

Limitations of the Study

It is important to understand the limitations of our sample and findings drawn from analyses of this sample of schools. For many of the design teams, these were the first schools to which they had pro-

---

[2]In addition, because the longitudinal sample focused on early-implementing schools, RAND collected data from a freshened sample of schools that began implementing NAS designs after 1995–96. However only four jurisdictions—Cincinnati, Memphis, San Antonio, and Washington state—agreed to participate in this data collection effort, and 46 schools in these jurisdictions responded to the principal and teacher surveys. Although we analyzed data from these schools, the analyses did not substantially change the results from those reported here. These results were not included in the set of reports on implementation, but provide some assurance of the robustness of our findings.

vided assistance with implementing their designs on a fee-for-service basis. In addition, at the beginning of scale-up in 1995, most of the design teams reported to RAND that their designs were still unfinished. As a result, the early years of implementation on which we report saw many changes in both the designs and the assistance provided as the teams and the schools gained experience.

The strategy that NAS developed for scale-up (NASDC, 1997) focused on a small number of jurisdictions that persuaded NAS that they possessed what NAS called "supportive operating environments" in which the designs could be implemented. In fact, for the most part, these districts did not possess such environments. They had limited understanding of whole-school reform and the sort of design-based assistance that NAS design teams were intending to provide. The districts, NAS, and the design teams collectively and individually invented procedures and policies for design teams and the assistance they provided as the implementation unfolded. For example, districts varied widely in the processes set up for matching schools and designs, the contracts set up with designs, the services to be acquired, and the ways they monitored implementation of the designs (Bodilly and Berends, 1999; Bodilly, 1998).

In short, the early years of scale-up continued to be a time of uncertainty. There was some chaos and a great deal to be learned on the part of NAS, designs, districts, and schools. Thus, this report documents experiences that may differ from those of schools beginning implementation today. NAS and the design teams might have matured due in large part to the lessons learned about the ways in which jurisdictions, design teams, and schools must work together (Bodilly and Berends, 1999; Bodilly, 1998).

While the fact that designs were evolving over time as they gained experience and adapted to local contexts makes a longitudinal evaluation difficult, we believe that the information obtained in following these schools still offers valuable lessons, particularly for CSRD schools adopting a variety of school-reform models in many differing environments. Thus, when interpreting the implementation findings, it is important to keep in mind these features of the population of schools we have studied.

IMPLEMENTATION LEVELS IN NAS SCHOOLS

Measuring Implementation in the Case Study Analysis

The study created an implementation scale based on common elements of the designs. These common elements were curriculum, instruction, assessments, student assignments, and professional development. We tracked progress on all these elements, as applicable. We rated progress in an element using a straightforward scale, as follows:

0 = **Not Implementing.** No evidence of the element.

1 = **Planning.** The school was planning to or preparing to implement.

2 = **Piloting.** The element was being partially implemented with only a small group of teachers or students involved.

3 = **Implementing.** The majority of teachers were implementing the element, and the element was more fully developed in accordance with descriptions by the team.

4 = **Fulfilling.** The element was evident across the school and was fully developed in accordance with the design teams' descriptions. Signs of institutionalization were evident.

Constructing a Core Implementation Index[3]

In our longitudinal analyses, we used a core implementation index to measure the average level of implementation in NAS schools. The core implementation index is a summative scale of teacher responses as to the degree to which the following described their school (on a

---

[3]In our earlier report, Berends and Kirby et al. (2001), we also developed a design team–specific implementation index that measures implementation of both shared and some unique aspects of the designs. The design team–specific index allowed us to measure implementation of each design on components that are unique to and emphasized by the design. The shortcoming of this index is that it is not directly comparable across designs because it varies both in terms of items and number of items included in the index. The details of this index are provided in the Appendix .

scale of 1–6, with 1 = does not describe my school, and 6 = clearly describes my school):[4]

- Parents and community members are involved in the educational program;

- Student assessments are explicitly linked to academic standards;

- Teachers develop and monitor student progress with personalized, individualized learning programs;

- Student grouping is fluid, multiage, or multiyear;

- Teachers are continual learners and team members through professional development, common planning, and collaboration; and

- Performance expectations are made explicit to students so that they can track their progress over time.

Teacher responses were averaged across a school to obtain the school mean level of implementation. We analyze this overall implementation measure for two reasons:

First, the core function of schools is teaching and learning. Therefore, we selected those teacher-reported implementation indicators that were related more directly to influencing what goes on in teachers' lives and inside classrooms. From an organizational perspective, classroom instruction is the core technology of school organizations and the primary mechanism through which learning occurs (Gamoran et al., 1995; Gamoran and Dreeben, 1986; Parsons, 1959). It is this core function of schools that the designs ultimately want to influence and it is this aspect of implementation that our overall implementation index aims to measure.

Second, we want to examine factors related to implementation, and this summary measure allows us to present our results in a parsimonious manner.

---

[4]The alpha reliability of this index was 0.81. The range of correlations for the individual items was 0.21 to 0.57.

However, measuring progress in implementation broadly across a wide set of schools in several partnering jurisdictions involved a number of challenges (Berends and Kirby et al., 2001; Kirby, Berends, and Naftel, 2001), including the uniqueness of the designs and the fact that the designs were still evolving. The Appendix contains a more detailed discussion of these issues.

In the analysis sample of NAS schools that we examine, small sample sizes for some design teams make traditional tests of statistical significance somewhat more difficult to apply. That is, with larger sample sizes we would have more power to detect differences and effects. Thus, we focus on what appear to be educationally substantive differences where appropriate.

Despite these challenges, evaluation remains an important component of any effort to change schools, and it is important to develop and refine sets of indicators that are informative not only for researchers, but for design teams, educators, and policymakers.

Thus, in order to address our questions about implementation stated above, we developed the core implementation index described earlier to broadly measure implementation of the *major*, shared components of the designs across the sites. The core implementation index is useful for understanding the progress of NAS schools during the scale-up phase.

Findings

In general, no matter which method we used—case study analysis or the core implementation index—we found that implementation levels were less than ideal in schools adopting the NAS designs.

Two Years After Scale-Up. RAND's early case studies found that schools varied considerably in the level of implementation achieved two years into the five-year scale-up effort. *Generally, about half of the 40 schools examined in the case study research were implementing at targeted levels (levels desired by teams, NAS, and districts) while the other half were below this level (Bodilly, 1998). The level of implementation varied by design team, district, and school characteristics.*

Four Years After Scale-Up. Schools responding to the longitudinal surveys showed similar findings with less-than-high levels of implementation, even after four years into the scale-up period. The following indicates the findings from the survey sample:

Implementation increased modestly from 1997 to 1999. The between-school variance decreased somewhat over time, and the within-school variance increased. In order to make it easier for the reader to gauge the magnitude of the changes over time, we calculated standardized z-scores based on the mean and standard deviation of the 1997 core implementation index. This allows us to represent changes using a common metric. The mean implementation index was 4.14 in 1997 with a standard deviation of 0.61. Thus, the standardized mean for 1997 is zero, with a standard deviation of 1.

Figure 4.1 shows the distribution of the core implementation index for all 71 schools in the longitudinal sample across the three years of data, using a standardized z-score based on the mean and standard deviation of the 1997 core implementation index.[5] The mean implementation index rose modestly by about 0.25 of a standard deviation in 1998, and by 0.29 of a standard deviation in 1999. The difference between 1997 and 1999 was statistically significant, using a paired t-test for means.[6]

The spread declined over time as well, as can be seen from the figure. Although not shown here, the variance in mean implementation among schools declined over time. The standard deviation declined from 0.61 in 1997 to 0.57 in 1998 and 0.52 in 1999. This decline was

------

[5]This graph and some of the others that follow are portrayed with box-and-whisker diagrams, which show the distribution of the particular indicator being examined. In a box-and-whisker diagram, the line in the box is at the median value—half the values fall above the line and half fall below. Each "box" captures the middle 50 percent of the distribution. The lines, called "whiskers," at each end of the box show the range of scores beyond the upper and lower quartiles. Outliers are indicated by the shaded circles. The box-and-whisker plot thus allows us to compare the centers (median or center of the box), spread (measured by the interquartile range or the height of the box), and tails of the different distributions.

[6]These are calculated as follows: The mean implementation index was 4.29 in 1998; thus the z-score for the 1998 mean is $(4.29 - 4.14)/0.610 \approx 0.25$. Similarly, the z-score for the 1999 mean is $(4.32 - 4.14)/0.610 \approx 0.29$.

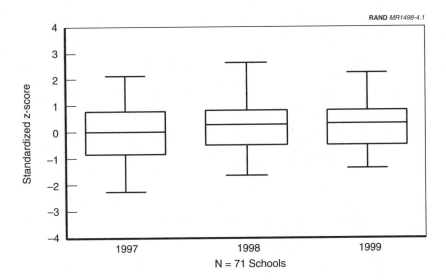

Figure 4.1—Standardized Z-Scores of the Overall Implementation Index (Based on 1997 Mean and Standard Deviation), 1997–1999

not statistically significant. However, the within-school variance increased over the same time period, suggesting that implementation did not become more "schoolwide" within a school.

In our multivariate analyses, we decomposed the variance in implementation into its variance components: within-school variance and between-school variance. The variance in implementation within schools was much larger than the variance between schools. In fact, only 18 percent of the total variance in reported teacher implementation was between schools; the remaining 82 percent was within schools. The between-school variance component declined from 27 percent in 1998 to 18 percent in 1999, with a corresponding increase in the within-school variance component. Such findings are not uncommon in analyses of school contextual effects on student and teacher outcomes (see Lee and Bryk, 1989; Gamoran, 1992; Berends and Kirby et al., 2001). However, because of such differences within schools, educators, design teams, and policymakers may need to think carefully about how to implement changes throughout the school.

Our multilevel models explained almost all of the between-school variance and about 31 percent of the within-school variance.

There were large differences in implementation by jurisdiction in 1999. We found large differences in the distribution of the core implementation index across the jurisdictions as well as design teams (Figure 4.2). In 1999, the mean implementation index was 4.32, with a standard deviation of 0.52. We calculated a standardized z-score for each jurisdiction and each design team, based on the 1999 mean and standard deviation for all schools.

Kentucky and Memphis ranked relatively high on this index with means that were 0.60 and 0.33 of a standard deviation higher than the mean while Washington state and San Antonio ranked the lowest, with means that were 0.77 and 0.87 of a standard deviation

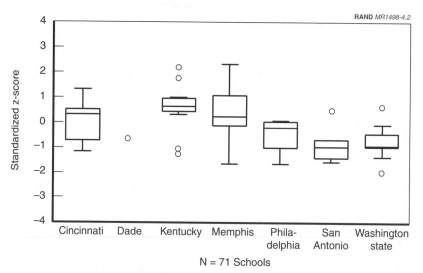

N = 71 Schools

NOTE: Sample sizes are Cincinnati (n = 10), Dade (n = 1), Kentucky (n = 13), Memphis (n = 24), Philadelphia (n = 6), San Antonio (n = 7), Washington state (n = 10).

Figure 4.2—Core Implementation Index (Standardized Z-Scores), by Jurisdiction, Spring 1999

lower than the mean.[7] Memphis schools also displayed the greatest spread in the data, as is evident from the long whiskers in the figure. Kentucky had a number of outliers, both high and low. Cincinnati also showed a great deal of spread, with schools having means that ranged from well below one standard deviation below the overall mean to well above one standard deviation above the overall mean. The differences between the highest and lowest jurisdictions were all statistically significant.[8]

There were large differences in implementation by design teams in 1999. Comparisons among design teams reveal that CON, RW, and NARE ranked comparatively high on the core implementation index while MRSH generally ranked the lowest, reflecting the ranking we found in 1998 (Figure 4.3). CON schools had a mean that was almost one standard deviation higher than the overall school mean while RW and NARE schools had means that were two-tenths and one-tenth of a standard deviation higher than the overall mean. MRSH schools had the lowest mean, over half a standard deviation below the overall mean. However, in terms of differences in means, none of these differences was statistically significant.

Implementation appeared to increase and deepen over the first four years after schools adopted designs, although at a decreasing rate. Figure 4.4 summarizes the actual relationship between years of implementation and the level of implementation for schools in our sample.[9] We see a sharp increase between the first and second years,

---

[7]The following is an example of how these effect sizes are calculated: The mean implementation index for Kentucky was 4.63; thus the z-score for Kentucky is $(4.63 - 4.32)/0.52 \approx 0.60$.

[8]Statistically significant here refers to the mean differences being significant at the 0.05 probability level or less. This is based on the multiple comparison test using the Bonferroni correction.

[9]In calculating the mean level of implementation for each group, we had more than one data point for some groups, based on the three years of data. For example, schools that had been implementing for one year in 1997 had been implementing for two years in 1998. We also had some schools that had been implementing for two years in 1997. In such cases, we used a weighted average of the mean level of implementation reported by these two groups of schools, where the weights were the number of schools in each group.

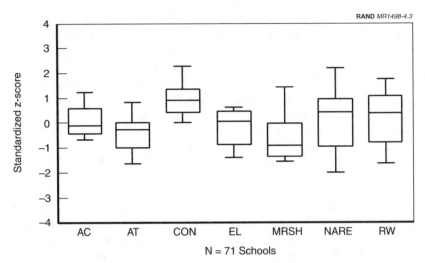

NOTE: Sample sizes are AC (n = 4), AT (n = 13), CON (n = 6), EL (n = 10), MRSH (n = 7), NARE (n = 19), RW (n = 12).

Figure 4.3—Core Implementation Index (Standardized Z-Scores), by Design Team, Spring 1999

modest increases from second through fourth years, and a sharp decrease in the fifth year. Schools with more than five years show higher levels of implementation, although the sample sizes are quite small.

Five Years After Scale-Up. *Even in schools selected by the* design teams *as high implementing, the level of implementation was quite low five years after scale-up.* In the course of gathering our sample, we learned that the various design teams, except RW, were not as knowledgeable about their schools as one might expect given their focus on design-based assistance. Information regarding schools' implementation levels was often outdated, overly optimistic, or simply missing. Although we had requested a sample of high-implementing schools, the levels of implementation across the

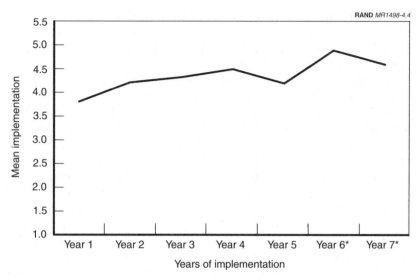

*Small sample size (2 schools).

Figure 4.4—Mean Implementation, by Years of Implementation, Longitudinal Sample

schools we visited tended to be low. The low levels of implementation were not a consequence of the newness of designs to schools because most schools in our sample had adopted their designs at least three years ago.

FACTORS AFFECTING IMPLEMENTATION IN NAS SCHOOLS

Several factors emerge from both the case study and survey research as fostering high-quality and coherent implementation in the types of schools in the sample, perhaps the most important of which is principal leadership. The findings are grouped into broad categories, earlier identified in our conceptual framework.

Designs and Design-Based Assistance

Designs and the assistance they offered clearly affected the level of implementation achieved.

Type of Design. Bodilly (1998) found that teams that placed greater relative emphasis on core elements of schooling (curriculum, instruction, student assignment, student assessment, and professional development) rather than a more systemic approach tended to have higher implementation. Similarly, the longitudinal survey found that overall certain designs had markedly higher levels of implementation: CON, NARE, and RW, while others such as MRSH had markedly lower levels of implementation. In the multivariate model, controlling for other factors such as prior implementation and school characteristics, we do not find many differences among designs, with two exceptions: CON schools and AC schools made steady progress over this time period. AC schools, which in 1997 were at the low end of the implementation index, have made marked progress in implementation over the two years. This may be due to unobserved characteristics of the designs themselves that make them easier or harder to implement in schools already facing several challenges in terms of poverty, lack of resources, and the capacity to implement designs—a critical issue for future research to address.

Of 13 schools that had been implementing for three or more years, implementation levels were higher in the RW schools, which implemented only the reading component of the RW design. RW schools achieved higher implementation levels than the other design schools in our sample because RW provided schools with virtually all of the necessary curriculum and pedagogy, requiring less initiative from teachers. It also provided frequent, consistent, and reliable implementation checks. Finally, RW, as a reading program rather than a truly comprehensive school design, was far less ambitious an initiative to take on than the other designs.

Importance of Clear Communication. Our findings highlight the importance of clear communication to teachers in facilitating higher implementation (Bodilly, 1998; Berends and Kirby et al., 2001; Kirby, Berends, and Naftel, 2001). Clear communication had a large and statistically significant effect on the level of implementation. Of course, this variable and the teacher support variable were correlated.

Design-Based Assistance. Bodilly (1998) found that two important contributors to design implementation were having a stable team with the capacity to serve a growing number of schools and design team support in the form of resources in encouraging high levels of implementation. The longitudinal study found that on average, schools that reported more resources for implementation (e.g., materials; professional development; time for planning, collaboration, and development; consultants to provide ongoing support; technology; and funding) had higher levels of implementation (Berends and Kirby et al., 2001).

Chun, Gill, and Heilbrunn (2001) reported that teachers they spoke with received training and some design-based assistance, but found that neither consistently met needs. Some teachers reported that the training provided over time was not sufficient. Moreover, the quality of training varied by design representative.

School Capacity

Strong Principal Leadership. Schools reporting having strong principal leaders had implementation levels over half a standard deviation above schools at the sample average. In addition, individual teachers' beliefs about principal leadership were important in explaining within-school variance in implementation. Our findings suggest that effective and supportive principal leaders are likely to both increase and deepen implementation in a school. For example, if most or all the teachers in a school view the principal as a strong leader, this is likely to reduce the variance within a school and help the design become more schoolwide. The importance of principal leadership for establishing effective schools has been emphasized by researchers for decades (Edmonds, 1979; Purkey and Smith, 1983; Rosenholtz, 1985), so it is not surprising that such leadership is critical for the implementation of NAS designs. While not surprising, the crucial role that principal leadership plays with respect to implementation should not be overlooked when adopting and implementing whole-school reforms.

Teacher Factors. Teachers' characteristics and their attitudes were also important determinants of level of implementation across the different analyses. For example, in the longitudinal survey, we found that teacher perceptions of students and their readiness to learn were all significantly related to teacher-reported levels of implementation. Teachers with a greater sense of efficacy—i.e., those who believed strongly that lack of basic skills was not a hindrance to their students' academic success, or that students can learn with the resources available—also reported higher implementation than those who felt otherwise. We acknowledge that teacher efficacy may not be entirely exogenous in our model—it is certainly plausible that higher implementation of designs may have increased teachers' capacity to work with their students and hence their sense of efficacy. If so, the relationship is not causal but correlational. Even so, we believe our findings underscore the importance of enhancing teachers' abilities to work in diverse settings and providing them with the resources and supports they need.

School Context

School Composition. Taking into account other factors related to teachers, design teams, and districts, we found that poverty and minority composition of students were related to implementation, both in a positive direction. Teacher-reported implementation levels were higher in higher-poverty schools and among schools with high percentages of minority students.[10] It is interesting and promising to find that schools serving largely poor or minority students reported more success at whole-school reform. This may be largely a question of motivation or determination to succeed on the part of the teachers and principals in these schools. It also offers an indication of the ability of some designs to help change these challenging schools. However, in our longitudinal analysis, the positive, separate effects of poverty and minority composition were largely wiped out in schools that ranked high on *both* poverty and minority composition.[11] Unfortunately, the small sample size prevented us from decompos-

---

[10]Schools that ranked 10 percentage points above the sample mean on either of these variables reported levels of implementation that were one-tenth of a standard deviation higher than schools at the sample mean.

[11]Because poverty and minority composition are strongly correlated (the correlation coefficient is 0.76), we introduced an interaction term to see whether the combined effect of high-poverty and high-minority composition was different from the effects of these two variables separately. The estimated effect of the interaction term was equal to the sum of the coefficients on poverty and minority separately and in the opposite direction; schools that were 10 percentage points higher in terms of poverty and minority composition, relative to the sample mean, reported implementation levels two-tenths of a standard deviation lower than schools at the sample mean. On net, the combined effect of poverty and minority composition (the interaction term) washes out the separate positive effects of these variables.

ing these results further, but it is clear that more work remains to be done to understand how these characteristics of schools affect implementation.

School Level. Bodilly (1998) also found that at the school level, implementation was higher in schools that were elementary schools; were well informed about the design they selected and allowed free choice of design; and were relatively free of strife and had stable leadership.[12]

Our discussion has focused thus far on the net influence of each factor. However, it is important to emphasize that schools often face a multiplicity of challenges, and the interaction among these factors can set these schools back considerably in their attempts to implement school designs. For example, Bodilly (1998) found that schools that were beset with a combination of two or more negative factors, such as internal tensions, leadership turnover, forced adoptions of designs, or poor understanding of designs, ranked very low on implementation. Thus, schools need stable leadership and capacity and commitment on the part of the teachers to make the designs work.

Selection Process

Teacher Support for the Model. This variable was important in explaining both within-school and between-school variance in implementation in the survey. Supportive teachers implemented at a higher level within a school; the greater the degree of overall school-

---

[12]Our earlier work (Berends and Kirby et al., 2001) also showed that some school demographics were related to implementation, notably size, school level, and student mobility, although the effect differed across the models. In the models where we did not control specifically for jurisdiction, characteristics of the schools appeared to be more important. Large schools had significantly lower levels of implementation (about one-fifth of a standard deviation lower). Secondary schools also reported lower levels of implementation, although the effect was significant in only one of the models. Student mobility had a negative impact on implementation, as one would expect. Schools with higher student mobility reported levels of implementation that were about one-tenth of a standard deviation lower that those with lower student mobility. In the later work (Kirby, Berends, and Naftel, 2001), these school demographics did not appear to be significant. One possible reason might be that, as time goes on, these school demographics do not play as important a role as leadership, teacher sense of efficacy and support for the model, and support from the design team and district.

level support, the higher the implementation. This highlights the importance of getting teachers behind the adopted model; supportive teachers tend to reinforce and enhance implementation, not merely at the individual teacher level but at the school level as well. Whether teachers voted to adopt the model was largely subsumed in the teacher support variable, and as such, did not have a separate effect on implementation. Similar results were found by Chun, Gill, and Heilbrunn (2001). Due to limited information and uneven design-based assistance, not all teachers ever fully understood or accepted their respective designs.

District Context

The district context also proved to be important in impeding or ensuring implementation. Our findings highlight the importance of stable district leadership, provision of adequate resources, and supportive rules and regulations.

Districts played several important roles in fostering/hindering implementation, including: initial matching and selection; encouraging support by the design team; and creating a supportive environment with political leadership, regulatory policies, and consistent funding stream (Berends, Bodilly, and Kirby, forthcoming).

At the district level, Bodilly (1998) identified several district and institutional factors that contributed to implementation. These were leadership backing and stability at the district level; centrality of the NAS initiative to the district's agenda; lack of crisis situations; history of trust and cooperation; availability of resources for transformation; school-level authority and/or autonomy; union support; district accountability; and assessment systems that were compatible with those of the designs.

The longitudinal survey (Berends and Kirby et al., 2001) showed that the level of implementation varied significantly across districts. In that analysis, we found that Memphis and Kentucky ranked high on these indicators of support and ranked high in implementation, while others, such as San Antonio and Washington state, lagged far behind.

In the case studies of 13 schools that had been implementing for three years or more, we found districts were supportive of their schools' efforts in the sense that they provided the necessary funds to implement their respective NAS designs. However:

- Most districts undermined their support to schools and teachers (perhaps unintentionally) by also requiring them to incorporate districtwide initiatives that in some cases conflicted with design approaches to curriculum and instruction;

- In addition, schools' capacity to carry out the reform was limited because districts had not granted schools the autonomy required by the designs;

- Following the lead of their districts more than the elements of their respective designs, teachers found themselves struggling to juggle multiple responsibilities and initiatives, resulting in even less time to learn about design features and engage in design-related activities.

FACTORS THAT CONTRIBUTED TO THE DECISION TO DROP THE DESIGN

As part of the longitudinal analysis, we conducted additional exit interviews with principals who reported dropping the NAS designs out of the original sample of 155 schools in either 1998 or 1999. We asked principals about the factors that contributed to the decision to drop the NAS design and what advice principals would give to schools on the verge of implementing a whole-school design. Thirty principals responded to the interviews,[13] and their responses offer some valuable insights. These responses also point to the importance of funding, supportive leadership at the district and state levels, and assistance from design teams in ensuring sustained implementation.

---

[13]It is difficult to calculate an attrition rate (i.e., schools that dropped the design as a percentage of the total sample) for the sample as a whole. Some schools that did not respond may well have dropped the design. Out of the 184 schools at the beginning of scale-up and excluding the 12 Pittsburgh schools that were later dropped from the study, at least 41 schools out of 172 had dropped the design, giving us a lower-bound attrition rate of approximately 24 percent.

Funding to pay for the design and for professional development for teachers was the primary reason for dropping the design, while lack of support from the district and the state ranked second. Schools were also unhappy about the amount of effort required on the part of teachers to implement the designs, and the materials or training provided by the design teams. Nine principals cited "other reasons," but on a closer reading, these reasons appeared to relate in some way to lack of funding, lack of support at the state level, and dissatisfaction with the assistance provided by the design teams.

About ten schools reported that they were planning to replace the design with some other reform effort. Seven schools reported that this new program was more curriculum-centered than the design, and four reported that this was another whole-school reform. Interestingly, although the schools were dropping the design, a little under half reported that they planned to continue some elements or aspects of the designs.

Principals were asked what advice they would give to schools that were considering adopting whole-school designs. Some of their comments are noteworthy:

> Make sure you know everything up front—costs, training, and ask for five-year commitments. Make arrangements for time.

> First consider what type of kids you are serving. . . . These programs do not fit every building. Make sure you have enough money for training. If you don't have the money, there's no use jumping into it.

> Do it systematically, be careful with selection. Make sure the selections are successful in a variety of different settings and have data to prove it. Make sure you have faculty buy-in.

> Make sure all teachers and stakeholders understand the need and design of the change. . . . After all, faculty is going to be doing it.

> Make sure you have funding and support from state and district.

Research the design thoroughly. Visit schools that have implemented the program. Call the state and see how long they project
the program's continuation.

Be patient in seeing significant change. With staff, people accept
change differently. Change takes time and new learning.

This advice resonates with findings discussed earlier.

SUMMARY AND POLICY IMPLICATIONS

NAS and the design teams partnered with schools and districts
that were characterized by a host of problems related to poverty,
achievement, and climate characteristics. To scale-up the designs or
replicate implementation in these sites proved difficult.

Level of Implementation

Four years after scale-up, schools reported relatively modest levels of
implementation, although average level of implementation across all
NAS schools did increase from 1997–1999 (two to four years after
scale-up). Achieving high levels of implementation, especially within
a school by all teachers, proved challenging. Even four years after
scale-up, there was considerable variance in reported implementation within a school. There were large differences in implementation
by jurisdiction, by design, and across schools.

Factors Affecting Implementation

It is clear that several factors need to be aligned for designs to be well
implemented in schools. Without strong principal leadership, without teachers who support the designs and have a strong sense of
teacher efficacy, without district leadership and support, and without
clear communication and provision of materials and staff support on
the part of design teams, implementation is likely to lag far behind.
These are sobering and important lessons for any efforts at school reform. They underscore the basic inequality among schools in terms
of capacity to undertake reform and point to the need for development of leadership and staff capacity as the precursor to reform, not

necessarily the result of it. In some instances, schools and districts may need to adopt a two-tiered approach to implementation— building up school capacity, particularly the skills and readiness of both the staff and students to implement change, and then attempting to implement the whole design throughout the school.

Chapter Five

IMPLEMENTATION OF NAS DESIGNS IN A HIGH-POVERTY DISTRICT

Mark Berends, JoAn Chun, Gina Schuyler,
Sue Stockly, R. J. Briggs

While the last chapter examined the relationship of district, design, school, and teacher factors to implementation in a longitudinal sample of schools across all NAS sites, this chapter focuses on implementation of NAS designs within a high-poverty district. Here we focus on the conditions in the district, schools, and classrooms that promote or inhibit design implementation and changes in teaching and learning within a particular district (see Berends et al., 2002).

In this chapter, we first describe the research questions and methodology of this classroom study and then the rationale behind conducting the study in the San Antonio district. Next, we provide contextual information on the district at the start of the initiative and reasons for implementing the designs. We then discuss the implementation of the designs according to the factors related to the adoption of the designs; district assistance; professional development offered; teacher support; and changes in classroom practice. We discuss student achievement in the next chapter.

RESEARCH QUESTIONS

In our research on San Antonio schools adopting NAS designs, we focused on the challenging educational environments that these schools faced, the high-stakes accountability system in which they operated, the process for adopting NAS designs, support for implementation including training and professional development, teacher support of the NAS designs, and changes in instructional practices.

Specifically, we were interested in the following research questions:

- Do the NAS designs extend beyond changes in school organization and governance and permeate classrooms? Do NAS teachers and students interact with each other and subject materials in ways that reflect the innovative curricular and instructional approaches of the design teams?

- What factors at the district, school, and classroom level are related to implementation of designs and changes in classroom instruction?

Of course, we were also interested in the relationships between these various factors and student achievement, which we summarize in the next chapter.

METHODOLOGY

The schools analyzed in this chapter were those involved in the early stages of the district's partnership with NAS; non-NAS classrooms and schools were also part of the study. The NAS designs being implemented in this district at the time of this study included CON, EL, MRSH, and RW. While RW is intended to address core subject areas, the RW design begins by implementing the reading program, Success for All. None of these schools in San Antonio planned on implementing the nonreading subject areas of the RW design.

We gathered a variety of data in the San Antonio classroom study, including: principal and teacher surveys conducted at the end of the 1997–1998 and 1998–1999 school years; interviews with district staff, design team leaders, local facilitators, principals, and teachers; classroom observations; illustrative examples of student work; data provided by the district on test scores and student and teacher demographic characteristics; and achievement data from a supplementary test administered to students (Stanford-9 reading). RAND collected these data on a sample of 4th-grade teachers and their students during two school years.

For analyzing changes in teacher practice between the 1997–1998 and 1998–1999 school years, we relied on a longitudinal sample of 40 teachers. In 1997–1998, we were also able to observe and gather classroom artifacts from 12 teachers in NAS and non-NAS schools, and in the following year, we were able to gather such data from about 19 teachers.

The analysis sample relating classroom conditions to student achievement consisted of over 60 teachers and roughly 850 students, but we also compared our results with all elementary schools (n = 64) and 4th-grade teachers (n = 279) and 4th graders (n = 3,820) within the district. In addition, this study relied on other RAND research on NAS that included site visits to schools and school districts to gather information about district and school administrators' and teachers' reports of the progress of the NAS initiative (Berends and Kirby et al., 2001; Kirby, Berends, and Naftel, 2001; Bodilly, 1998, 2001). A brief description of these data collection efforts appears in Table 5.1 (for a more detailed description of the methodology for this study see the Appendix and Berends et al., 2002).

LIMITATIONS

As with the implementation studies described in the previous chapter, the schools in the San Antonio classroom study were also some of the first schools to which design teams were providing assistance on a fee-for-service basis. The design teams were also evolving (Bodilly, 2001), and NAS and the design teams continued to alter their strategies over the time period examined during this particular study.

For the San Antonio classroom study, district staff assisted RAND in selecting teachers academically and demographically representative of its elementary schools. In light of this sample selection, our findings must be interpreted with care. The small number of schools inspires caution as does the even smaller percentage of teachers observed and interviewed. Confidence in the generalizations, however, lies in the fact that we were able to compare some of our results with the teachers and students in all district schools. Because we were able to draw on a variety of qualitative and quantitative data, we were able to compare findings from these data sources to check the robustness of the findings reported.

Table 5.1

Types of Data in RAND's Classroom Study of San Antonio

Type of Data	Information Provided
Teacher survey	Design team program characteristics Instructional strategies Professional development activities Teacher background Classroom climate and other characteristics
Teacher logs of classroom activities	Design team program characteristics Instructional strategies
Observations of classroom instruction	Design team program characteristics Instructional strategies
Teacher interviews and focus groups	Design team program characteristics Instructional strategies Design team implementation benchmarks Professional development activities Common planning time Resources for implementation
Principal and instructional guide interviews	NAS design implementation School climate and other characteristics Professional development activities Resources for implementation
Design team interviews	Design team program characteristics Instructional strategies Design team implementation benchmarks NAS design implementation Professional development activities Resources for implementation
District interviews	NAS design implementation Professional development activities District policies Resources for implementation
Student characteristics and performance	Individual students' TAAS mathematics and reading scores longitudinally linked across grades 3, 4, and 5 (also linked to teachers and schools) Stanford-9 administered to 4th graders in spring 1998 and spring 1999 (linked to teachers and schools) Students' demographic and individual characteristics

In addition to the teacher surveys, test scores, and other quantitative data, our multiple classroom observations, conversations with teachers and school administrators, examination of lesson plans, and analysis of student work revealed that design implementation is greatly affected by the environments of the district and the schools. As will be revealed in detail, the designs themselves were only one means brought in by the district to reform its academically troubled school system.

CHOICE OF DISTRICT

We undertook this study during the early years of NAS's scale-up phase. We could not predict ahead of time which districts would be more successful in implementing design-based assistance reforms than others. But, early indications showed that understanding district context would prove important. In addition, by concentrating on one cooperative district, we might be able to more directly track changes in teacher-student interactions and eventual student performance associated with design adoption.

At the time this study was undertaken, NAS had entered into partnerships with selected districts. NAS already knew that the districts did not provide quite the environments originally envisioned as supportive of whole-school reform. Nevertheless, two districts were judged by NAS as being especially supportive in terms of commitments by the district superintendents: Memphis and San Antonio. Rather than trying to understand what happened in an unsupportive district and measure outcomes there, we attempted to choose a more supportive one. Thus, we chose San Antonio because of its level of support at the time and its willingness to participate in the study. Due to previous agreements among Memphis City Schools, the University of Memphis, and RAND, we were unable to extend the design and methods of our San Antonio classroom study to Memphis.

Events soon revealed that San Antonio's district policies were much less supportive than initially anticipated—the substance of this chapter. The changes we document in San Antonio provide lessons for all reforms in high-poverty, high-stakes accountability settings. Thus, they deserve special attention. Furthermore, as can now be seen, NAS has not been successful in implementing its designs and maintaining a supportive environment in any of the districts it partnered with originally. The larger issue is whether a supportive environment for design-based assistance is possible anywhere under current district policy environments.

SAN ANTONIO CONTEXT

While NAS was busy starting up in July 1991, the San Antonio school district struggled to raise its students' achievement levels and meet the challenges it faced. At the time, productive communication proved problematic, as did the effective utilization of district staff. Much energy was expended on the management of day-to-day organizational affairs. According to several central office administrators, instructional practice was too often addressed last. In the words of one, "The school district was perceived as backwater, lowperforming, not doing anything, in decay."

Prior to the new superintendent's arrival there was no sense of a unified curricular vision across the district, let alone among the various feeder schools. Individual schools had in place a wide variety of curricular and instructional programs, with little coherence among them. When school staff was asked what instructional strategies were in place, a typical response tended to include 12 to 14 different programs. Classrooms basically functioned in isolation. Though people at the district level were responsible for the various programs, there was no expectation for entire schools or even a majority of classrooms to adopt them.

This diversity and range of programs across school campuses made it difficult to know what students were being taught and how learning was being assessed within classrooms across the district. Moreover, without a unified curricular trajectory, the same topics were at times observed being taught at a variety of grade levels. As one district staff member stated:

> We had a lot of redundancy in the curriculum and we had a total lack of direction, in part because each school in this district very much did its own thing. . . . I walked [through] a 3rd-, a 5th-, a 7th-, and a 9th-grade classroom. Within the same ten-day period they were all doing the solar system . . . everybody was doing exactly the

> same thing. The mobiles were hanging in every room. . . . The test
> was the same.

When the new superintendent came on board, significant changes occurred in the district. The superintendent proceeded to focus on five district goals: increasing student achievement, fostering collaboration and communication, strengthening parent and community involvement, building an infrastructure for professional development, and providing appropriate school facilities to all students.

To facilitate the realization of the district's five new goals, the superintendent set out to build an infrastructure to support instruction. Upon learning that teachers and principals could use more central office support and that the efforts of the district office were not optimally coordinated, the new superintendent set out to reorganize. She began by eliminating certain central office positions, creating new ones, and reallocating resources to better serve schools. Her vision was to create a blend of site-based and central operations management.

> You know, we have to come to terms with what really makes sense
> to be consistent districtwide and what really the schools should be
> able to decide.

She felt that there should be consistency across the district with respect to operations such as uniform policy, transportation, and discipline. The superintendent believed all schools should focus on instructional matters as much as possible.

Pressures to Improve State Test Scores

The press to increase student achievement and improve test scores in San Antonio schools was clearly evident during the time of our study. To this end, the district, under the superintendent's leadership, established an Office of Curriculum and Instruction responsible for developing a sequential, standards-aligned curriculum across grade levels in all schools throughout the district. The subjects covered on the Texas Assessment of Academic Skills (TAAS), namely mathematics and reading, were given primary attention. Additionally, the district partnered with New American Schools to help tighten its focus and to encourage school improvement.

Suddenly, schools were not only exposed to, but required to, implement many ideas at once, naturally resulting in some confusion and resistance on the part of school staff.

The emphasis on increased student achievement not only called for greater student learning, it heightened the district's focus on improved TAAS performance as well. Tied to the Texas system of school accountability, TAAS scores provided measures of achievement readily reported to and understood by administrators and teachers alike. The act of addressing targeted skills enabled educators to work toward specific academic goals during a time of great change in the district. Successful TAAS performance not only became the goal easiest to visualize but in fact the *single* goal to attain. Schools paid a price for this, however. According to teachers, the focus on TAAS tended to mute creativity and channel all activities toward preparation as the test approached. Some teachers reported preparing their students for TAAS from day one of the school year by incorporating test-taking strategies and TAAS vocabulary into their lessons.

> We are very TAAS-focused at the beginning of the year. A lot of us would think in that direction from the beginning when you start learning how to highlight in the book and pick out what is important. There are a lot of strategies that we teach that start off from the very beginning in all the lessons. (RW school.)

> I think TAAS takes up pretty much the day, and I think as teachers we get bogged down with those worksheets and don't come up with other creative ways to implement the objectives that they test on in TAAS. So I think we're very worksheet-oriented because I think when the children do get that test booklet, it won't be in the form of a game, it won't be in the form of a project. But it would be in paper/pencil test. (EL school.)

In addition, lack of time during the school day—a chronic issue—became even more problematic in light of teachers' needs to balance TAAS preparation with other instruction. Many teachers reportedly coped with the multiple demands on their time by putting aside other activities to focus almost exclusively on TAAS as the test dates grew closer.

> Come January, MRSH is over here, on the side. . . . From January
> through the end of February, which is when we have our writing
> TAAS, we write compositions . . . we write all day, every day in the
> month of February. So then MRSH is out the window. . . . Maybe
> once a week we could do that, but you can't teach a unit once a
> week. And so it just doesn't happen. Okay, as soon as that's over
> (TAAS writing), like March 1st, then we're cramming for the TAAS
> formatted math and reading. . . . And we do that for two months
> solid.

During the 1998–1999 school year, schools administered as many as
four district-directed TAAS simulations, after which teachers were
required to analyze the results and pinpoint their students' weaknesses.

> [Y]ou . . . have assessments schoolwide that you have to do and
> figure out the percentage of students passing and write out a pass
> plan on how you can get those students who did not pass up to
> passing mode. You have to turn it in, a sheet with every student's
> name as to what objectives they have passed and what objectives
> they've failed.

> We give a TAAS simulation and if your class is extremely weak in a
> certain area, it is your [the teacher's] responsibility to boost that one
> target area.

In many classrooms, bar graphs were posted, revealing individual
students' scores on each subtest. Interestingly, two low-performing
TAAS schools were "encouraged" by the district to suspend all activity that did not directly stress TAAS skills. For one school, this meant
neglecting its NAS design altogether. Another school suspended all
design activity after spring break to prepare intensively for TAAS.
According to teachers, they were told to do so by the school administration, who received this "suggestion" from the district.

At several schools, teachers remarked that 1998–1999 was the first
school year they were explicitly asked to "teach to TAAS." The
administration disliked having to make such a request, but felt that
their schools had no substantial say in the matter. Schools feared
being placed on lists that threatened their existence. Moreover, a
district policy enacted at the start of the 1998–1999 school year based

teachers' evaluations in part on their students' TAAS scores. According to one teacher:

> [The district] has just about threatened to disown schools that were doing EL because we weren't concentrating on TAAS. And TAAS is the be-all, end-all. . . . But we're seeing scores that are not acceptable.

Whether or not schools were directly told to focus on TAAS preparation, teachers at all schools in our sample reported feeling pressure to "teach to TAAS" given the high-stakes nature of the test.

To help students perform better on TAAS, teachers not only spent time on reviewing the skills that would be tested, but also the art of test-taking. This included teaching test-taking strategies and exposing students to vocabulary, wording, and format.

> And then we practice with bubbles, transferring back and forth. And they've got to have a, b, c, d, e, and f. . . . And they really have to practice and practice and practice with that. And I don't know why it is so hard. . . . I would like to know why it is so difficult for them to make the transfer. (MRSH school.)

> It's *how* to read and understand what it's asking because if you understand what the TAAS is looking for, you can figure out how to answer it. . . . As we teach skills we teach strategies with it and figure out exactly which strategy is appropriate for this question. (RW school.)

It is within this context of high-stakes accountability, challenged schools, and high expectations for school improvement that the NAS designs were introduced to and implemented in schools.

NAS'S ESSENTIAL ROLE IN THE DISTRICT'S REFORM STRATEGY

While restructuring instructional leadership, rethinking the delivery and content of professional development, introducing instructional strategies to teachers, pushing state standards, and refocusing the district's attention on instruction and student achievement, San Antonio district administrators simultaneously reviewed national reform efforts and programs. Central office administrators seriously examined and eventually decided to implement the reform ideas of NAS—particularly NAS's approach to comprehensive school reform. Convinced that the designs could play an important role in the district's efforts to bring about increased student achievement, the NAS designs became an important piece of the reform package in the district. Viewing NAS designs as the framework and glue to tie the multiple district initiatives together, the central office expected to monitor the progress of design implementation and support the schools in their efforts.

The superintendent viewed designs as the needed catalyst to force schools to examine change from within. She did not want the piecemeal practice of reform to continue within the district's schools, where only certain classrooms or subject teachers engaged in new practices. Not only did she view the NAS designs as the outside galvanizing force for change, she also had hopes that the designs would help sustain the district's efforts to engage in comprehensive school reform. Others in the central office thought, too, that the NAS designs could "provide a wholeness and integration and stimulate teachers to think or rethink what they were doing." The designs also were seen as one way to help shift teachers' thinking as isolated agents of instruction to members of a community of learners: "When you've got a whole-school design, everybody plays, everybody's part of the planning process."

As time passed, it became clear to central staff members and design team representatives alike that greater communication was needed between them. The district took the initiative by arranging quarterly meetings to be attended by all design representatives and several central office administrators and staff members. These meetings began in the 1998–1999 academic year. Central office staff were hired or reassigned to provide schools with instructional leadership. At the district level, four people were hired to serve as *Instructional Stewards*, or area superintendents. The Instructional Stewards were required to report directly to the superintendent. Each was held accountable for his or her own Learning Community, a specified group of elementary, middle, and high schools. The primary responsibility of the Instructional Stewards was to support schools and provide instructional guidance. The Instructional Stewards were expected to provide support by assisting the analysis of school data such as TAAS results and supervising the development of campus improvement plans. They were to study the campus plans of every school in their respective Learning Communities to assess their viability as well as commitment to San Antonio district goals.

In the words of one Instructional Steward, "Curriculum, instruction, assessment, is what we're all about." Another reported that Instructional Stewards were "responsible for supporting the principals, of evaluating them, of helping them to determine the priority needs within their schools and supporting them in accomplishing whatever it is they needed to accomplish."

It was important to all involved to determine how best to align the designs with the district's plan for professional development and emphasis on state-developed academic standards. There had been confusion regarding this because in some cases the district initiatives directly conflicted with the principles of various designs. Moreover, when there was overlap between district and design ideas regarding instructional practice, the teachers often did not know which to follow.

The district context described so far is important when understanding the results of our San Antonio classroom study. In what follows, we discuss some of our results as they relate to the adoption of designs, the assistance provided by the district for implementation, professional development, teacher support, and instructional practices in NAS and non-NAS classrooms.

FINDINGS

Adoption of Designs

Upon talking with teachers, principals, and district staff, it became clear that the process by which teachers learned about NAS designs varied from school to school. Teachers at some schools reported being exposed to all the designs supported by the district—CON, EL, MRSH, and RW. Others heard about only a select few. A number of schools in our sample sent a select group of teachers to design presentations. These teachers then came back to their schools to share what they learned with their colleagues so that all could vote on their design of choice. Some schools had teachers visit actual design schools and report back to their colleagues. In some cases, teachers listened to the presentations of design representatives at their own schools. In the MRSH schools, the principals introduced the design to their teachers after each visited a demonstration site. Though teachers at these schools were told about at least one other design, MRSH seemed to be the one favored as it was introduced.

Regardless of the number of designs to which each school was introduced, all teachers across our sample were given the opportunity to vote. At many of the schools exposed to multiple designs, teachers first discussed the suitability of each to their respective campuses and then approved the design most favored through a vote. In some cases, all presented designs were listed as choices. Early on, in accordance with the district, initially at least 60 percent of all teachers and school staff had to vote in favor of a given design for it to be implemented.

Across our sample, teachers reported feeling pressure to choose a design. Given that in time all district schools would have to take on a design, teachers never had the choice to reject design adoption altogether. Not only was there pressure to take on a design—several teachers stated that they were given little time to learn about and decide upon a design. According to one of our MRSH teachers: "I remember that it was a rush, rush thing . . . and I know that at the time we voted on it, we had no idea what it was. . . . All we were told was the teacher would have a lot of input." As one of the teachers at an EL school stated, "Truthfully, I felt that we could have and should have looked at other designs. But because of the time constraints, we had to immediately decide, and we did not get an opportunity to look at as many designs as there are out there."

Teachers reported choosing designs that seemed to match their schools' visions and instructional approaches. For many this meant going with the design that required the least change. Teachers at one CON school, for example, stated that this design suited them best given that they already had reworked their curriculum and were unwilling to rewrite it.

> As a staff, what we were looking for was something that would fit what we already have. . . . We weren't willing to chuck all the work

that we had already done. . . . Co-NECT allowed us to keep the curriculum that we had and perhaps enhance it with technology.

At one of our RW schools, teachers stated that having to write thematic-based units turned them off to their other choices. In the case of our EL schools, the design principles and project-based approach to instruction appealed to teachers and school staff.

Thus, while teachers were attracted to certain aspects of NAS designs and were given the opportunity to vote to adopt a particular design, the time constraints to make a decision inhibited a greater understanding of what teachers could accomplish with a NAS design in place.

District Assistance for Design Implementation

All schools in the district, regardless of being NAS or non-NAS, received increased support for teachers in the form of *Instructional Guides*. The Guides assumed responsibility for handling all curricular issues on campus and for keeping abreast of the latest instructional strategies and techniques. When needed, they assisted teachers in classrooms by modeling skills, for example. Instructional Guides also helped to identify and locate resources. Not only did they tutor and test students, they provided training to school staff as well. Furthermore, they worked closely with their respective principals, serving to facilitate communication between teachers and administrators. Given their many roles, Instructional Guides tended not to spend as much time in classrooms as they would have liked. Many reported that a good chunk of their time was spent away at training sessions. Instructional Guides at NAS schools attended both district in-services and design training.

Instructional Guides received a great deal of credit for enabling the district office to push forward and implement ideas very rapidly. Quarterly meetings attended by Instructional Guides and central office staff served to further the budding lines of communication. During these meetings, Guides reportedly discussed what was working at their schools, what upset teachers, what needed to be improved upon, and what additional support systems were necessary.

When asked whether the district supported their schools' design implementation efforts, most teachers indicated that it did so passively. The central office allowed schools to choose from a selection of designs, for example. Additionally, it did not dictate how to proceed with design implementation. Most importantly, the district provided the funds to enable comprehensive school reform. Clear to teachers, however, was that the central office's emphasis was on test results. Thus, teachers in design schools were required to implement the district's mathematics and reading initiatives in addition to their reform models of choice. In this way, support from the central office for design implementation was conditional.

> It's left up to the campus and the grade levels on how . . . to integrate all of this information. So I don't want to say that the district doesn't support the design. They do, but they support just as much the things that the district is implementing onto the campuses as well.

Professional Development

Professional development is a crucial element for school improvement (Bodilly, 2001; Garet et al., 1999). One of the challenges facing NAS schools has been that districts, not schools, control the resources for professional development. Districts also differ in the amount of funding they have to focus on specific professional development efforts for NAS design implementation. Moreover, some designs stress the importance of specific design team training for implementing the designs (e.g., MRSH and RW). Others (e.g., CON and EL) emphasize the importance of long-term development of teachers' capabilities and professionalization, which in turn should contribute to ongoing school improvement. Whatever the approach, the availability of resources for design team training, district training, and overall professional development efforts for design implementation remains a challenge within districts that have competing goals, objectives, and incentives for teacher professional development.

Design Team Assistance. Besides the district and the Instructional Guides, design teams provide another important source of support for implementation. Design teams assist implementation by providing schools and teachers with support such as training, professional development, and materials (Bodilly, 1998; Glennan, 1998). Teachers' responses to our surveys provided a broad picture of how all design schools were progressing in implementation, and changes that occurred from one year to the next. Some of these responses between the spring of 1998 and 1999 for a small number of teachers surveyed across two school years appear in Table 5.2.

For instance, in 1998 a relatively high proportion of teachers in the NAS schools (58 percent) agreed that their respective design team had clearly communicated "its program to school staff so that it could be well-implemented." By 1999, the percentage of teachers reporting clear communication by design teams was markedly higher—88 percent.

Training by Design Teams. As for the actual design training, however, there was little regular, consistent assistance provided, according to teacher interviews across design schools. Over time, there was even less contact between teachers and their respective design representatives.

In large part, this had to do with the fact that these representatives serviced numerous schools, making it difficult for them to be attentive to any one. It also appears that from the start, strong relationships rarely were established, making it unlikely that teachers would rely on their respective design representatives for external technical support and assistance. In some schools, design representatives turned over, disrupting what rapport had been established. Several teachers in our sample saw their design representatives so infrequently that they didn't even know their names. The RW schools should have received the most regular design assistance given that each had one facilitator on campus to meet its needs. Additionally, the program included a series of implementation visits conducted by RW consultants. At one of our RW schools, however, the Instructional Guide took on the RW facilitator role as well, making it very difficult for her to efficiently address issues pertaining to the design team reading program.

Few design representatives entered classrooms on a regular basis. Teachers reported that visitors to classrooms tended to be district staff. The teachers were given little, if any, outside "expert" support that enabled them to objectively assess their progress and growth as design teachers. Teachers reported that when in need of help, they tended to turn to their colleagues or Instructional Guides first. Across design schools, teachers did not have enough interaction with their respective design representatives to feel their absence.

In addition, teachers reported on our surveys that their participation in design-related professional development meetings/conferences declined from one year to the next. In 1998, 62 percent of teachers reported participating in these types of activities more than twice during the past 12 months; 50 percent of teachers reported doing so in 1999. The percentage of teachers who reported attending workshops or courses related to their NAS design also decreased from 50 percent in 1998 to 39 percent in 1999 (see Table 5.2).

In part, these decreases may be due to design teams emphasizing teacher training more during the initial stages of implementation. However, the decline may also be a signal that the level of implementation itself was declining in these schools because the district was shifting its focus away from NAS efforts.

Consistent with the survey results, interviews and observations revealed that teachers at EL, CON, and MRSH design schools saw their respective design representatives with little regularity—an impediment to design implementation. Regardless of their schools' adopted designs, teachers reported the need for more concrete, hands-on training that would enable them to better understand design processes.

District Training and Professional Development. In addition to training by design teams, teachers at NAS schools also received the district's professional development, as did their colleagues from non-NAS schools. Much of the in-service professional development revolved around the district's reading and math initiatives. Teachers at RW schools attended reading in-services provided by the design rather than the district. More workshops having to do with language arts were offered during the 1998–1999 school year. Teachers attended technology training and workshops concerning state standards and curriculum alignment as well. Relatively speaking, few social studies or science workshops were provided.

Table 5.2

**Percentage of Longitudinal Sample of NAS Teachers Who Reported
Design Team Communication, Professional Development,
and Support in Spring 1998 and Spring 1999**

	Spring 1998	Spring 1999
NAS design team clearly communicated its program	58	88
Attended design-related professional development meetings/conferences in past 12 months	62	50
Attended workshops or courses related to NAS design in past 12 months	50	39
Strongly support the NAS design team program	54	25
Strongly or somewhat oppose the NAS design team program	15	43

NOTE: Percentages are based on teacher reports in a longitudinal sample of 40 teachers—26 NAS teachers responded to the survey items in this table; 14 non-NAS teachers did not respond to these NAS-specific questions.

Because NAS teachers were obligated to attend as many of these various in-services as their colleagues in non-NAS schools, the amount of training activities served only to heighten frustrations. All of the designs except RW required teachers to develop units and write curriculum. While encouraging schools to implement NAS designs, the district simultaneously constrained their ability to do so by telling teachers what to teach and how.

The district and design teams did not tend to coordinate their efforts with respect to professional development, so teachers were left on their own to merge the information they received from each. This was not easily done without modifying the essence of each design. Not only did this effort burden teachers' workload, but it also led to confusion as to what to prioritize.

Teacher Support for the NAS Designs in San Antonio

Over the two school years we conducted research, one indication of changes in NAS implementation came from an item that asked teachers how strongly they supported or opposed the NAS design team program in their school. In 1998, 54 percent of teachers indicated that they "strongly support a NAS design team program" in their school, but this fell to 25 percent in 1999. The proportion of teachers indicating that they strongly opposed or somewhat opposed NAS designs in their school increased from 15 percent in 1998 to 43 percent in 1999 (see Table 5.2).

Clearly, the central office played an active role in initiating change across the district as did design teams in their select schools. The actions of the central office made it difficult for NAS teachers to view design implementation as a district priority. Consequently, these teachers were not able to fully commit to the ideas described in their respective design literature. Some feared that the NAS initiative, too, like many others that had been introduced over the years, would fade away in time. Furthermore, aspects of designs such as EL, MRSH, and CON overwhelmed many teachers. The task of writing curriculum was not an activity readily undertaken or easily accomplished by many, given their lack of time and experience.

During interviews, teachers reported variation with respect to levels of design implementation within their schools. Implementation in individual classrooms depended in large part on teachers' feelings about the designs, their willingness to invest time and energy, and their particular strengths and weaknesses. One teacher in the sample stated that within her school, differing levels of competency existed among teachers. The task of having to write curriculum "exacerbated the unevenness."

Another teacher reported that within her school, some of her colleagues were more engaged in design implementation than others. Another teacher stated:

> You have to have your commitment factor. Some people are very committed to it and other people are not, so that affects how you're going to implement it.

A number of teachers believed that NAS designs alone did little to help children who lacked solid academic foundations. Due in large part to other district activities that were pushed, some came to view designs as hands-on, project oriented approaches to education that built *on*, not *up*, basic skills. One teacher at an EL school indicated that her students needed more structure. She stated that many came from unstructured home environments and thus needed more orderly classroom experiences.

> [I]t would work probably better with a group of kids that are on grade level, that have a lot of self-control. . . . If they come from a home where there is no structure, [and] they come into a classroom where there is no structure . . . that's the problem. But I really feel, and I might be wrong, that this works with a different population much better than what it has worked with our students.

Teachers at a CON school stated that their design units had to be "modified" to address their students' basic skills needs. At RW and MRSH schools, teachers expressed less doubt about the potential of NAS designs to bring about desired change in school achievement. This may have to do with the fact that their respective designs either gave them a curriculum to follow (RW) or topics to develop and standards to incorporate (MRSH).

INSTRUCTIONAL PRACTICES

We examined a variety of survey questions about both the skills students are expected to demonstrate and the particular instructional strategies teachers use in their classrooms. Since NAS designs tend to emphasize higher-order, analytic thinking skills over more basic skills, we might expect teachers in NAS classrooms to report lower levels of memorization and higher levels of other types of critical-thinking skills (Bodilly, 2001). We sorted teacher responses about student tasks and teacher practices according to more-conventional or reform-like categories of instruction. While some of the reports are based on teacher surveys, which may be subject to problems of response biases due to exposure to reform jargon (Mayer, 1999; Burstein et al., 1995), we believe the following comparisons are informative. Moreover, to check the robustness of our findings we also relied on our observational data, interviews with teachers, and examination of student work to further our understanding about what instructional practices occurred across elementary classrooms in the district.

Conventional Instructional Practices

Figure 5.1 shows mean responses on a four-point scale (almost never to every lesson) in which teachers were asked, "How often do you have students memorize facts or problems?" Memorization tended to be emphasized more by non-NAS teachers, but only in 1998. The slight increase in NAS responses in 1999 may be due to the increased pressures schools were experiencing to switch to more basic skills instruction to prepare for the TAAS.

We also asked teachers to indicate how often they used particular instructional strategies in their classes, using a five-point scale, ranging from never to almost every day. Responses from teachers in NAS and non-NAS schools varied only slightly in both years when it came to reporting on conventional instructional strategies such as:

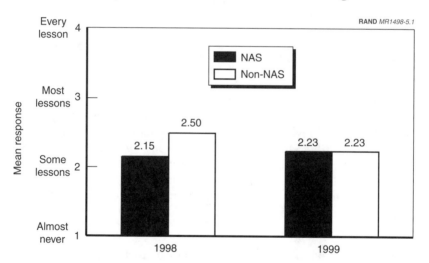

NOTE: Means are based on teacher reports in a total sample size of 40 teachers—26 NAS and 14 non-NAS.

Figure 5.1—Average Teacher Response for Having Students Memorize Facts or Problems in the Typical Lesson in NAS and Non-NAS Schools, Spring 1998 and Spring 1999

- Work individually on written assignments/worksheets in class;

- Practice or drill on computational skills;

- Read textbooks or supplementary materials; and

- Work on next day's homework in class.

With the exception of the last item, well over 90 percent of all 40 teachers reported using these strategies at least once or twice a week. Between 21 and 29 percent of teachers indicated having students work on their next day's homework in classes that often.

In general, teachers in the NAS schools indicated less reliance on more-conventional instructional strategies than teachers in non-NAS schools. Teachers in non-NAS schools were much more likely to use conventional instructional strategies such as lecturing, administering a test over a full class period, and administering quizzes.

Reform-Like Instructional Practices

Teachers responded to several survey items asking about how often students were requested to demonstrate analytical and higher-order thinking skills, using a four-point scale (almost never to every lesson). We found few differences in NAS teachers' responses compared with non-NAS teachers when asked how often students use library sources, brainstorm ideas for written work, debate ideas, apply concepts or skills from earlier lessons, judge and critique their own and each others' work, reflect, relate the material to their life or their community, draft and redraft work, and work in teams toward a common goal.

We used a number of survey items measuring instructional strategies to construct a composite for reform-like instructional practices. Responses from two scales were standardized—to indicate (1) how often teachers used the instructional strategies with this class (a 5-point scale ranging from never to almost every day) and (2) how often teachers had students demonstrate skills (a 4-point scale ranging from almost never to every lesson). The following items were included in the reform index:[1]

- Have students listen to an outside speaker/expert;

- Have students perform research projects;

- Use manipulatives to demonstrate a concept;

- Have students work with manipulatives;

- Have small groups work on problems to find a joint solution;

- Have the whole class discuss solutions developed in small groups;

- Have students work on problems for which there is no obvious method of solution;

- Have students represent and analyze relationships using tables and graphs;

- Have students respond to questions or assignments that require writing at least a paragraph;

- Have students keep a journal;

- Summarize main points of today's lesson;

- Have students work on projects in class;

- Have students explain their reasoning; and

- Have students represent and analyze relationships using tables, graphs, or charts.

Teachers' responses for this reform-like instructional composite are provided in Figure 5.2. While the average use of reform-like instructional practices increased for NAS and non-NAS teachers between 1998 and 1999, teachers in NAS schools reported higher levels than their counterparts in non-NAS schools. For example, in 1999, 54 per-

---

[1]The alpha reliability for this index was 0.77 for both 1998 and 1999. The range of correlations for the individual items was 0.17 to 0.20 in both years.

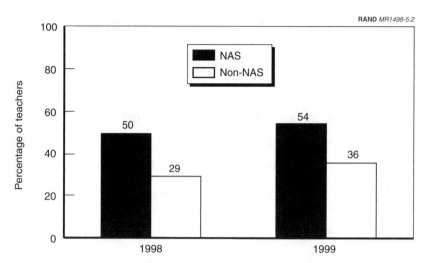

RAND *MR1498-5.2*

NOTE: Percentages are based on a total sample size of 40 teachers—
26 NAS and 14 non-NAS.

**Figure 5.2—Percentage of Teachers Who Reported Using Reform-Like
Instructional Practices at Least Once or Twice a Week in NAS and Non-NAS
Schools, Spring 1998 and Spring 1999**

cent of NAS teachers reported using practices in the reform-like
composite at least once or twice a week compared with 36 percent of
non-NAS teachers.

While NAS teachers tended to report more reform-like instructional
practices, one might expect that the enactment of such practices
might differ due to the unique features of each NAS design. Given
the unique aspects of designs and their respective emphases on student work products, one would reasonably expect to see differences
in classroom appearance, setup, and student work displays across
design schools. While such displays are a simple way that teachers
can give the impression of superficial compliance to implementing a
reform, we found even these displays were less apparent in the second year than the first year of our study. In the first year, design elements were often clearly identifiable. In MRSH classrooms, standards were posted next to student work. Word walls and team score
sheets were posted in RW classrooms. Rich classroom libraries were

found in CON classrooms and student work linked to themes and a multidisciplinary perspective was posted in hallways and classrooms.   Displayed throughout EL classrooms were expedition themes, student-developed rubrics, and drafts and redrafts of student writing.

In year two of our study, the growing influence of the central office on classroom affairs was reflected in the other types of postings found on classroom walls.   Across our sample schools, identical posters outlining the writing and reading processes, math definitions, and district-developed rubrics were commonly found taped to classroom walls.   In every classroom, word walls were found as well as postings of student work on bulletin boards.   Classrooms across our sample looked alike in other ways as well.   The district provided all classrooms with six computers and at least one printer.   All computers were loaded with the same programs.   The same trade books were found in every room.   In most classrooms, desks were commonly arranged in clusters of four to six.   Teachers across schools reportedly rearranged students quite regularly to enable classmates to get to know one another.

One could tell that classrooms were part of given designs only because teachers advertised this fact through posters.   In MRSH classrooms, various standards tended to be posted on bulletin boards next to displays of student work.   In EL classrooms, design principles were often found taped to walls.   CON classrooms tended to be less-distinctively marked.   The selection of student work on display as well as reading-related posters clearly distinguished RW classrooms from the rest.   The appearance of classrooms as well as the work displayed revealed teachers' efforts to comply with both the district's demands and those of their selected designs.

Classroom observations revealed a schism with respect to design implementation.   The designs per se were not the source of teachers' problems.   The difficulties arose out of the struggle to merge district demands with design practices while maintaining the integrity of the designs.   All teachers indicated in their talks with us that they perceived passing TAAS scores to be the bottom line.   With this in mind, the teachers were left on their own to figure out how to incorporate district initiatives into their lesson plans in the spirit of their designs.   To determine whether NAS teachers and students actually interacted with each other and subject materials in ways reflective of design teams' curricular and instructional theories, classroom activities were examined with care.

As mentioned earlier, to address the demands of the TAAS, the district implemented specific mathematics, reading, and language arts programs in addition to the NAS designs. In the spring of 1996, all schools were implementing *Everyday Mathematics*—developed by the University of Chicago School Mathematics Project. The district expectations were that all schools throughout the district would follow a similar pace, and the district developed pacing guides to ensure that this would happen. In addition, San Antonio elementary schools implemented a reading program that involved a 90-minute reading block. By the 1998–1999 school year, elementary schools districtwide were not only expected to schedule two 90-minute blocks of uninterrupted instructional time for reading and math, respectively, but teachers were also required to manage time within these blocks in prescribed ways. Though not to the same degree, the district structured language arts activities (spelling, grammar, and writing) as well, totaling approximately 70 minutes of instruction time per day. Thus, roughly four hours of instructional activities were mapped out for all the district's elementary school teachers to follow (RW teachers were exempt from the district reading program).

Not surprisingly, then, our analyses revealed few differences in teacher perceptions of instructional environments between NAS and non-NAS schools. Some changes were evident. For example, teachers in NAS schools reported instructional strategies and classroom practices that could be categorized as reform-like (e.g., discussion in small groups to find a joint solution to a problem, project-based learning, use of manipulatives), rather than conventional (e.g., drill and skill and individual worksheets). In other areas, fewer differences were found. For instance, both NAS and non-NAS teachers reported similar use of instructional materials, though more teachers in NAS than non-NAS schools perceived inadequate materials to be a problem. The more substantial differences we found were not between NAS and non-NAS schools, but between 1998 and 1999, which is likely a reflection of the dramatic level of change within the district itself. That is, while the implementation of NAS designs was not high relative to other schools and jurisdictions (see Berends and Kirby et al., 2001; Kirby, Berends, and Naftel, 2001), implementation of NAS designs was higher in 1998 than it was in 1999.

Interviews revealed that though the district was supportive both financially and philosophically of NAS designs in its schools, it unwittingly hindered design implementation at all schools except RW by establishing an ever-growing presence in the daily classroom affairs of its teachers. The paucity of communication between the district and design teams failed to create the kind of supportive operating environment called for by NAS. Moreover, the limited communication between teachers and their respective design representatives served to weaken implementation as well. Not knowing how to integrate central office initiatives with design aspects, teachers tended to compromise designs by selecting and modifying only those elements that could coexist with district actions.

> I just think that [the district] is trying to do too many things. Maybe they feel that our schools are very low so they are doing all these other things without really giving us a chance to test it. . . . They are doing all these things without realizing that it's overkill. It's way too much.

SUMMARY AND POLICY IMPLICATIONS

Many schools across the country are now attempting NAS-like reforms using federal funding provided by such programs as Title I and the CSRD program. Schools adopting comprehensive school reforms confront many of obstacles during implementation and thereby face continuing challenges in improving student achievement. This is important to remember when setting expectations for school improvement under new federal, state, and local programs— particularly when implementing strategies and interventions in high-poverty, low-performing settings.

Our findings are consistent with Porter and Clune's scheme for better educational policy (see Porter et al., 1988; Porter, 1994; Clune, 1998). They posit that educational policies such as comprehensive school reform are likely to influence teachers and students to the extent to which they are specific, powerful, authoritative, consistent, and stable. *Specificity*, or depth, is the extent to which the comprehensive school reform provides detailed guidance or materials to help schools and teachers understand what they are supposed to do (e.g., materials that describe the stages of implementing the design and ongoing, clear assistance strategies to further promote implementation). *Power* refers to the rewards or sanctions attached to the whole-school reform, such as teachers receiving bonuses or greater autonomy if they comply with implementing the design. *Authority* refers to the degree to which the reform policy is seen as *legitimate* and as having the *support* of those who are responsible for implementation. If respected groups or policymakers have strong positive views toward whole-school reform and if teachers support its implementation, the design is likely to have greater influence in changing teaching and learning. *Consistency* or *alignment* refers to the extent to which the set of whole-school interventions and strategies are aligned with a common mission and vision, both within the school and the district. *Stability* refers to the reform being sustained over time in a coherent, consistent manner. Policymakers and educators might use these dimensions as a means for thinking critically about the comprehensive school reform being considered and whether the conditions exist for it to succeed.

Thinking carefully about the factors necessary to promote high-quality implementation and coherence with other educational policies and reforms and ensuring that these factors are present and aligned in schools is the only way in which comprehensive school reform can succeed in improving the learning opportunities of all students, especially those in high-poverty settings.

Chapter Six

NAS DESIGNS AND ACADEMIC ACHIEVEMENT

Mark Berends, Sheila Nataraj Kirby, Scott Naftel,
Christopher McKelvey, Sue Stockly, R. J. Briggs,
JoAn Chun, Gina Schuyler, Brian Gill, Jodi Heilbrunn

The overall mission of NAS is to help schools and districts significantly raise the achievement of large numbers of students with whole-school designs and the assistance design teams provide during the implementation process. This chapter provides policymakers and researchers some understanding of the performance progress that NAS made within the partnering jurisdictions during the scale-up phase. This chapter focuses specifically on the following research questions:

- Did NAS schools make gains in test scores relative to all schools in their respective jurisdictions?

- What were the achievement gains across grade levels of individual students in NAS schools compared with non-NAS students?

Before turning to the findings, we must explain what this analysis is and what it is not, so we provide some background on the analysis. We then present our findings using school-level test scores. After that, we discuss the relationship, or lack thereof, between school-level aggregate scores and school-level implementation as we measured it in Chapter Four. We go on to present the findings on student-level test scores in San Antonio and Memphis. Finally, we cover findings from the final set of case studies and others' work before providing a general summary (more details of the methods we used appear in the Appendix).

BACKGROUND OF THE ANALYSIS

A major presumption behind the NAS concept was that each design would be responsible for evaluating its own efficacy. The RFP required evaluation section in the proposal and NAS itself constantly promoted self-evaluation or third-party evaluations for each of the teams. The teams turned out to vary in their ability in this regard and in the energy they spent on it.

NAS requested that we examine the progress teams made toward the goals of improving student performance in the schools undergoing scale-up in the partnering jurisdictions. NAS was not interested in progress made outside of the scale-up sites. Thus, RAND was not asked to evaluate each team's efficacy in improving schools and student outcomes in all of their respective sites. Rather, our work is confined to schools using designs in the partnership districts during the scale-up phase.

While RAND and the Annenberg Advisory Panel recommended NAS develop a set of assessment instruments geared to measure the types of performance the design teams expected, this advice was not taken for several reasons. First, NAS might not have had the resources available for this type of undertaking. Second, the design teams did not agree on a set of assessments, and several did not have assessments in place to examine. Third, and perhaps most important, the partnering districts insisted that the schools be held accountable to the state- or district-mandated assessments. For the most part, NAS and its design teams were concerned that these existing tests were not intended to measure critical-thinking skills or complex reasoning skills on which many of the designs focused (Mitchell, 1996). Even so, NAS and the design teams agreed to partner with these districts and to accept the state- and district-mandated tests as the means of measuring improved performance. It was thought by many at the time that the designs would minimally be able to show progress in these areas, so there should be no concern. Finally, because these were whole-school designs, the schools were an important focus for our analyses. Districts expected average school test scores to improve as a result of implementation of the design.

RAND tracked test score results in partner districts from 1995 to 1998. We focused on evidence based on school- and student-level achievement. For the *school*-level results, we examined whether NAS schools made gains in reading and mathematics scores relative to all schools in their respective jurisdictions. At the *student*-level, we focused attention on two supportive school districts—San Antonio and Memphis—to understand whether NAS designs were related to student achievement compared with non-NAS schools. The results from San Antonio also enable us to control for other relevant student, classroom, and school characteristics within a multilevel framework.

The performance trends portrayed span only a few years, and several design developers and school reformers emphasize that it takes several years to expect implementation to take hold throughout the school (Sizer, 1992; Hess, 1995; Levin, 1991; Darling-Hammond, 1988, 1995, 1997). In addition, our results clearly show the wide variation in implementation both within schools and among jurisdictions and design teams. Thus, because of this variation in implementation, one should not expect robust performance results across the NAS sites. However, it is important to examine trends in performance to set realistic expectations for meaningful schoolwide improvement.

MONITORING ACADEMIC PROGRESS WITH SCHOOL-LEVEL TEST SCORES

When examining school-level achievement, we analyzed data on trends in mathematics and reading scores for NAS schools and the associated jurisdiction for selected grades in elementary, middle, and high schools, where relevant. Because we were concerned about the variability that particular grade test scores show within a given school, we generally aggregated across NAS schools, using grade enrollment as weights. Thus, the comparisons being made are generally between NAS schools and the district or the state.[1]

---

[1]The comparison we make here between NAS schools and the district averages uses absolute gains. In addition, we also calculated and compared percentage gains in test scores for the NAS schools and the jurisdictions. The results were not substantially different from those presented here. Moreover, although not reported here, we compared the gains in test scores of the individual NAS schools with their past performance to see if the schools made *any* gains over time. Again, the results did not differ from those discussed in this section.

Moreover, it is important to note that some of the designs do not specifically have curriculum and instruction materials per se, and even some design teams that do may not have been implementing that particular design component. This should be kept in mind when examining the results that follow. However, mathematics and reading are central to improving student learning for large numbers of students. These subject area tests are also central to the account-ability systems of the jurisdictions in which NAS schools are located. Thus, we focus on these two subject areas.

The fact that NAS schools began implementing at different times makes clear comparisons of gains over time difficult. Wherever pos-sible, we show data for the baseline and baseline plus two years. For some late implementing schools, we show the baseline and baseline plus one-year data. (For more details on these results and the tests used by the various jurisdictions see Berends and Kirby et al., 2001.)

For these results, we relied on the tests administered by the districts as part of their accountability system. While not ideal, these were the tests the jurisdictions, NAS, and the design teams expected to influ-ence during the course of the NAS scale-up strategy. In its initial re-quest for proposals, NAS's intent was for "break the mold" schools. NAS was not interested in incremental changes that led to modest improvement in student achievement compared to conventional classrooms or schools. Rather, the achievement of students was to be measured against "world class standards" for *all* students, not merely for those most likely to succeed. Moreover, design teams were to "be explicit about the student populations they intend to serve and about how they propose to raise achievement levels of 'at risk' students to world class standards" (NASDC, 1991, p. 21).

If such ambitious effects on student achievement occurred, these large test score changes would be reflected in school-level scores. Yet, to fully understand the test score trends of NAS schools three years into scale-up, it is important to keep in mind several issues when examining school-level scores.

First, differences in achievement between schools are not nearly as great as the achievement differences within schools. For the past 30 years, a finding on student achievement that has stood the test of time is that about 15–20 percent of the student differences in achievement lie *between* schools; most of the achievement differences (80–85 percent) lie *within* schools (Coleman et al., 1966; Jencks et al., 1972; Lee and Bryk, 1989; Gamoran, 1987, 1992). Understanding the differences between schools remains critically important for making changes that maximize the effects of schools on students. However, it is also important to understand the limitations of schools—no matter what the school reform—in explaining the overall differences in student achievement (Jencks et al., 1972).

Second, when examining the grade-level scores over time (e.g., 4th-grade scores between 1995 and 1998), these are based on different cohorts of students taking the tests. These scores are often unstable because some schools have small numbers of students taking the test in any given year, and these scores are more likely to vary from year to year with different students taking the test. Districts and states use such scores in their accountability systems, and over a longer period of time, they provide some indication of a school's performance trends.

Third, while establishing trends in the NAS schools relative to other schools within the same district is informative, it is important to remember the variety of family, school, district, and design team factors that influence these scores. Research on student achievement has consistently found that individual family background variables dominate the effects of schools and teachers (Coleman et al., 1966; Jencks et al., 1972; Gamoran, 1987, 1992), and such effects are not controlled for when describing school-level test scores. More-specific information than districts typically collect or make available is necessary to understand the relative effects of these factors on student achievement.

Fourth, the ways districts report their scores to the public are not always amenable to clear interpretations over time. For example, several districts changed their tests during the scale-up phase, and the tests in some cases have not been equated, so the test scores are not directly comparable over time. Moreover, in some instances, the form in which test score information is reported (for example, median percentile rank) makes it difficult to detect changes in the tails of the distribution. Wherever possible, we have tried to obtain specific test score information at the school level to clarify the interpretations that can be made.

Fifth, the way that we summarize school performance—comparing whether the NAS schools made gains relative to the jurisdiction—may miss some significant achievement effects that could be captured if student-level data were available and comparable across the jurisdictions. That is, our indicator will only reflect large achievement effects of designs. The data provided by the districts do not support more fine-grained analyses to understand smaller, statistically significant effects on student-level achievement scores, particularly for certain groups of students (e.g., low-income or minority students or students with limited English proficiency).

Comparing NAS Schools with District Averages: Setting Expectations

NAS schools were predominantly high-poverty and high-minority, and many faced challenges related to student mobility.[2] It could be argued that comparisons with the district average are unfair to these schools, particularly if they fail to capture smaller, albeit significant, achievement effects.

However, it must be pointed out that NAS and the design teams agreed to be held accountable to district assessments and to improve student learning for substantial numbers of students. Because of these expectations, NAS requested that RAND examine the progress of these NAS schools relative to the district averages to understand whether the NAS expectations of dramatic improvement were met.

Sample of NAS Schools for Performance Trend Analyses

The sample of NAS schools for which we have data on test scores is larger than the sample of schools used for the implementation analysis. Of the 184 schools in the original sample, we have data on 163 schools. Some schools were dropped from the sample because

---

[2]When examining trends in school performance, it is important to consider the state and district accountability system (Berends and Kirby, 2000; Miller et al., 2000; Koretz and Barron, 1998). For example, different exclusion rules for special population students could result in different rates of achievement growth across jurisdictions and bias outcomes for particular groups of schools. However, the comparisons made here are between NAS schools and the jurisdiction average. Therefore, all the schools are supposed to be subject to similar testing provisions and administration.

they were not implementing: This was true of the Pittsburgh schools and about 12 schools in Dade. Some of our schools were K–2 schools for which there was no testing data available and other schools were missing data on test scores.

Our analysis of performance trends focused on whether NAS schools made gains in test scores relative to their respective jurisdictions.

Overall, the results are mixed (see Table 6.1). Of the 163 schools for which we had data, 81 schools (50 percent) made gains relative to the district in mathematics and 76 schools (47 percent) made gains in reading.

Differences in School Performance by Jurisdiction

Among the four jurisdictions with ten or more implementing NAS schools, Memphis and Kentucky schools appear to be the most successful in terms of improvement in mathematics, while Cincinnati and Washington state do better in reading (Table 6.1).

Differences in School Performance by Design Team

Examining school performance results by jurisdiction inevitably brings up the question: Which design teams appear to be the most successful in improving student test scores? In many ways, this is an unfair question. School performance and implementation vary importantly across jurisdictions. Given:

- the importance of district environments and support in implementation of the designs;

- the uneven implementation of designs across the jurisdictions;

- the uneven distribution of designs across jurisdictions and small sample sizes for some designs;

- the variation in testing regimes; and

- the possible lack of alignment between assessments and design team curriculum, instruction, and goals,

it is difficult to compare "success" rates of various designs in a meaningful and fair fashion. Nonetheless, NAS and the design teams agreed to be held accountable to district standards, and NAS expected dramatic achievement gains across design teams.

Thus, we present the performance summary results by design to help set expectations for those implementing comprehensive school reforms (see Table 6.1). The results vary across the two subject areas. For example, for the eight AC schools, five made progress relative to the district in mathematics, but only two did so in reading. With the exception of ATLAS and EL schools, about half of the other design team schools made progress relative to the district in mathematics; in reading, fewer than half of AC, CON, and NARE schools made gains relative to the district. RW was the most consistent, with ten out of 21 schools making progress in both reading and mathematics relative to the district. Of the 11 MRSH schools, seven made progress in mathematics and eight in reading.

Once again, we warn that these results need to be interpreted in the context of district environments. Because of the wide variation in implementation and environments that occurs within schools and among jurisdictions, one should not expect robust performance results across the NAS sites after only a couple of years at most. In addition, better and longer-term performance data at the student level are needed in order to make conclusive judgments about designs and their effects on student achievement, controlling for important school, classroom, and student characteristics.

THE LINK BETWEEN IMPLEMENTATION AND PERFORMANCE AT THE SCHOOL LEVEL

One of the goals of the RAND analysis plan is to monitor progress in implementation and performance in NAS schools and to understand the factors that relate to higher implementation and higher performance. Such findings will not only inform New American Schools, but also the CSRD program now under way.

However, as the above section has made abundantly clear, we do not have good, sustained, and coherent measures of school-level achievement scores that are comparable across jurisdictions and across design teams. The summary tables we show above compared gains in NAS schools with changes in the district test scores—any gains—but as we detailed in each section, sometimes the compar-

Table 6.1

NAS Schools Making Gains Relative to Jurisdiction, by Jurisdiction and Design Team, Three Years into Scale-Up

	Number of schools	Number making gains in test scores relative to district
Jurisdiction		
Math		
Cincinnati	18	9
Dade	11	6
Kentucky	51	30
Memphis	30	16
Philadelphia	19	7
San Antonio	12	4
Washington state	22	9
Reading		
Cincinnati	18	10
Dade	11	5
Kentucky	51	22
Memphis	30	11
Philadelphia	19	11
San Antonio	12	7
Washington state	22	11
Design Team		
Math		
AC	8	5
AT	24	9
CON	17	10
EL	16	4
MRSH	11	7
NARE	66	36
RW	21	10
Reading		
AC	8	2
AT	24	15
CON	18	6
EL	15	8
MRSH	11	8
NARE	66	27
RW	21	10
Overall		
Math	163	81
Reading	163	76

isons were across one year, sometimes across two years, and often covered different time periods, where cohorts of schools were involved.

Our data do not show any clear linkage between implementation and performance in NAS schools. This was disappointing and runs counter to conventional wisdom. If the theory of action underlying comprehensive school reform is correct and if these models are implemented in a sustained coherent fashion, then higher implementation should be related to improved outcomes. As Stringfield et al. (1997, p. 43) conclude in *Special Strategies for Educating Disadvantaged Children,* "We know that some programs, well implemented, can make dramatic differences in students' academic achievement." Yet, Stringfield et al. go on to point out the critical challenge in educational reform that has existed in this country for decades:

> [A]fter a third of a century of research on school change, we still have not provided adequate human and fiscal resources, appropriately targeted, to make large-scale program improvements a reliably consistent reality in school serving students placed at risk. (p. 43.)

We offer some hypotheses for the failure to find a link between implementation and performance when examining school-level aggregates. First, despite schools reporting implementation of designs, it remains relatively early for expecting deep implementation that would dramatically affect performance gains. As Sizer (1984, p. 224) points out, "Schools are complicated and traditional institutions, and they easily resist all sorts of well-intentioned efforts at reform." Moreover, as several design developers and school reformers have pointed out, schoolwide change can take more than five years for a school to accomplish meaningful change (Sizer, 1992; Hess, 1995; Levin, 1991; Darling-Hammond, 1988, 1995, 1997).

Some of the design teams emphasize that it takes several years to expect implementation to take hold throughout the school (Bodilly, 1998; Smith et al., 1998). Only with coherent implementation would one expect school test scores to consistently increase throughout the school. Our analysis shows a large number of NAS schools near the midlevel implementation points on scales for the wide array of indicators considered here. Moreover, there is a great deal of variation among teachers within the NAS sites. While there is a range in implementation levels observed in our analysis, it is probable that implementation is not deep enough throughout the schools at this point to raise student scores across grade levels. Over time with more-specific test score information and additional measures of implementation, the empirical link might be observed. This remains an open question.

Second, the nature of our dependent variable—a simple 0/1 variable—does not allow for any gradations in student performance. Had we been able to calculate effect sizes, perhaps we would have seen a link between implementation and performance.

Third, the analysis sample may have failed to find evidence of the link between implementation and student performance, perhaps because of measurement error in our indicators. Although our implementation indicators appear to be credibly constructed and to track well with Bodilly's findings, they may fail to capture important aspects of implementation that are linked to school performance. The great variability that we see within schools in implementation adds to the difficulty in measuring mean implementation levels in a school. The summary measures examined in this study may not have the power to distinguish fully between schools with higher and lower levels of implementation. As we noted in Chapter Four, the majority of the schools' implementation levels were at the midpoints on our scales, and there was a great deal of stability between 1997 and 1999 (i.e., both in mean levels and within-school variance) (see also Kirby, Berends, and Naftel, 2001; Berends and Kirby et al., 2001).

MONITORING ACADEMIC PROGRESS WITH STUDENT-LEVEL TEST SCORES

The ultimate aim of school reform efforts and implementation of NAS designs is to substantially improve student performance. As we pointed out, analysis of grade-level aggregate scores within NAS schools compared with the district are fraught with problems for which it is difficult to control with available data. However, other analyses of student test scores in what were two ostensibly supportive NAS districts—San Antonio and Memphis—reveal that significantly raising student achievement scores, sustaining them over time, and attributing them to design team activities presents a substantial challenge as well.

Student Achievement in San Antonio

As described in the previous chapter, elementary school students in San Antonio take the TAAS. Given the available data, we conducted two sets of analyses: First, for the entire district we examined the effects of student, teacher, and school characteristics on the 4th-grade TAAS reading and mathematics scores, controlling for prior achievement. Data provided by the San Antonio district and other sources allowed for construction of a data set containing more than 3,800 4th-grade students in about 280 classrooms in all 64 elementary schools in the district. Individual 4th graders' TAAS reading and mathematics scores were regressed against students' prior achievement and student, teacher, classroom, and school characteristics using multilevel models to partition the variation in reading and mathematics achievement into student and classroom components. Second, we analyzed student achievement in a subsample of over 800 students in 63 classrooms for which teachers completed our survey.

The results at the district level provide the context for the subsample. Data gathered from the teacher surveys help inform the district analysis on the impacts of teacher practices and perceptions of student achievement. In addition, these students were administered the Stanford-9 open-ended reading test, making possible an independent measure of student performance without the "high stakes" implications of the TAAS.

After controlling for all of these student, classroom, and school characteristics, we fail to find a significant effect of implementation of NAS designs in San Antonio.[3] This same result came up in estimations of a variety of other model specifications, using other regres-

---

[3]Because students are nested within classrooms, which are nested within schools, we relied on multilevel modeling techniques to provide more accurate estimates of student-, classroom-, and school-level effects (see Bryk and Raudenbush, 1992; Bryk, Raudenbush, and Congdon, 1996; Singer, 1998; Kreft and De Leeuw, 1998). Further details are available in Berends et al. (2002).

sion techniques such as ordinary least squares, three-level linear models and probit models, where the dependent variables were binary indicators of passing or failing scores.[4] This is not surprising since we are examining effects on spring 1998 scores, and many of the designs had not been in place that long. In addition, implementation was not deep in these schools, given the conflicting reforms that overshadowed implementation of NAS designs in these schools. As such, we would not expect to find effects of implementation on student achievement.

Because instructional conditions varied more between NAS and non-NAS schools during the 1997–1998 school year, we wanted to examine whether such variation in instructional conditions was related to student achievement, controlling for other student, teacher, classroom, and school characteristics. We first examined relationships in all 4th-grade classrooms in the district and then in the sample of classrooms for which RAND gathered additional survey data on classroom instruction and a supplemental reading test (Stanford-9) (see Berends et al., 2002).

We did not find that instructional conditions promoted by reforms such as NAS—including teacher-reported collaboration, quality of professional development, and reform-like instructional practices—were related to student achievement net of other student and classroom conditions.

However, we did find significant effects of principal leadership on the TAAS reading and mathematics scores by 0.15 and 0.21 of a standard deviation gain, respectively. Principal leadership in our analysis was measured by teacher reports about principals who clearly communicated what was expected of teachers, were supportive and encouraging of staff, obtained resources for the school, enforced rules for student conduct, talked with teachers regarding instructional practices, had confidence in the expertise of the teachers, and took a personal interest in the professional development of teachers. Chapter Four described how our previous analyses have shown the importance of principal leadership in implementing the designs

---

[4]For example, additional analyses of longitudinal student achievement growth models from grades 3–5 do not show significant effects of NAS classrooms and schools compared with non-NAS comparisons.

(Berends and Kirby et al., 2001; Kirby, Berends, and Naftel, 2001). In our San Antonio classroom study, we found a link between principal leadership and student achievement in NAS and non-NAS schools, indicating that leadership is important for academic achievement in general, and to implementation in particular.

Student Achievement in Memphis

Memphis was another supportive district of NAS designs during the scale-up phase. The superintendent provided significant resources toward designs and was committed to NAS's scale-up strategy to widely diffuse the designs within the district. In fact, her leadership during her tenure in Memphis resulted in her being honored as national superintendent of the year.

Memphis has used the Comprehensive Test of Basic Skills, version 4 (CTBS/4) since 1990. This is a commercial, multiple-choice test that measures skills in reading, mathematics, and other subject areas. In the spring of 1998, Memphis adopted the CTBS/5 Complete Battery Plus (Terra Nova). This latter version of the CTBS as tailored to the State of Tennessee is also a multiple-choice test, but concentrates on higher-order thinking skills to a greater extent than the previous CTBS/4. Scores have been equated across the two tests. Produced by CTB/McGraw-Hill, both forms of the test contain items developed specifically for students in Tennessee.

Tennessee has a sophisticated testing and assessment program called the Tennessee Value-Added Assessment System (TVAAS), which enables the tracking of the academic progress of every student in the state in grades 3–8 and beyond (as high school testing is implemented) in science, math, social studies, language arts, and reading (see Sanders and Horn [1994, 1995] for more details on this system and the methodology used to measure student progress). TVAAS reports annually on the gains that students made in each grade and each subject grouped by achievement levels. These reports have information on the three most recent years as well as the three-year average gains. The state monitors all school systems that are not achieving national norm gains; those systems

> achieving two or more standard errors below the national norms must show positive progress or risk intervention by the state. Each

school and system is expected to achieve the national norm gains regardless of whether its scale scores are above or below the national norm. (Sanders and Horn, 1994, p. 302.)

The raw data for TVAAS are the scaled scores from the CTBS/4 and now CTBS/5, which form a part of the Tennessee Comprehensive Assessment Program (TCAP). All students in grades 2–8 are tested yearly; this information is linked to the school and the teacher by subject area and grade. The longitudinal nature of the data allows each student to serve as his or her own "control." TVAAS uses statistical mixed-model methodology to estimate a multivariate, longitudinal model of student achievement and then to aggregate these data to the classroom or the school level. The gain scores of a school's students are estimated and compared with the national norms. Thus, deviations from the national norms can be calculated to see how the school is doing with respect to a national sample of students.

The index of student achievement used in the analyses is the Cumulative Percent of Norm (CPN) mean. This measures the percent of national (expected) gain attained by the school in the reported grades (Bratton, Horn, and Wright, 1996). For example, if a school had a CPN equal to 75 percent in 5th-grade reading, then the average gain of the 5th-grade students in the school was 0.75 of the expected year-to-year gain based on a national sample.

Ross et al. (1998, 1999, 2000, 2001) provide an examination of the relative performance of restructuring elementary schools in Memphis from 1995 to 1998 (see Figure 6.1). They compared gains in the restructuring schools on the TCAP with non-restructured (NR) elementary schools and the state. Their results show that by 1998, both cohort 1 (in year 3 of implementation) and cohort 2 schools (in year 2 of implementation) demonstrated "small, nonsignificant advantages over the NR schools" (Ross et al., 1999, p. 3). An additional important finding is that higher-poverty schools appeared to derive the greatest benefits from these reforms. Their overall conclusion is that although the effects have varied by year and by cohort, restruc-

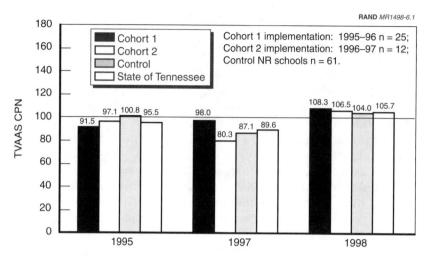

NOTE: Figure taken from Ross et al. (2001).

**Figure 6.1—Memphis City Schools TVAAS Results for All Subjects
Cumulative Percent of Norm, Mean Across Grades 3–5**

turing shows promise in raising achievement in Memphis elementary schools.[5]

Yet, despite these relatively more-promising results Memphis has decided to drop the designs in favor of more curriculum-specific re-

---

[5]In our analysis, we found less positive results (see Berends and Kirby et al., 2001) when comparing the NAS-only designs with the district. We worked with Steven Ross of the University of Memphis and William Sanders of the University of Tennessee, who provided the supplementary results in our research. The data we examined for mathematics and reading for elementary schools were somewhat different from Ross et al. (1998, 1999, 2001) for several reasons. First, we compared the NAS schools with the district, and they compared the NAS school designs with "non-restructured" schools between 1995 and 1998. Second, Ross et al. also included some non-NAS schools in their analyses. Third, to be consistent to what we did for other jurisdictions, we compared Memphis NAS schools with the district, using base year of implementation to two years after implementation. Had we used the 1998 results for cohort 1, our results would have looked more similar to Ross et al. Fourth, we also examined secondary schools, where the picture seems somewhat more mixed: It varied by year and the most recent year is the least encouraging, with NAS schools well below the district average.

forms.[6] The former superintendent who brought in the NAS designs and provided significant support for them—about $12 million over six years—took another position. The incoming superintendent announced to the school board that the whole-school reform models would be discontinued in favor of new districtwide curriculum, beginning with a reading program in fall 2001. Similar to the situation in San Antonio, there were concerns about the effectiveness of designs and their ability to teach students more fundamental reading and writing skills. Apparently, recent score results in Memphis did not help in that they were not nearly as positive as in the past year (Ross, S. M., personal communication).

FINDINGS FROM CASE STUDIES

Similar to what we found in our quantitative analyses, the case study work offered some provocative, but inconclusive, information that might lead one to assert that a variety of factors other than design implementation account for the differences in test score gains between the matched pairs of schools that were the focus of the study (Chun, Gill, and Heilbrunn, 2001). These factors include student and family characteristics; stability, experience, and morale of the teaching force; and test preparation programs. Moreover, several factors likely contribute to the absence of a relationship between design implementation and test score results. These include:

- Tests that fail to capture the range of student learning outcomes targeted by NAS designs;

- Pressure on schools to raise test scores immediately and dramatically (which promotes the use of skills-oriented curricula at odds with ambitious, interdisciplinary designs); and

- Low levels of implementation across the board—an absence of truly comprehensive reform.

---

[6]This information is from an article in *The Commercial Appeal* by Aimee Edmonson entitled "Watson Kills All Reform Models for City Schools" (June 19, 2001). See also NAS's response in a press release of June 28, 2001—"New American Schools' Statement on Memphis Superintendent's Decision to Drop Comprehensive School Reform" (http://www.newamericanschools.com/press/062801.phtml).

SUMMARY AND POLICY IMPLICATIONS

Our analysis of performance trends across the set of schools three years into scale-up focused on whether NAS schools made gains in test scores relative to their respective jurisdictions.

- Among the four jurisdictions with ten or more implementing NAS schools, Memphis and Kentucky schools appeared to be the most successful in terms of improvement in mathematics, while Cincinnati and Washington state did better in reading.

- In total, of the 163 schools for which we have data allowing us comparisons in performance relative to the district or state, 81 schools (50 percent) made gains relative to the district in mathematics and 76 schools (47 percent) made gains in reading.

Because of the wide variation in implementation and environments that occurs within schools and among jurisdictions, it may have been too early to expect robust performance results across the NAS sites. However, our implementation analysis shows little increase in level of implementation over time and continuing within-school variation in implementation. Thus, one might expect design adoption to never have any lasting impact on student performance. In addition, better and longer-term performance data are needed in order to make conclusive judgments about designs and their effects on school performance.

The detailed classroom study of San Antonio allowed us to examine whether variation in instructional conditions was related to student achievement, controlling for other student, teacher, classroom, and school characteristics:

- As expected because of the early stages of implementation, elementary students in NAS schools did not significantly differ in their achievement growth compared with students in non-NAS schools.

- More importantly, we did not discover that instructional conditions promoted by reforms such as NAS—including teacher-reported collaboration, quality of professional development, and reform-like instructional practices—were related to student achievement net of other student and classroom conditions.

- However, we did find significant effects of principal leadership on the TAAS reading and mathematics scores.

Evidence from Other Studies

At this point in comprehensive school reform, there is only limited evidence about the effectiveness of design-based models from studies that rely on rigorous comparative evaluation designs. For example, Herman et al. (1999) find only two models were able to provide convincing results in terms of raising student achievement levels. In addition, in evaluations of the Comer's School Development Program, Cook and his colleagues at Northwestern University (see Cook et al., 1999; Cook et al., 1998) found no effect of the model on student achievement in Prince George's County, Maryland, but found small positive effects on students (less than one-tenth of a standard deviation) in Chicago schools. These Cook et al. studies were based on randomized experimental longitudinal designs, and both point to the importance of further longitudinal studies that carefully examine the approaches of design-based assistance providers and the variation in implementation and performance that is likely to occur. Cook et al. (1998) also point to the importance of district-level support and expectations for improving instruction and achievement. Other studies have shown that raising achievement levels in dramatic fashion within urban school districts is a formidable challenge (see Fullan, 2001; Bryk et al., 1998; Orr, 1998).

The evidence reported here suggests variation in implementation and performance and describes a number of factors related to implementation. The evidence suggests that design teams, districts, schools, and teachers have a great deal of work to do to fully implement designs on a broad scale before we can expect to see dramatic, or even significant, improvements in student outcomes. Whether large numbers of schools can implement whole-school designs in a sustainable fashion that can improve student achievement across grade levels remains an open question.

Chapter Seven

THE FUTURE OF WHOLE-SCHOOL DESIGNS: CONCLUSIONS, OBSERVATIONS, AND POLICY IMPLICATIONS

Mark Berends, Susan Bodilly, Sheila Nataraj Kirby

The NAS effort, as we mentioned earlier, offered an unprecedented opportunity to study and understand a dramatic attempt at whole-school reform from its inception—one based on an experimental approach of research and development, demonstration, and scale-up. Analyzing the initiative over this past decade has offered a broad perspective on the issues facing different parties to the reform effort: founders, developers, district administrators, principals, and teachers. Perhaps more importantly, RAND's findings from monitoring the NAS effort over this past decade offer important and sobering lessons for federal, state, and local policymakers attempting to improve failing schools through comprehensive school reform. This final chapter provides a retrospective on the following:

- The unique nature of the RAND approach to evaluating the NAS initiative, its strengths and weaknesses;

- The contributions of NAS to educational reform;

- The implications of the RAND analyses to the external change agent theory of action; and

- Implications for the current federal CSRD policy.

UNIQUENESS OF THE RAND APPROACH

While NAS has been a unique effort, the analyses performed by RAND concerning NAS have also been unique. The scope of the NAS effort was remarkable: capitalizing seven teams; pushing for a scale-up effort in ten districts; and undertaking a scale-up effort in hundreds of schools. The RAND analysis had just as remarkable a scope. It covered the evolution of NAS and its teams from inception to 1998. It tracked implementation and performance in over one hundred schools from 1996 through 1999. It combined an action-oriented approach with formative assessment methods conditioned on the developmental nature of the intervention. For that reason, the RAND analyses focused heavily on the development of designs and their implementation strategies. These two issues are overlooked in more-summative research designs. This approach enabled NAS and RAND to draw strong connections between the conditions of implementation and outcomes.

This uniqueness had both strengths and weaknesses. Its strengths were that it provided in-depth information on implementation and systemic issues that few other studies of reforms have provided, and it uniquely identified both the collage of actors and activities that needed to be successfully meshed for the effort to prove successful and the important conditions under which the innovations could flourish.

On the other hand, it did not provide as clear and compelling evidence on outcomes as one might have desired, especially if the sponsors were interested in significant improvements for selected groups of students. Given the developmental nature of the intervention, the measures and controls were not and could not be geared for this. Furthermore, the teams themselves often did not provide the proof of their theories of learning that would have complemented the RAND efforts and strengthened the entire analytical impact. However, the framework and methods were strong enough to show that dramatic improvements expected by NAS and the partnering districts did not exist for most schools.

The RAND approach worked well under these very special circumstances: a developmental intervention; a client needing information for improvement quickly; and the stipulation that the results had to be dramatic to continue with the effort. However, sponsors interested in more-specific and careful measures of more fully developed interventions would not benefit by this approach.

THE CONTRIBUTION OF NEW AMERICAN SCHOOLS

NAS accomplished several of the goals it had set for itself and in the process made several important contributions to educational reform that need to be kept in mind.

NAS funding and leadership led to the deliberate development of functioning design teams. When NAS started, few whole-school designs existed. Judging from the initial proposals, there were few organizations capable of design development or of thinking in terms of whole-school approaches. NAS funding eventually took seven designs from ideas on paper to firmly developed and functioning teams whose designs have been adopted in multiple sites in the educational marketplace. In essence it proved that teams could be deliberately created and developed over time.

NAS showed that initially dependent external change agents could be moved toward self-sufficiency over time. NAS undertook a very systematic venture capital approach. It weeded out teams it thought were not moving toward strong self-sufficiency or showing the results it wanted, while it provided capacity-building funds for those that were moving in its preferred direction. It provided assistance to teams in their development to allow them to become self-sustaining. Perhaps most notably, NAS encouraged federal funding, in the form of advocating for the CSRD program, to allow for growth in the market for the teams. In the end, NAS still provides some funding through loans for capacity building, but the remaining design teams otherwise operate independently in the marketplace of school reforms.

NAS explicitly sought scale-up of the reform initiative. Foundations and others have sought to create self-sustaining programs. Few have been able to do so, but some have been successful. NAS went a step further and deliberately pushed toward a scale-up strategy from the very beginning. NAS can take credit for deliberately spreading, or scaling up, a variety of designs in many different school settings. The creation of the CSRD funding is just one manner in which NAS still promotes the concept of scale-up of design-based assistance for whole-school reform.

NAS explicitly made analysis and good consumer education a part of its efforts. A major purpose behind the RAND analyses was to offer critical and timely analysis of the NAS operations. NAS has always been very supportive of this effort and an avid consumer of the RAND information, using it to help identify problems and solutions to improve the initiative. From the beginning, NAS has emphasized the importance of quality assurance among its teams. It continues to promote this idea through the *Guidelines for Ensuring the Quality of National Design-Based Assistance Providers* and by creating and spinning off the Education Quality Institute.

Our review of the NAS experiences indicated that this deliberate effort did succeed in some important ways, and the approach of providing venture capital with specific goals could be used as a policy instrument in the future when innovative approaches and new actors are desired. In addition, NAS actions as a change agent have significantly influenced policy in its areas of interest.

IMPLICATIONS FOR THE EXTERNAL CHANGE AGENT THEORY OF ACTION

We began our discussion by indicating the RAND's analyses focused on the theory of action inherent in the NAS initiative, not on the efficacy of each design. We return here to that theory as a way to draw conclusions about the NAS initiative. RAND findings provide mixed evidence to support several hypotheses underpinning NAS's theory of change:

- The initial NAS hypothesis, that by adopting a whole-school design a school could improve its performance, was largely unproven. We found specific positive examples of schoolwide implementation and improvement under certain conditions; however, negative examples were found under more-common conditions. Our general findings were of weak implementation and lack of strong improvements in school performance. The RAND analyses provide neither clear support for nor evidence against the contention of some that whole-school design approaches are superior to more programmatic approaches to school reform (Slavin, 1997a, 1997b, 1999, 2000; Pogrow, 1998, 2000a, 2000b; Slavin and Madden, 2000; Fashola and Slavin, 1998).

- NAS's and RAND's hypothesis that designs alone are not helpful to schools and that schools need assistance in implementation was proven correct. Teachers and school administrators clearly reported higher levels of implementation associated with strong assistance from design teams. But, just as importantly and consistent with the implementation literature, conditions at the schools and within the districts and the manner of selection also proved important to implementation and outcomes.

- The scale-up hypothesis that a district that converted 30 percent of its schools using whole-school approaches would become high-performing and not revert to unproductive practices was disproved. Districts, such as Memphis, reverted back to their former status quickly with changes in administrations.

- The scale-up hypothesis that a district needs to provide a supportive environment was dramatically proven by the negative case of San Antonio. Without a supportive environment the designs did not flourish.

In general, we conclude that the theory of action was largely underdeveloped and underspecified. The causal chain of events leading to strong implementation and outcomes has proven to be far more complex than that originally considered by NAS and one that remained largely outside of its control and influence. This finding is in keeping with the literature on implementation indicating the complexity of the change process.

Based on our experience with NAS, we offer the following implications for future efforts to bring about whole-school reforms through external agents.

Externally developed education reform interventions cannot be "break the mold" and still be marketable and implementable in current district and school contexts. NAS attempted to have both "break the mold" designs and designs that would appeal and be implemented nationally. It faced and still faces a fundamental market issue. The evidence of our evolution analysis and the implementation analyses all point to the fact that schools did not have a ready place for these designs. Schools were not by and large fertile ground for "break the mold" ideas, often because of a lack of capacity or local, state, or district regulations. Rather, the designs had to change to be suitable to school conditions or simply not be implemented. Design team calls for significant school autonomy over budget, staffing, curriculum, instruction, and assessments often did not fit into the institutional infrastructure that schools faced. Under these conditions the designs often settled for approaches that called for marginal improvements over time. In order for the design to be well-implemented, the district and school contexts have to change to allow for "break the mold" school-level ideas to flourish.

External interventions need to address systemic issues that can hinder implementation. The relatively weak implementation of the designs in scale-up was associated with several systemic factors: lack of teacher capacity to undertake the designs, especially in terms of time and subject area expertise; lack of principal leadership; and an incoherent district infrastructure that did not match the needs of design implementation. Improved district support appears difficult to obtain, but perhaps feasible with a significant resource outlay and strong relationship between a NAS-like organization and a district (not just the superintendent). The requirements for teacher capacity and principal leadership for design implementation appear more problematic. It is those very schools lacking in these qualities that theoretically would most benefit from external assistance interventions. This implies the design concept did not focus on the important dimensions of school improvement when attempting to increase school effectiveness. Greater attention to building basic teacher capacity and effective principal leadership for transition should be the focus of reform, at least for low-performing, high-poverty schools.

A rush to scale-up when interventions are not completely developed weakens results. NAS designs and teams were not ready to scale up when NAS called for this move in 1995. NAS was not ready for this scale-up either. It had not fully developed its concepts of school matching, district partnerships, or a supportive district environment to the point where it could ensure its designs would thrive in a scale-up activity. Many of the problems associated with the scale-up phase are attributable to pushing toward full-scale production before all the kinks in the product were worked out. However, these problems are likely to persist partly because developers are under financial pressures to scale up their interventions before they are thoroughly evaluated and partly because districts and schools are under severe political pressure to adopt external solutions—whether proven or not—as a means of addressing the lackluster performance of their students. Venture firms like NAS must weigh the benefits of waiting until development is complete against the costs of waiting to enter the field with a new product when interest is high. The consequences of not waiting should be taken seriously. Failures in implementation due to a rush to get into schools result in a continuing weakening of the trust between teachers and administrators and between parents and the education community.

A key component of successful implementation is consistent, clear, and frequent communication and assistance between design developers and schools, particularly teachers. Implementation tended to be very low in schools where teachers reported they did not understand the design, see the design team members often, or receive strong assistance. Case studies pointed to the importance of the selection process in establishing firm positive relationships between the external agent and the school staff; in addition, they highlighted the importance of communicating with and involving all teachers in the school, not just the "leads." The external agents struggled to provide high levels of assistance, but could not always do so given the leap in capacity required from demonstration in a few, often nearby, sites to scale-up in many schools across the country. A reasonable inference from our research is that a strong, trusting relationship between a school and an external agent is a prerequisite for strong implementation of complex interventions that require significant changes in behavior. If funders and developers expect teachers to change behavior significantly, then they need to invest considerable time and effort to build trusting relationships with teachers.

Monitoring site progress, self-evaluation, and reflection are necessary if external developers are to be successful and to improve their offerings over time. Our work throughout the development and demonstration phases indicated that most of the teams had not created the feedback loop or data needed to further develop their designs and offer meaningful support packages to the schools. This affected their ability to produce the desired results. In later phases, most did not collect adequate information about their implementing sites to allow for proper support or even to hazard a guess as to implementation levels in schools. This ran counter to the emphasis placed by NAS on quality assurance and its continuous calls for self-evaluation by the design teams. In part, this is a resource issue—the push to scale-up left the developers with few resources for evaluation. In part, it is a priority issue—developers want to spend money on development of the ideas they are committed to, oftentimes whether or not they are effective, and may see evaluation as less important or too expensive. But, unless systems for tracking progress in schools and understanding school-level concerns are created and used for improving the external intervention, then the effort cannot succeed over the long term. This capacity must be deliberately built into the development effort and continuously maintained.

The typical outcome measures used in public accountability systems provide a very limited measure of student and school performance. Years of evaluations indicate that the best way to measure whether an intervention is having an effect is to measure variables most closely associated with the interventions. This truism would lead evaluations away from using district and state test score data toward a richer set of assessments and indicators for whole school reform. However, the conditions in the scale-up phase worked against this. First, the external agents had not developed convincing indicators of progress; in fact, they had to be asked to develop benchmarks for progress by the districts because indicators of progress did not always exist. Second, districts insisted their tests be used as the sole indicator and NAS promised dramatic improvements in this single indicator. In short, in the developmental phases of an intervention, the assessment instruments needed to adequately measure progress do not exist. The assessment measures that do exist—district-mandated tests—do not adequately measure the impact of innovative approaches.

This tension will be a constant hindrance to understanding the impact of innovative approaches unless alternative indicators and assessments are developed in ways that are well aligned with what the reforms are trying to do. Few reforms will show strong results when they are geared toward improving students' complex thinking and mastery of difficult subject matter, but are measured by simplistic tests. We will not be measuring what is important, but measuring what is easy to measure. The high-stakes testing regimes currently in vogue and the overwhelming emphasis given to improved test scores on state- or district-mandated tests as *the* measure of improvement do not bode well for many innovative reform efforts.

IMPLICATIONS FOR CURRENT POLICY: A CAUTIONARY NOTE

Currently, many schools throughout the country are attempting whole-school reform requiring significant changes in teacher and administrator behaviors using the federal funding provided by such programs as Title I and the CSRD program. RAND's program of studies of NAS has identified the conditions needed to make these efforts successful including: teacher support and sense of teacher efficacy; strong and specific principal leadership abilities; clear communication and ongoing assistance on the part of design developers; and stable leadership, resources, and support from the district.

The RAND analyses indicate these conditions are not common in the districts and schools undertaking CSRD—schools with similar characteristics to those NAS served in the scale-up phase. Because the target of the federal Title I and CSRD funds is primarily high-poverty schools, schools most likely to be affected by the CSRD program are also schools that are most likely to face very fragmented and conflicting environments, difficult and changing political currents, new accountability systems, entrenched unions, serious lack of slack resources in terms of teacher time, and demoralized teachers given the fluctuating reform agenda and the difficult task of improving student performance under these types of conditions (for a description of CSRD schools see Kirby et al., in review). These schools will face many obstacles during implementation of whole-school designs, and because of this, whole-school designs will face continuing challenges in significantly raising the achievement of all students.

Given this, federal and state policymakers need to think critically about their current stance of simultaneously promoting high-stakes testing; the implementation of comprehensive school reforms that promote innovative curriculum and instructional strategies; and the implementation of multiple other concurrent reforms. This is especially the case when confronting reduced state and local budgets during a time of retrenchment.

The implementation of high-stakes testing regimes precludes the adoption of rich and varied curricula that challenge students and motivate them toward more in-depth learning experiences. It certainly prevents adoption of such curricula when other more basic skills reforms are mandated on top of the design-based curriculum. High-stakes tests become a two-edged sword in this environment. On the one hand, high-stakes tests motivate schools to increase performance and often to seek out new curriculum and instructional strategies associated with comprehensive school reforms. On the other hand, those very same tests provide disincentives to adopt richer, more in-depth curriculum—even when mandated.

Concurrently, these same districts are facing new and growing pressures to see the performance of their lowest achieving schools increase substantially, and these schools are frequently high-poverty, high-minority schools that receive Title I funds. For example, some of the key Title I provisions involve states establishing rigorous standards for what students should know (content standards); establishing performance standards for how well students should know the content; and developing assessments to measure school and/or student progress toward these goals. By the spring of 2001, all states were required to have such assessments in place to comply with Title I policy, with additional testing and accountability requirements emerging from recent federal legislation.

If districts react to this pressure with past behaviors, they will likely promote the failure of whole-school reforms. In the past, districts have sought to increase accountability, while also mandating a series of reforms, without providing for the slack needed to implement them. For instance, some districts are mandating reading and math programs with specified professional development routines, increased teacher and principal accountability based on inappropriate test regimes, and further reductions in school-level budgets. Simultaneously, they encourage schools to adopt schoolwide models without much review of effectiveness or fit with the district policies or school needs. The result will be, as it was in the scale-up districts, continued fragmented, incoherent policies not supportive of whole-school interventions.

In short, we anticipate continuing conflicts between whole-school design or model adoption and district and school contexts as well as political pressures rushing schools and external assistance providers into partnerships that are not well thought through. If districts continue in this manner, the outcome will be neither short-term gains, nor long-term success. Expectations regarding the ability of schools to make meaningful changes with the assistance of externally developed designs in this fragmented and unsupportive environment are not likely to be met. This may well lead policymakers to abandon what could be a promising vehicle for whole-school reform without having given it a chance.

DRIVEN BY RESULTS AND A DECADE OF EXPERIENCE

by New American Schools

Comprehensive school reform "arguably holds out the greatest hope of producing categorical change" in schools.[1]

The best available information and our own experiences suggest comprehensive school reform (CSR), while not problem-free, has great potential for success and has become the dominant school reform model in the nation's classrooms. However, its ability to reach large numbers of schools and students depends in no small part on changes in the culture of school systems and, above all, a move from policies dominated by the quick fix of the day to practices driven by results and continuous improvement. The nation should continue to invest in CSR with an eye toward improvement, given the promise shown. Now is not the time to move on to the "new, new thing." This is especially true, given the recent passage of the Elementary and Secondary Education Act, which requires educators to meet tougher accountability standards or risk sanctions and corrective action imposed by states and the federal government. Congress's willingness to make permanent the Comprehensive School Reform Demonstration (CSRD) program, to increase its funding level this year, and to identify CSR as a strategy low-performing schools should consider for school improvement is a recognition of what has been accomplished to date.

---

[1] "Better By Design: A Consumer's Guide to Schoolwide Reform," a report by the Thomas B. Fordham Foundation

During the past decade, New American Schools (NAS) has evolved from a developer and supporter of specific whole-school reform efforts to an organization dedicated to successful and wide-scale implementation of comprehensive improvement strategies that have been proven to work or have exceptional promise. This evolution presented many challenges that provide insights into what is needed to ensure sustained improvement efforts. Our contribution to RAND's *Facing the Challenges of Whole-School Reform: New American Schools After a Decade* is an attempt at articulating what we have learned and where we are headed, with the hope it will contribute to a continuous process to improve and grow. It also is in keeping with the NAS tradition of looking critically at our actions and learning from our mistakes. RAND has been an invaluable partner in this endeavor.

Without RAND's insightful findings and strategic advice, we would have lost our way on the road to continuous improvement. As a result of our ten-year relationship with RAND, we are committed to rigorous, ongoing evaluations of all that we do to ensure quality design and delivery of programs and services for schools and students. While we did not always agree with RAND and its evaluation approaches, we respected and valued its role in improving public education and, specifically, comprehensive school reform. We extend special appreciation to Tom Glennan, Susan Bodilly, and Mark Berends, all leaders in comprehensive school reform research.

We have learned many lessons about what is needed to increase student achievement through the successful implementation of comprehensive improvement plans in classrooms. Arguably, the most important lessons focus on school readiness, district policies and practices, quality controls, evaluations, and community support. We have taken these lessons and built a strategy around them to achieve our decade-long mission of increasing student achievement. While our mission has not changed, many of the activities we now undertake are different from what they were ten years ago or even two years ago.

This chapter explains why we have chosen this strategy. First, it reviews NAS's history. Then, it discusses the important concept of comprehensive school improvement that includes CSR designs or models. It then turns to a description of the lessons learned and our current areas of interest.

NEW AMERICAN SCHOOLS: 1991–2001

In 1991, New American Schools, a nonprofit corporation formed by the chief executives of some of our country's most successful businesses, planned to develop "a new generation of American schools." NAS organized a five-year research and development competition that ultimately provided 11 independent organizations with funding and technical assistance to develop "comprehensive school designs." Over time, NAS invested more than $130 million in the organizations, now known as design teams. They created models that reorganize an entire school around a unified vision and a shared plan for higher student achievement; quality professional development for teachers, principals, and other school personnel; greater parental and community involvement; ongoing evaluation of progress and performance for continuous improvement; and closely tied networks of like-minded educators.

Beginning in 1991, NAS contracted with RAND to develop and manage an independent evaluation of our work. During the past ten years, RAND's evaluative studies, critical feedback, and reports have helped NAS to identify and define the weak links and missing components of comprehensive reform strategies for schools and school districts and later would contribute substantially to new service offerings provided by NAS to states, school districts, and schools, including charter schools.

In 1996, NAS urged seven of the design teams to adopt a national dissemination strategy based on fee-for-service. We supported this strategy by providing the seed capital and technical assistance to help them operate like professional service firms, financially independent of NAS. With NAS as a partner, they entered into agreements with a group of major school districts across the country to implement their models or designs in at least one-third of the districts' schools. About that time, NAS began to finance the design teams on the basis of loans rather than grants through a self-sustaining investment program that eventually became the Education Entrepreneurs Fund. Today these design teams work in almost 4,000 schools and operate totally independently from NAS.

In 1997, Congress passed the CSRD program, in response to NAS's and others' initial successes and the long-term potential for CSR to improve public education. Since its passage, approximately $900 million has been appropriated to help schools and districts start up CSR efforts. As a result, hundreds of organizations have begun to offer school reform services and products.

In 1999, NAS joined hands with other organizations to help educators and parents decipher the differences among organizations offering CSR programs and services. NAS sponsored an independent blue-ribbon panel composed of leaders across the spectrum of public education—from Chester E. Finn, Jr., of the Thomas B. Fordham Foundation to Sandra Feldman of the American Federation of Teachers—to craft and endorse guidelines to help schools, teachers, parents, and others determine which of these organizations and service providers truly offered quality CSR services.

In 2001, we built on the work of the blue-ribbon panel by helping to form the Education Quality Institute (EQI), an independent organization whose aim is to help consumers of education products and services select programs that meet locally defined needs and adhere to quality guidelines, are research based, and have been proven to work.

Importantly, that same year, we shaped a decade's worth of classroom experience, extensive research, and independent evaluations into a coherent set of consulting and operational services, products, and tools, offered through two divisions within New American Schools: the NAS Service Network and the Education Entrepreneurs Fund. These offerings support and partner with the design teams as well as many other quality providers of comprehensive services working in schools. But, the primary objective is to help educators at all levels create the environments necessary for quality comprehensive school improvement to take root and flourish.

COMPREHENSIVE SCHOOL IMPROVEMENT: A SYSTEMS APPROACH, NOT JUST A CSR DESIGN OR MODEL

At this point, it is important to draw a distinction between individual CSR designs or models and comprehensive school improvement. The former is an approach offered by an organization at the school level; the latter is a broad systemic strategy for improvement that includes CSR designs. Comprehensive school improvement supports improved student achievement through the coherent alignment of CSR designs or models with policies and practices at the state and district levels related to school leadership and governance, curriculum and instruction, professional development, accountability and evaluation, resource allocation, and community engagement, among other areas.

Numerous studies, particularly the RAND reports, have found that the success of any design is the joint product of efforts by the design's developer, the school, and the school district. As a systemic strategy for increasing student achievement, comprehensive school improvement involves the use of a design as well as external support to achieve student performance objectives; a commitment by teachers and staff to the model—often in the form of a vote; investments of teacher time and district funds; the involvement of the superintendent's senior staff to align district policies to reinforce those investments; the engagement of the community and parents; and means of measuring the quality of design implementation and student outcomes. States and outside organizations, such as NAS, that work with designs and local educators also can influence the outcome of this joint effort.

Models, whether "home grown" or nationally developed, are a necessary part of this strategy—they drive change at the school level, but the model or design and its developer are only one part of the equation. *Models must be implemented to be effective.* Successful implementation requires that the individual design be aligned to the school's needs and that the school's teaching staff freely commits to the design and is given the time to train and implement it. The design's developer also must provide the necessary school-level assistance in implementation. Importantly, the implementation process, including the technical assistance, needs to be fully financed. Finally, the Board of Education and the central office must give high priority to the support of design implementation in all of its policy processes.

At the national level, comprehensive school improvement involves evaluating these multiparty implementation processes across districts with the best available information, identifying what works and what does not, determining why, directing investment and purchasing decisions to designs or models that do work, throwing out what does not work, and repeating this cycle. Here is where federal and state education policies, philanthropy, and organizations, such as NAS, can have high leverage and direct influence. Over time, this system will assure a winnowing that leaves the best models or designs at the top.

LESSONS LEARNED

1. Applied research and continuous evaluation is key to identifying and disseminating best practices to increase student achievement. However, poorly conducted research does more harm than good and unfairly stigmatizes schools and students.

Underlying all reform and improvement initiatives is an assumption that performance and results will be assessed in a fair and accurate manner; however, current approaches to measuring and evaluating student and school performance often are misleading and unfair. As a result, news accounts of school rankings do not offer a complete picture of what is happening in classrooms. Teachers cannot develop the individualized instruction needed for student improvement. School leaders cannot be fairly judged by the public on their ability to increase student achievement.

Traditionally, evaluation staffs in central offices determine the performance of individual schools by comparing the average scores of students in a particular grade in one year with the average scores of a different set of students in that same grade in the next year. The typical year-to-year comparison of averages in a grade says more about the students—and especially their socioeconomic status—than the quality of the classrooms in which they sit. Few districts actually look at how the same group of students improves over time. Yet, this is the best way to determine what schools add to student learning.

This type of comparison is generally known as a "value-added" approach. While not perfect, it offers significant improvements in precision and accuracy over most current evaluation techniques employed by districts today, including some of those used by RAND in its studies of the NAS-affiliated designs. It also permits evaluators to control for important variables such as student mobility, socioeconomic status, and prior achievement levels. Evaluation systems must allow districts and schools to measure year-to-year progress as well as measure student achievement in comparison to absolute standards. A system enabling understanding of both is a powerful driver of change and improvement.

Through the Services Network, we now offer assistance to educators in evaluation techniques, as they collect, use, and manage student-level data to ensure that fair and accurate information is driving decisionmaking in and outside the classroom.

2. Individual schools and teachers need assistance to help them prepare for change. At the same time, superintendents and others must recognize that while all schools can improve, they do not all need an external change agent to reform or improve.

It seems like an obvious statement, but it cannot be emphasized enough: If schools and teachers do not believe they need to change and are not prepared to rethink and restructure what they do, no amount of money or muscle will force it upon them. We have learned that prior to making substantive changes to curriculum or instruction, schools and districts need assistance in planning for and preparing for more effective teaching and learning programs as well as long-term change and continuous improvement.

We also now recognize that while all schools in a district may need assistance to build their capacity for continuous improvement, they all do not necessarily need an externally developed design or model to reform or improve. Outside providers are not for everyone, although together they offer a broad range of consumer choice and individually provide real opportunities for tailoring. Some schools can and always have done it themselves.

Still, ties to a national model can offer enormous benefits, even for high-performing schools. Even a highly competent staff might reasonably elect to buy and tailor a compatible design rather than build it from scratch; students might benefit from a thoughtful, research-based design faster. External models also provide a means of maintaining a school's coherence in the face of staff and principal turnover. Moreover, existing models provide a ready-made network of like-minded school staff, connected by local, regional, and national meetings, as well as the Internet. And design "brands" do offer a simple means by which high-performing schools can help parents and teachers understand the school's education program and philosophy, thus fostering good matches of the school with prospective employees and students.

3. Investing in schools alone is necessary but not sufficient for meaningful and sustained improvement. States and school districts must develop policies and practices that support the school improvement processes and become embedded into a district's culture to ensure they last beyond one dynamic superintendent.

NAS has learned that a school-by-school improvement strategy is a necessary but not sufficient approach for creating sustained improvement in student achievement. Teachers, students, and other school staff interact within systems of federal, state, district, and school policies and practices that comprise and shape the conditions under which teaching and learning take place. In the broadest terms, the conditions we are concerned about have to do with *opportunities, capacities, and incentives* for improvement. The extent of their alignment is what New American Schools means by *system-level coherence*.[2] Unfortunately, many urban schools operate under relatively incoherent conditions, both programmatically at the school level—with multiple competing improvement efforts under way simultaneously,[3] and at the district and state levels—with evaluation, accountability, scheduling, professional development, decentralization, and compensation policies that are not aligned with schools' improvement efforts. Briefly stated, this is what opportunities, capacities, and incentives mean to NAS:

Opportunities for improvement pertain to the level of flexibility schools have to be creative in taking corrective action. Strategies that

---

[2]Several education researchers have written about the concepts of opportunities, capacities, and incentives as well as levels of coherence in educational systems (see, for example, Paul Hill, Christine Campbell, and James Harvey [2000], *It Takes a City: Getting Serious About Urban School Reform*, Brookings Institution Press, Washington, DC; Anthony Bryk et al. [1998], *Charting Chicago School Reform: Democratic Localism as a Lever for Change*, Westview Press, Boulder, Colo.).

[3]See, for example, F. M. Newmann, B. Smith, E. Allensworth, and A. Bryk, "School Instructional Program Coherence: Benefits and Challenges," Consortium on Chicago School Research, January 2001.

promote increased opportunity include various forms of decentralization such as site-based budgeting, performance-based contracts to manage groups of schools within existing systems, and public charter schools that operate entirely outside the traditional district. Other opportunities for improvement include district and school policies that give educators a freer hand through new allocation of resources and innovative scheduling of the school day and year.

Capacities for improvement pertain to the knowledge, skills, and abilities of those who lead, direct, and administer change: top officials at district and school level, teachers, staff, parents, and other members of the community. Examples of strategies that build capacities include the implementation of whole-school reform models; training and leadership development strategies; and investments in information technology.

Incentives for improvement pertain to the structure of accountability and compensation systems. Incentive-based strategies include establishing rewards for meeting federal, state, district, and school expectations for academic achievement, and consequences for failing to do so.

The mission of the Services Network is to align education policies and practices to foster strong organizational performance and high student achievement. The Services Network operates on the principle that coherence among opportunities, capacities, and incentives can be achieved both by transforming existing school systems—the school district as we know it today—and by creating new systems of schools operating under charters or contracts. Both approaches are vital dimensions of a comprehensive national strategy for improving education.

To accomplish its mission, the Services Network offers an integrated set of *State and District Services* and *New School Services* through strong internal capacity and best-in-class strategic partners. Each set of services includes four components: (1) needs assessment, (2) strategic planning, (3) implementation assistance, and (4) quality assurance and feedback. To assist its clients, the Services Network draws on its capacity in key competency areas, which include:

District Redesign

- Leadership and management
- Professional development
- Resource allocation
- Community engagement
- Charter and contract school arrangements

Accountability and Evaluation

- Accountability policy development
- School review and evaluation
- Information management and analysis

Special Education

- Interpretation of federal, state, and local law and funding streams
- Student assessments
- Program design and implementation
- Management of the Individualized Education Program (IEP) process
- Development of Medicaid reimbursement processes

Charter and Contract Schools

- Authorizer application and approval processes
- Accountability plan development and monitoring
- School start-up coordination help on facilities, personnel, budget, and data systems

Governance Training

- Authorizer renewal and revocation decisions processes
- Lessons from new schools for district redesign

4. Most schools and districts need sustained, high-quality support from external organizations to build capacity and leadership at the local level.

While most schools and districts need and want assistance from external organizations to help them improve student performance, the providers of these services and products, mostly nonprofits, often lack the capital and business expertise to offer large numbers of schools sustained, high-quality work *simultaneously*. They also lack the capacity to link and partner with other quality providers. As a result, NAS is supporting education providers through its Education Entrepreneurs Fund. The Fund provides financial resources, technical assistance, and consulting in business planning and marketing to help promising education organizations and companies deliver consistently superior programs and assistance to a growing network of schools over time. Currently, the Fund makes investments in design teams to help them improve their offerings to schools and make them available to more schools. For example, design teams have used loans to pay for up-front operating expenses in classrooms, while they wait for payment from schools recently added to their client list. These loans provide the necessary cash flow to give design teams the flexibility to work with the school system's billing cycle and the ability to add the staff and systems necessary to expand their work to larger numbers of schools. Investments also have been used to improve design teams' technology offerings, curriculum materials, and school-level technical assistance.

The Fund also seeks to make nonprofit organizations more accustomed to thinking and operating like businesses, helping them benefit from business and marketing models as well as long-term strategic plans. This function falls under the Fund's Education Entrepreneurs Network, whose mission is to help providers and other "education entrepreneurs" turn promising ideas or small-scale classroom techniques and tools into products, programs, and services that can be widely used in school settings. Entrepreneurs in the field of education are breaking new ground every day in classrooms, demonstrating their work can raise student learning. For example, foundations often fund the creation and initial development of an innovative program that has met with success in a few classrooms; however, little support is available to help nonprofits actually launch the resulting product or service into the larger education marketplace. By providing technical, marketing, and business assistance, the Network fills this role and helps nonprofit organizations expand beyond a few pockets of excellence. It also stimulates mutually productive partnerships among education providers, creating a more efficient marketplace that ultimately brings high-quality products and services to those students who most need them.

5. Educators, parents, and the larger school community must have a way to measure the performance of these outside organizations that consult and/or provide services and products to schools.

Parents, business and community leaders, and other members of the public need a resource to help them make well-informed decisions, based on trusted research, instead of political whim and opinions of interested parties. This has become increasingly difficult. Today more than 300 organizations receive payment for their services through the federal CSRD program; however, we have no real quality standards in place. Quality should not be confused with perfection—it is a process of continuous improvement; evaluating, throwing out what doesn't work, and focusing on what does. Our experience suggests that in the absence of good information about which programs can be relied upon to do good work, the good, the bad, and the ugly are thrown together in an undifferentiated mass that schools, districts, and the public cannot hope to untangle. When consumers can't trust anyone, they trust no one.

In 1999, to address the need for useful and reliable consumer information on CSR providers, NAS sponsored a blue-ribbon panel of notables from across the political and philosophical spectra of public education to develop and endorse a set of rigorous quality guidelines. This year NAS, along with the Council for Basic Education, helped create the independent EQI, a *Consumer Reports* for education. Much more work needs to be done to make these guidelines the industry standard and EQI the recognized standard-bearer of quality; however, a first step has been taken, and we welcome involvement by all who care about quality in public education.

Had the guidelines, EQI, or something like them been in place during the past few years, educators and the public would have been better informed about issues around quality, evaluations, performance, and related topics. Consistent with this lesson, NAS now only seeks partnerships with providers who focus on student performance, commit to independent quality reviews, and allocate resources to assure continuous improvement within their organization and within partner schools.

6. The policies that shape public education are inherently political. As such, we must build broad community understanding and support for school redesign.

To ensure community engagement is informed by research rather than empty rhetoric, we must commit ourselves to communicating fair and accurate information on a regular basis and to involving key stakeholders in the decisionmaking process. We learned that school improvement efforts must be built on a broad base of support, rather than the tenure of one charismatic leader. In some districts implementing comprehensive school reform models, schools demonstrated a healthy return on the considerable investment of district funds and staff time, but neither the broader district systems supporting the CSR strategy nor the designs themselves were embedded sufficiently in the school systems and within their stakeholder groups to assure the strategy's continuation in the absence of leadership commitment. In many school systems, it is far easier for district leaders and the central office to go back to the old ways than to continue the redesign effort.

But, for the work to succeed over the long term, the endorsement of a more permanent decisionmaking body—the community as a whole—must be cultivated. Today NAS stresses the importance of community involvement through the Service Network's offerings, which help educators and school leaders develop and implement an intensive and substantive engagement plan with parents, teachers, community and business leaders, and others around school improvement strategies.

THE FUTURE OF NEW AMERICAN SCHOOLS

As a leader in comprehensive school improvement strategies, NAS is proud of its record and the accomplishments of the CSR design teams. We believe they are among the best school reform programs widely available today. However, we should be counted among the first to recognize that no silver bullet exists for school improvement. NAS has never defended setbacks as success, nor have we celebrated successes as miracle cures. Instead, throughout the RAND evaluation effort, we have openly published our own and the design teams' mistakes and failures, while embracing them as opportunities for improvement rather than reasons to abandon our work.

We operate as a learning organization, dedicated to continuous improvement, putting these values into practice:

Quality. We will work only with education providers who have demonstrated results of higher student achievement, increased student attendance, decreased dropout rates, greater parental and community involvement, and other indicators of success.

Scale. We will work to move beyond a few islands of excellence by supporting promising and proven programs that can be replicated to ensure large-scale implementation of successful comprehensive school improvement strategies.

Sustainability. We will work to ensure continuous improvement by helping the best strategies sustain their impact and become permanent features of the public education landscape.

Comprehensiveness. We will work to promote the alignment, consistency, and durability of school improvement strategies, avoiding the adoption of disparate programs that are disjointed in practice.

Collective action. We will work to get education providers to join together for the common goal of improved student performance and, importantly, network best-in-class providers to help develop a unique, coherent set of services and products that can easily be matched to meet the specific challenges facing any school or school district.

Choice. We will work to ensure that educators, parents, and community leaders are able to select from a diverse portfolio of high-quality options to determine what improvement strategy is best for their students and unique needs, especially for those schools and students most in need.

New American Schools' mission is to help the country raise achievement for all students through the implementation of comprehensive school improvement strategies at the school, district, state, and national levels. Our mission is far from complete. As we reach our tenth anniversary, NAS continues to break new ground, transitioning from a largely grants-driven initiative to a professional services organization. Bolstered with the accomplishments of the past decade, New American Schools is uniquely positioned to link and deliver superior, research-based education services that together give states, districts, and schools the tools and assistance needed to ensure that all children succeed at high levels.

METHODOLOGY FOR THE STUDIES ON IMPLEMENTATION AND PERFORMANCE

CASE STUDIES TWO YEARS INTO SCALE-UP (BODILLY, 1998)

Sample

Resources allowed the development of 40 school-level case studies with the intent of performing longitudinal analysis across each school over a two-year period. New American Schools was working with ten jurisdictions, including three state jurisdictions, with specific districts in those states, and seven independent districts.[1] We chose six of these jurisdictions to study in the first year of implementation.[2] We used seven in the second year.[3] That choice was in part determined by the evident progress made in getting the initiative under way in each jurisdiction.

---

[1]This includes selected districts within Kentucky, Maryland, and Washington state, and seven districts: Cincinnati, Dade, Memphis, Pittsburgh, Philadelphia, San Antonio, and San Diego.

[2]In the first year, we chose to study the six jurisdictions that had schools that were beginning implementation that year. These included: Cincinnati, Dade, two districts in Kentucky, Memphis, Pittsburgh, and two districts in Washington state.

[3]In the second year, NAS's relationship with some districts changed; thus, the district sample changed. We added two jurisdictions (Philadelphia and San Antonio) and dropped one (Washington state), making seven jurisdictions in the second year: Cincinnati, Dade, two districts in Kentucky, Memphis, Pittsburgh, Philadelphia, and San Antonio. Five jurisdictions stayed the same over the entire study and two new ones were added in the second year.

In choosing schools to study, we attempted to get at least four schools for each design team, to be able to track differences both among designs and among districts. However, each team does not work in each jurisdiction, and each team is implementing in different numbers of schools. For example, AC had less than 20, the fewest schools, while RW had more than 100 schools implementing at least the *Success for All* portion of the design. Neither were the teams uniformly dispersed throughout all districts. For example, Cincinnati had only CON, EL, and RW schools.

Table A.1 shows the sample for the second year of scale-up. Of the 40 schools we visited in 1997, we had also visited 30 in the previous year. Ten were visited only once. Seven of these ten were visited only once because they were added when we added districts in the second year. Those schools were in San Antonio and Philadelphia.

We attempted to make the choice of schools within a district random. In at least one case, we had little choice but to leave the selection to the district.[4] While not random, our sample was fairly representative of NAS schools in general. The sample included urban and

Table A.1

RAND Sample for Site Visits

	AC	AT	CON	EL	MRSH	NARE	RW	Totals
Cincinnati			2	2			2	6
Dade	1		2		2		2	7
Kentucky						4		4
Memphis	2	2	1	2	2		2	11
Philadelphia		3	1		1			5
Pittsburgh						3		3
San Antonio				2	2			4
Totals	3	5	6	6	7	7	6	40

[4]For example, the state of Florida put a group of Dade County schools on a probation list because of low performance against a set of state indicators. Dade County mandated that all schools on this list adopt the RW design and be off limits to researchers. Thus, this group could not be included in the sample, leaving us with no choice as to which RW schools to include—the only two RW schools not on the state probation list.

rural schools and districts; elementary, middle, and high schools; and schools that were well-resourced and schools that were not.

Data Sources and Collection

We used many sources and types of information:

- Structured interviews (a set of predefined questions, both open- and closed-ended) by telephone about resource usage and in person during field visits. The structured formats varied by type of respondent.

- Observations of activities in schools. These observations were not formal or extensive. We toured each of the schools, sat in on several randomly selected classes, and observed special events at the school scheduled for the day, if they had applications to the design. In several instances we were able to observe critical friends' visits taking place, teacher group meetings, etc.

- Archival data, including documents produced by design teams, schools, and districts describing their efforts; plans by these parties for transformation; and local news releases or newspaper items concerning the local education scene, local political issues, NAS, design teams, or schools using NAS designs.

- Numerical data on each school's enrollment, demographics, test scores, etc.

The major data collection in the field took place during two waves of site visits in spring 1996 and in spring 1997. The latter established the level of implementation of the 40 schools at the end of the second year of scale-up. All interviews probed for the reasons behind differing levels of implementation.

We attempted to ensure that two researchers visited each school for approximately one day. One researcher spent a day at the district collecting information and performing interviews. All interviews had a structured format, with a mix of factual closed-ended questions and open-ended questions. Interviews were translated into condensed formatted sheets that covered specific variables identified to be of interest and coded for later analysis. Specific issues, such as resource usage and the matching process between design teams and schools, were explored using structured phone surveys.

The analysis used a combination of quantitative and qualitative measures. We used the qualitative data to develop a quantitative measure for the dependent variable, the level of implementation.

Measuring the Dependent Variable

The implementation analysis used an audit-like approach to establish the level of implementation in each school. Schools associated
with each team were assessed over common areas of schooling we
call "elements" (see Table A.2). By *common*, we mean that each design included specific changes to that element from "typical" practice. These common elements were curriculum, instruction, assessments, student assignments, and professional development. But
within each element of schooling, the teams varied significantly in
what they attempted to accomplish.

Three elements remained, but were not held in common among the
teams: staff and organization, community involvement, and standards. That is, not all teams aspired to make significant changes in
these areas. Together with the five common ones, these are the eight
elements that make up what we refer to as the "school-level component" of the designs. We also tracked progress on these three elements, as applicable.[5]

The specifics of each element for each design team were originally
determined by a document review and interview with the design
team during the demonstration phase. The elements were sharp-
ened in scale-up by a request from NAS and several districts for design teams to create "benchmarks" of progress for their designs that
schools and districts could use to understand where they were

---

[5]Our analysis of design documents shows that, in fact, the teams have more elements
than these eight. Additional elements include governance changes, integrated technology in the classroom, and integrated social services. In scale-up, with the emphasis
on developing a supportive environment within the district, these elements became
part of NAS's jurisdiction strategy: all of the governance, integrated social services,
and technology. We thus still tracked them, but not as part of the school-level designs.
Instead, we tracked them as part of the jurisdiction's supportive environment that
NAS was to encourage and support.

Table A.2

Elements of Designs

Element	Description
Curriculum	Usually, the knowledge bases and the sequence in which they are covered, whether defined by traditional subject areas or in more-interdisciplinary fashion.
Instruction	The manner in which the student acquires knowledge and the role of the teacher in this process.
Assessments	The means for measuring progress toward standards, either at the school or student level.
Student Grouping	The criteria or basis for assigning students to classes, groups, or programs.
Professional Development	Includes opportunities to develop curriculum and instruction, to develop expertise in using standards, to collaborate with others, and to enter into networks or prolonged discussions with other teachers about the profession. Several teams also planned extensive on-the-job practice, coaching in the classroom, and teaming in individual classrooms, as well as schoolwide forums to change the ways in which teachers deliver curriculum and instruction permanently.
Community Involvement/ Public Engagement	The ways parents, businesses, and others participate in schools and vice versa.
Standards	The range of skills and content areas a student is expected to master to progress through the system and the levels of attainment necessary for schools to be judged effective.
Staff and Organization	The configuration of roles and responsibilities of different staff. Changed organizational structures and incentives encourage teachers to access both staff in-services and professional growth opportunities.

going and when and to determine whether they were making reasonable progress. The benchmarks developed varied significantly from team to team as one would expect; however, all gave descriptions of what teams expected by the final year of a three-year implementation cycle.

We relied on two types of evidence of progress. First, we looked for evidence of implementation in keeping with the benchmarks and expectations provided by the team. Second, we interviewed district and school-level staff to understand their views of the design and how much they had changed their behaviors and to gain descriptions of the level of implementation. We asked how much their jobs had changed so far in relation to where they understood the design to be taking them.

Creating a Scale

The following paragraphs describe the construction of the dependent variable of the analysis—the level of implementation observed.

Level of Implementation

We rated progress in an element using a straightforward scale, as follows:

0 = **Not Implementing.** No evidence of the element.

1 = **Planning.** The school was planning to or preparing to implement.

2 = **Piloting.** The element was being partially implemented with only a small group of teachers or students involved.

3 = **Implementing.** The majority of teachers were implementing the element, and the element was more fully developed in accordance with descriptions by the team.

4 = Fulfilling. The element was evident across the school and was fully developed in accordance with the design teams' descriptions. Signs of institutionalization were evident.[6]

Application and Development of a Summary Dependent Variable

We initially applied these levels of implementation to each element that a design team intended to change in a school.[7] For *each element included in a design*, a score was given based on the observations and interviews conducted at the sites.[8] We then developed an average score for each school to use as a summary variable. First, we summed across the elements of design identified for each design team. For the five common elements, we totaled the values for each element and then divided by five to arrive at a school implementation level.[9] No weighting was attached to particular elements. For assessment of more elements, we summed across those included in the design and divided by the appropriate number (from five to eight). We assigned schools to the above categorizations based on the average score.[10]

---

[6]Implementation analysis often calls this level of implementation *institutionalizing* or *incorporating*, implying a level of stability and permanence. Our research indicates that the transience of the school and district political context often prevents institutionalization. We have thus used *fulfilling* to imply that the elements are present as the design teams intended, but we make no claim as to permanence.

[7]The reader should note that the use of numbers in the above scale does not imply interval-level data. The intervals between these points are not known. For example, a school with an average score of two is not halfway done with implementation. Neither is it twice as far along as a school scoring a one. The leap from planning to piloting might be far less formidable than the leap from implementation to the full vision of the design. In fact, a school scoring a three might take several more years to finish the design fully. The score indicates only what a school has accomplished in the way of implementation, as denoted in the above description.

[8]Reliability between raters was a potential issue in the creation of these scores. Reliability was increased by each rater performing this operation on a sample of schools that they and other raters had visited. The raters then exchanged scores and discussed discrepancies and how to resolve them.

[9]These five elements are curriculum, instruction, assessments, student grouping, and professional development.

[10]In assessing the total score of a school, the following intervals were used: A 0 or less than 0.8 was "not implementing;" a score equal to or greater than 0.8, but less than 1.6, was "piloting," etc.

LONGITUDINAL ANALYSES OF IMPLEMENTATION AND PERFORMANCE (BERENDS AND KIRBY ET AL., 2001; KIRBY, BERENDS, AND NAFTEL, 2001)

The Population of New American Schools for the Longitudinal Evaluation

The original sample of schools consisted of those schools initiating implementation of NAS designs in eight jurisdictions that NAS named as its partners during scale-up in either 1995–96 or 1996–97. These eight jurisdictions include:

- Cincinnati;

- Dade;

- Kentucky;

- Memphis;

- Philadelphia;

- Pittsburgh;

- San Antonio; and

- Washington state.[11]

The choice of these jurisdictions reflected RAND's desire to obtain a sample including all the designs that were participating in the scale-up phase and the judgment that the costs of working in the additional jurisdictions would not yield commensurate benefits. While jurisdictions and their support of the NAS reform will no doubt continue to change over time, these jurisdictions reflected a range of support for implementation—from relatively supportive to no support at all (see Bodilly, 1998).

---

[11]At the time we decided on the longitudinal sample of schools, Maryland and San Diego were not far enough along in their implementation to warrant inclusion in RAND's planned data collection efforts. Since then, several of the design teams report that they are implementing in Maryland and San Diego.

The 1998 Final Analysis Sample

Our aim was to collect data on all the NAS schools that were to be implementing within the partner jurisdictions. NAS believed that as of early fall of 1996, there were 256 schools implementing NAS designs across these eight jurisdictions. However, based on conversations with design teams, jurisdictions, and the schools, the sample was reduced to 184 schools for several reasons:

- There were 51 RW schools in Dade that were low-performing and on the verge of serious sanctions, so the district promised these schools that they would not be burdened with researchers.

- An additional 21 schools declined to participate because they did not want to be burdened with research, were not implementing, or had dropped the design.

Thus, for our surveys of teachers and principals, the target sample was 184 schools (see Table A.3).

Of the 184 schools in our 1997 sample, we completed interviews with 155 principals. Based on our interviews with principals in the spring

Table A.3

1997 Target Sample for RAND's Longitudinal Study of Schools: Principal Interviews and Teacher Surveys

| Jurisdiction | Design Team | | | | | | | |
	AC	AT	CON	EL	MRSH	NARE	RW	Total
Cincinnati			5	5			6	16
Dade	5		4	1	3		4	17
Kentucky						51		51
Memphis	5	5	5	5	4		9	33
Philadelphia		12	4		2			18
Pittsburgh						12		12
San Antonio			8	5				13
Washington state		8				16		24
Total	10	25	18	19	14	79	19	184

of 1997, most of these schools reported they were indeed implement-ing a design.[12] Yet, some were not. Figure A.1 shows that 25 of the 155 schools (about 15 percent) reported that they were in an ex-ploratory year or a planning year with implementation expected in the future. About 85 percent (130/155) of the schools for which we had teacher, principal, and district data reported implementing a NAS design to some extent.[13]

Because our interest is in understanding the specific activities that are occurring within the 130 schools that were implementing a NAS design to some extent (the non-white areas of Figure A.1), we limited our analysis sample to these 130 schools.

In the spring of 1998, all 184 schools were once again surveyed. The completed sample size consisted of 142 implementing schools. However, the overlap between the 1997 and 1998 samples was in-complete. For purposes of this analysis, which is partly longitudinal in nature, we limited the analysis sample to schools that met two criteria:

- Schools were implementing in both 1997 and 1998; and

- Schools had complete data (i.e., from teachers and principals) in both years.

Of the 130 schools implementing in 1997 for which we had complete data, seven had either dropped the design or had reverted to plan-ning, and another 17 had missing or incomplete data. Thus, 106 schools met both criteria. Figure A.2 shows the derivation of the sample.

---

[12]The first question we asked principals was about the status of the school's partner-ship with a NAS design. Principals could respond that they were in an exploratory year (i.e., the school has not committed to a design yet); in a planning year (the school has partnered with a design team and is planning for implementation next school year) in initial implementation for part of the school (i.e., a subset of the staff is im-plementing); continuing implementation for part of the school; in initial implementa-tion for the whole school (i.e., all or most of the staff are working with the design); or continuing implementation for the whole school.

[13]These were schools that had complete principal data, at least five teachers respond-ing to the teacher surveys, and complete district data.

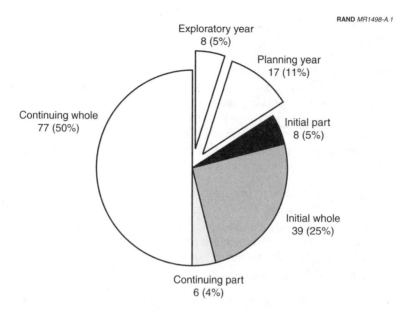

RAND *MR1498-A.1*

Figure A.1—Principal Reports of Implementation Status, Spring 1997

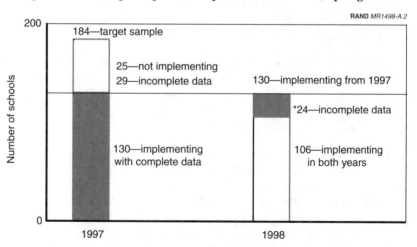

*6—dropped design, 1—reverted to planning, 17—missing principal or teacher data.

Figure A.2—Derivation of the Sample Analyzed in
Berends and Kirby et al. (2001)

Of these 106 schools, there were two schools in Pittsburgh that we later discovered were not implementing and had dropped the design. In fact, throughout RAND's monitoring of the schools in Pittsburgh, there were severe budget crises. RAND's site visits and principal phone interviews consistently revealed that NAS implementation in Pittsburgh was not taking place (also see Bodilly, 1998). As a result, these two schools (and Pittsburgh) were excluded from the analysis; our final sample for the analysis for the implementation study three years after scale-up consisted of 104 schools across seven jurisdictions.

The average school size for the 104 schools was 662 students, but the standard deviation of 434 was quite large. Eighteen percent of the schools had fewer than 400 students. The distribution of the 104 schools across levels revealed that 64 percent were elementary schools, 14 percent middle schools, and 14 percent high schools. Eight percent were mixed levels.

Teachers in our sample were mostly female (84 percent), mostly white (68 percent), and the majority had a master's degree or above (52 percent). More than three-fifths were over 40 years old, mirroring the national teacher profile. Teachers also reported that, on average, they had been in their current school for seven years.

As of spring 1998, 40 percent of the 104 schools reported two years of implementation, 35 percent of the schools reported three years of implementation, and 25 percent of schools reported four years or more of implementation. More than half of the NARE schools reported four or more years of implementation.

The various criteria we used to define the sample all biased the sample to some extent in a positive direction in terms of expected implementation. RAND's sample of NAS sites is drawn initially from a set of NAS schools that expressed interest in implementing designs in districts that had formed a partnership with New American Schools. In addition, we chose schools where principals reported they were implementing the designs either partly or wholly for at least two years in 1998. This was done to ensure some degree of comparability across schools in terms of where they were in implementing designs. But, omitting schools that reported they were not implementing or had just started implementing in 1998 from the sample made our analysis relatively more likely to find effects of designs on teaching and student achievement, where they existed.

The 1999 Final Analysis Sample for Examining Implementation Trends

Among the 104 schools that formed the longitudinal sample for the three-year scale-up study, we obtained complete data (i.e., from principals and at least five teachers in the school in 1999) on 71 schools. Principals in ten of the 104 schools reported that they had dropped the design but the attrition in the sample was largely due to nonresponse (13 schools were missing principal data as well as some teacher data; ten schools had fewer than five teachers responding to the survey). Thus, the analysis sample for the second study consisted of 71 schools in which principals reported that they were implementing designs in all three years (1997, 1998, and 1999) and which had complete data in all three years.

Table A.4 compares respondents with nonrespondents. In terms of jurisdictions, nonresponse was higher among schools in Washington state, Cincinnati, and Kentucky; in terms of design teams, non-response was higher in CON, EL, and NARE schools. Schools that had been implementing for three and five or more years in 1998 were disproportionately represented among the nonrespondents. Non-responding schools tended to be less poor than responding schools, and to have lower proportions of minority students. However, as measured by the 1998 survey, these schools reported fairly similar levels of overall implementation of NAS designs as the responding schools and the within-school variability in reported implementation was the same. Despite the high attrition and somewhat differing characteristics of the nonrespondents, the patterns of implementation we found were remarkably similar to the findings of the earlier study (Berends and Kirby et al., 2001) based on the 104 schools.

The distribution of the 71 schools in the longitudinal sample by jurisdiction and design team is shown in Table A.5. In the longitudinal sample, a little over one-quarter of the schools were NARE schools, primarily located in Kentucky, while ATLAS, RW, and EL each accounted for 15–18 percent of the sample. AC, CON, and MRSH had

Table A.4

**A Comparison of Respondents and Nonrespondents in the 1999
Longitudinal Sample, Based on 1998 Data**

Selected Characteristics	Nonrespondents	Respondents
Number of schools		
Cincinnati	6	10
Dade	3	1
Kentucky	7	13
Memphis	5	24
Philadelphia	1	6
San Antonio	2	7
Washington state	9	10
Design team		
AC	1	4
AT	4	13
CON	6	6
EL	6	10
MRSH	0	7
NARE	13	19
RW	3	12
Years implementing in 1998		
2 years	11	31
3 years	13	22
4 years	4	13
5 years	5	5
Percentage		
Percent elementary schools	60.6	66.2
Mean percent students eligible for free/reduced-price lunch	58.5	66.3
Mean percent minority students	52.7	63.0
Total number of schools	33	71

the smallest number of schools in the longitudinal sample. All 71 schools had been implementing for three or more years by 1999. About 44 percent of the sample had been implementing for three years; a little over 30 percent for four years; and the remaining one-fourth of the sample for five years or more (most of these were NARE schools).

Table A.5

Distribution of the 1999 Longitudinal Sample, by Jurisdiction and Design Team

Jurisdiction	Design Team							
	AC	AT	CON	EL	MRSH	NARE	RW	Total
Cincinnati			3	2			5	10
Dade	1							1
Kentucky						13		13
Memphis	3	4	3	4	3		7	24
Philadelphia		5			1			6
San Antonio				4	3			7
Washington state		4				6		10
Total	4	13	6	10	7	19	12	71

Teacher Sample

The sample size of teachers who responded to the survey was approximately 1,700 in 1997, and 1,500 teachers in both 1998 and 1999. The average response rate among teachers in these schools has fallen over time in the 71 schools, from 73 percent in 1997 to 59 percent in 1999. The interquartile range for response rates, representing the middle 50 percent of the distribution, was 41–75 percent. Response rates were generally lower in 1998 compared with 1997, but response rates in 1999 were comparable with those of 1998 in most jurisdictions.

Measuring Implementation Within and Across Designs

Challenges of Constructing Indices to Measure Implementation. Measuring progress in implementation broadly across a wide set of schools in several partnering jurisdictions involved a number of challenges.

First, each design is unique. Attempting to develop a common set of indicators that measures implementation *across* designs is difficult, particularly when design teams adapt their programs to the local needs of the schools (Bodilly, 2001). However, despite their differences, design teams do aim to change some key conditions of schools in common ways, such as school organization, expectations for student performance, professional development, instructional strategies, and parent involvement.[14]   We attempted to draw on these commonalities to guide the construction of an index that could be used to broadly measure "core" implementation across designs.

Second, the difficulties of constructing indices that capture the key components of a design are compounded by the fact that these design components may themselves be evolving (see Bodily, 2001). For example, design teams may change their implementation strategies because of lessons learned during development and implementation experiences in various sites.

Third, even if one developed measures on which there was general agreement that they fully captured the key facets of designs, the local context introduces a great deal of variability that must be taken into account (Bodily, 1998; Bodily and Berends, 1999). For example, while a design may focus on project-based learning over several weeks of the semester, this may be superseded by district-mandated curricula that take priority over significant portions of each school day.

Fourth, because the index is so general, it may be measuring more than just reform implementation.[15] Each of the components is a characteristic of effective schools, so schools may be pursuing these separately as school goals or as part of a district initiative. An increase in any one of these measures may not necessarily mean higher implementation of the model. For example, it may be that the design is helping the school to better attain these goals, or even that the school has been more successful in meeting this goal over time, independent of the model.

Fifth, it is important to note that all the implementation results are based on teachers' responses to surveys. The usefulness of what we can learn and infer from the analyses is heavily dependent on the quality of the data that are obtained from these surveys. In some in-

---

[14]With the recent support of the federal CSRD program, schools need to make sure that their plan covers these areas. If one particular design team or CSRD model does not cover these and several other areas of school improvement, then schools need to adopt more than one design or model (see Kirby et al., in review).

[15]We thank one of our reviewers, Amanda Datnow, for making this point.

stances, what we find has been validated by RAND's early case studies and other research (Bodilly, 1998; Ross et al., 1997; Datnow and Stringfield, 1997; Stringfield and Datnow, 1998), but for some indicators, all we have are teacher-reported survey measures.

Sixth, in the analysis sample of NAS schools that we examined, small sample sizes for some design teams made traditional tests of statistical significance somewhat more difficult to apply. That is, with larger sample sizes, we would have more power to detect differences and effects. Thus, in the school-level descriptive analyses, we focused on what appeared to be educationally substantive differences where appropriate.

Despite these challenges, evaluation remains an important component of any effort to change schools, and it is important to develop and refine sets of indicators that are informative not only for researchers, but for design teams, educators, and policymakers.

Implementation Indices. We developed two implementation indices:

1. A core implementation index that broadly measured implementation of the *major*, shared components of the designs across the sites; and

2. A design team–specific implementation index that measured implementation of both shared and some unique aspects of the designs.

The core implementation index was useful for understanding the progress of the NAS schools during the scale-up phase. The design team–specific index allowed us to measure implementation of each design on components that are unique to, and emphasized by, the design. The shortcoming of this index is that it was not directly comparable across designs, because it varied both in terms of items and number of items included in the index, and thus was not strictly comparable across design teams.

We should reiterate that this design team–specific index was not designed to measure *all* the unique aspects of the designs. Indeed, we could not construct such a measure with the available data, given that this was a broad study of NAS schools, not a detailed case study of one particular design. As a result, the design team–specific index measures what we consider to be some of the key components of the designs.

Constructing a Core Implementation Index. The core implementation index is a summative scale of teacher responses as to the degree to which the following described their school (on a scale of 1–6, with 1 = does not describe my school, and 6 = clearly describes my school):[16]

- Teachers are continual learners and team members through professional development, common planning, and collaboration;

- Student assessments are explicitly linked to academic standards;

- Teachers develop and monitor student progress with personalized, individualized learning programs;

- Performance expectations are made explicit to students so that they can track their progress over time;

- Student grouping is fluid, multiage, or multiyear; and

- Parents and community members are involved in the educational program.

Teacher responses were averaged across a school to obtain the school mean level of implementation.

The professional life of teachers refers to the roles and relationships in which the teachers participate during the school day. In effect, when referring to restructuring schools, particularly those in poor, urban areas, this involves overhauling the conditions under which teachers work by changing their responsibilities and tasks and by developing a more professional culture in schools (Newmann et al., 1996; Murphy, 1992; Sykes, 1990; Wise, 1989). In contrast to teachers working in isolation without contact with their colleagues (see Louis and Miles, 1990; Lortie, 1970), design teams aim to build a collaborative environment for teachers. Thus, it is important to understand

---

[16]The alpha reliability of this index was 0.81. The range of correlations for the individual items was 0.21 to 0.57.

the extent to which teachers collaborate and engage in activities together, such as professional development, common planning time, and critiquing each other's instruction.

Each of the designs aims to bring all students to high standards, even though each may differ in the process to attain this goal. To monitor whether designs are making progress toward this end, critical indicators might include the degree to which (a) student assessments are explicitly linked to academic standards, (b) teachers make performance expectations explicit to students, and (c) the curriculum and performance standards are consistent and coherent across grade levels.

Most of the designs are concerned with shaping student experiences within classrooms to further their academic achievement growth. NAS designs embrace alternative instructional strategies that involve different relationships between teachers and students and between students and subject matter. Yet, again, each design differs somewhat in the specific nature of these activities. Conventional classrooms are often characterized as teachers talking *at* students and filling their heads with knowledge, with students responding with the correct answers at appropriate times (see Gamoran et al., 1995; Sizer, 1984; Powell, Farrar, and Cohen, 1985). In contrast, design teams tend to emphasize alternative instructional practices such as students working in small groups, using manipulatives, engaging in student-led discussions, or working on projects that span a long period of time (e.g., a marking period or semester).

The design teams also address a particular set of instructional strategies revolving around student grouping arrangements. How students are grouped for instruction and the effects of this on student achievement are subjects of heated debate among educators and researchers (see Slavin, 1987, 1990; Gamoran and Berends, 1987; Oakes, Gamoran, and Page, 1992; Hallinan, 1994; Oakes, 1994). Yet, most researchers agree that alternatives to inflexible grouping arrangements are worth further exploration. Thus, the NAS designs have experimented with such alternative student groupings. For example, students within an EL or CON design may have the same teacher for a couple of years. RW emphasizes flexible uses of grouping by organizing students according to their achievement levels in reading for part of the day and mixing achievement levels for other subjects. These groupings are assessed every eight weeks or so to see if students would be better served by being placed in a different group. In short, each of the designs is sensitive to the issue of ability grouping and is working with schools to group students in more-effective ways.

Conventional wisdom suggests that the parent-child relationship and parent involvement in the child's education are critical components of school success. The NAS designs have embraced this issue as well. Several of the designs aim to have individuals or teams within the schools serve as resources to students and families to help integrate the provision of social services to them (e.g., ATLAS and RW). Other designs emphasize students applying their learning in ways that directly benefit the community (e.g., AC, EL, and NARE). Of course, each design desires that parents and community members be involved in positive ways in the educational program.

Table A.6 presents the means and standard deviations of the core implementation index across the 71 schools for 1997, 1998, and 1999.

Constructing the Design Team–Specific Implementation Index. As we mentioned above, designs vary in their focus and core components. As a result, we constructed a design team–specific implementation index that included the six core items of the core implementation index and items that were specific to each design team. Table A.7 lists the specific items included in the specific index constructed for each design team.

Again, the specific measures listed may not have captured all the unique features of the designs. Moreover, the wording of the survey items was more general to broadly compare schooling activities across design teams. Nonetheless, the design team–specific indices created here provide additional information about implementation of some of the unique features of the design teams. Such information was helpful for examining changes over time in the teacher-reported implementation, including changes in the means and variance within and between schools.

Berends and Kirby et al. (2001) reported results for both the core implementation index and the design team implementation index.

Table A.6

Means and Standard Deviations of the Core Implementation Index and Its Components, 1997–1999

	Mean 1997	Mean 1998	Mean 1999	Change, 1997–1999	SD 1997	SD 1998	SD 1999	Change, 1997–1999
Parents and community members are involved in the educational program	3.80	3.85	3.90	0.10	0.79	0.93	0.90	0.11
Student assessments are explicitly linked to academic standards	4.42	4.63	4.79	0.37	0.68	0.64	0.62	−0.06
Teachers develop and monitor student progress with personalized, individualized learning programs	4.01	4.14	4.19	0.18	0.68	0.64	0.62	−0.06
Student grouping is fluid, multiage, or multiyear	3.62	3.79	3.80	0.18	1.25	1.28	1.12	−0.13
Teachers are continual learners and team members through professional development, common planning, and collaboration	4.77	4.87	4.88	0.10	0.60	0.62	0.51	−0.09
Performance expectations are made explicit to students so they can track their progress over time	4.23	4.39	4.43	0.20	0.63	0.53	0.55	−0.08
Core Implementation Index	4.14	4.29	4.32	0.18	0.61	0.57	0.52	−0.08

Table A.7

Survey Items Included in the Design Team–Specific Implementation Index, by Design Team

Survey Items	AC	AT	CON	EL	MRSH	NARE	RW
Core Items							
Parents and community members are involved in the educational program	√	√	√	√	√	√	√
Student assessments are explicitly linked to academic standards	√	√	√	√	√	√	√
Teachers develop and monitor student progress with personalized, individualized learning programs	√	√	√	√	√	√	√
Student grouping is fluid, multiage, or multiyear	√	√	√	√	√	√	√
Teachers are continual learners and team members through professional development, common planning, and collaboration	√	√	√	√	√	√	√
Performance expectations are made explicit to students so they can track their progress over time	√	√	√	√	√	√	√
Design Team–Specific Items							
The scope and sequence of the curriculum is organized into semester- or year-long themes	√						
Students are required on a regular basis to apply their learning in ways that directly benefit the community	√						
Students frequently listen to speakers and go on field trips that specifically relate to the curriculum	√						
This school is part of a K–12 feeder pattern that provides integrated health and social services to improve student learning		√					
Students are required by this school to make formal presentations to exhibit what they have learned before they can progress to the next level		√					

Table A.7—continued

Survey Items	AC	AT	CON	EL	MRSH	NARE	RW
Consistent and coherent curriculum and performance standards have been established across the K–12 feeder patterns		√					
Most teachers in this school meet regularly with teachers in other schools to observe and discuss progress toward design team goals			√				
Technology is an integrated classroom resource			√		√		
Students engage in project-based learning for a significant portion of the school day (i.e., more than one-third of the time)			√				
Technology is used in this school to manage curriculum, instruction, and student progress			√		√		
A majority of teachers in this school stay with the same group of students for more than one year				√			
Students frequently revise their work toward an exemplary final product				√			
There are formal arrangements within this school providing opportunities for teachers to discuss and critique their instruction with each other				√			
This school has the authority to make budget, staffing, and program decisions					√		
Curriculum throughout this school emphasizes preparation for and relevance to the world of work						√	
Students are monitored according to annual performance targets established by the school as a whole						√	
Student assessments are used to reassign students to instructional groups on a frequent and regular basis							√

Table A.7—continued

Survey Items	AC	AT	CON	EL	MRSH	NARE	RW
Students are organized into instructional groups using block scheduling for specific curricular purposes							√
This school has specific activities aimed directly at reducing student absenteeism							√
Students who are not progressing according to expectations are provided with extended days and/or tutors							√
This school has a coordinator, facilitator, or resource specialist assigned on a full- or part-time basis							√
Alpha Reliability Index	0.83	0.80	0.87	0.88	0.90	0.85	0.87

Kirby, Berends, and Naftel (2001) reported results for the core implementation index only because the findings were similar across the two indices.

Measuring Performance in NAS Schools

Monitoring Academic Progress with School-Level Test Scores. As previously stated, because of resource constraints, jurisdictions' hesitancy to have additional testing, and established agreements between NAS and the partner jurisdictions, it was not feasible in RAND's evaluation of NAS to administer a supplemental, common test to the students within the participating schools. Thus, we relied on the tests administered by the districts as part of their accountability system. While not ideal, these were the tests the jurisdictions, NAS, and the design teams expected to influence during the course of the NAS scale-up strategy. In its initial request for proposals, NAS's intent was for "break the mold" schools. NAS was not interested in incremental changes that led to modest improvement in student achievement compared with conventional classrooms or schools. Rather, the achievement of students was to be measured against "world-class standards" for *all* students, not merely for those most likely to succeed. Moreover, design teams were to "be explicit about the student populations they intend to serve and about how they propose to raise achievement levels of 'at risk' students to world class standards" (NASDC, 1991, p. 21).

If such ambitious effects on student achievement occurred, these large test score changes would be reflected in school-level scores. Yet, to fully understand the test score trends of NAS schools three years into scale-up, it is important to keep in mind several issues when examining school-level scores.

First, differences in achievement between schools are not nearly as great as the achievement differences within schools. For the past 30 years, a finding on student achievement that has stood the test of time is that about 15–20 percent of the student differences in achievement lie *between* schools; most of the achievement differences (80–85 percent) lie *within* schools (Coleman et al., 1966; Jencks et al., 1972; Lee and Bryk, 1989; Gamoran, 1987, 1992). Understanding the differences between schools remains critically important for making changes that maximize the effects of schools on students. However, it is also important to understand the limits of schools—no matter what the school reform—in explaining the overall differences in student achievement (Jencks et al., 1972).

Second, when examining the grade-level scores over time (e.g., 4th-grade scores between 1995 and 1998), these are based on different cohorts of students taking the tests. These scores are often unstable because some schools have small numbers of students taking the test in any given year, and these scores are more likely to vary from year to year with different students taking the test. Districts and states use such scores in their accountability systems, and over a longer period of time, they provide some indication of a school's performance trends.

Third, while establishing trends in the NAS schools relative to other schools within the same district is informative, it is important to remember the variety of family, school, district, and design team factors that influence these scores. Research on student achievement has consistently found that individual family background variables dominate the effects of schools and teachers (Coleman et al., 1966; Jencks et al., 1972; Gamoran, 1987, 1992), and such effects are not controlled for when describing school-level test scores. More-specific information than districts typically collect or make available is necessary to understand the relative effects of these factors on student achievement.

Fourth, the ways districts report their scores to the public are not always amenable to clear interpretations over time. For example, several districts have changed their tests during the scale-up phase, and the tests in some cases have not been equated, so the test scores are not directly comparable over time. Moreover, in some instances, the form in which test score information is reported (for example, median percentile rank) makes it difficult to detect changes in the tails of the distribution. Wherever possible, we have tried to obtain specific test score information at the school level to clarify the interpretations that can be made.

Fifth, the way that we summarize school performance—comparing whether the NAS schools made gains relative to the jurisdiction—may miss some significant achievement effects that may be captured if student-level data were available and comparable across the jurisdictions. That is, our indicator will only reflect large achievement effects of designs. The data provided by the districts do not support more fine-grained analyses to understand smaller, statistically significant effects on student-level achievement scores, particularly for certain groups of students (e.g., low-income or minority students or students with limited English proficiency).

Measure of School Performance. The analyses of performance in NAS schools focused on one main research question—Did NAS schools make gains in test scores relative to all schools in their respective jurisdictions?

To answer this question, we collected data on trends in mathematics and reading scores for NAS schools and the associated jurisdiction for selected grades in elementary, middle, and high schools, where relevant. Because we were concerned about the variability that particular grade test scores show within a given school, data were generally aggregated across NAS schools, using grade enrollment as weights. Thus, we compared NAS schools with the district or the state. However, in a couple of cases, the test score information did not lend itself to aggregation. In these cases, we provided trends for each NAS school in the sample.

The comparison we made between NAS schools and the district averages used absolute gains. In addition, we also calculated and compared percentage gains in test scores for the NAS schools and the jurisdictions. The results were not substantially different. Moreover, we compared the gains in test scores of the individual NAS schools with their past performance to see if the schools made *any* gains over time. Again, the results were not substantially different from those obtained using absolute gains.

It is important to note that some of the designs do not specifically have curriculum and instruction materials per se, and even some design teams that do may not have been implementing that particular design component. However, mathematics and reading are central to improving student learning for large numbers of students. These subject area tests are also central to the accountability systems of the jurisdictions in which NAS schools are located. Thus, we focused on these two subject areas.

The fact that NAS schools began implementing at different times makes clear comparisons of gains over time difficult. Wherever possible, we collected data for the baseline and baseline plus two years. For some late implementing schools, we were only able to get baseline and baseline plus one year data. (See Berends and Kirby et al. [2001] for more detail on each of the tests used by the various jurisdictions.)

Earlier, we showed that the NAS schools in this sample were predominantly high poverty and high minority, and many faced challenges related to student mobility.[17] It could be argued that comparisons with the district average are unfair to these schools, particularly if they fail to capture smaller, albeit significant achievement effects.

However, it must be pointed out that NAS and the design teams agreed to be held accountable to district assessments and to improve

---

[17]When examining trends in school performance, it is important to consider the state and district accountability system (Berends and Kirby, 2000; Miller et al., 2000; Koretz and Barron, 1998). For example, different exclusion rules for special population students could result in different rates of achievement growth across jurisdictions and bias outcomes for particular groups of schools. However, the comparisons made here are between NAS schools and the jurisdiction average. Therefore, all the schools are supposed to be subject to similar testing provisions and administration.

student learning for substantial numbers of students. Because of these expectations, NAS requested that RAND examine the progress of these NAS schools in comparison with the district averages to understand whether NAS's expectations of dramatic improvement were met.

Sample of NAS Schools for Performance Trend Analyses

The sample of NAS schools for which we have data on test scores is larger than the sample of 104 schools used for the implementation analysis. Of the 184 schools in the original sample, we have data on 163 schools. Some schools were dropped from the sample because they were not implementing: This was true of the Pittsburgh schools and about 12 schools in Dade. Some of our schools were K–2 schools for which there were no testing data available and other schools were missing data on test scores.

CASE STUDIES FIVE YEARS AFTER SCALE-UP

In order to better understand the relationship between implementation and performance, we conducted a case study of matched schools, matched on the basis of design, district, grade span, years of implementation, and implementation level (as measured by our surveys but validated by the design teams). One school was high-performing and the other was not. Although we attempted to get a total of 20 schools, only 13 schools participated in the study (five matched pairs and a triplet): two ATLAS, two CON, five MRSH, and four RW schools. One to two researchers spent a day at each school conducting interviews with principals, groups of teachers, and district officials. We collected data from the design teams about the schools as well as data from the district and the schools themselves on student test scores; demographic and program descriptors; other school programs and interventions; level of implementation; district support of the design; and perceptions about the causes of different levels of performance increase.

METHODOLOGY FOR SAN ANTONIO CLASSROOM STUDY (BERENDS ET AL., 2002)

The San Antonio district has over 90 percent of its students eligible for free/reduced-price lunch; most of the students in the district are either Hispanic (85 percent) or African American (10 percent); and approximately 16 percent of the students in the district are classified as having limited English proficiency. Since 1994, the proportion of San Antonio students failing to earn passing rates on the TAAS in each school year has consistently been the highest or second highest in the county.

It is within this context of high poverty and low student performance that elementary schools in San Antonio began the process of adopting NAS reform models. Of the 64 elementary schools in the district, three schools began implementation during the 1995–1996 school year, nine schools the following year, and 20 schools during the 1997–1998 school year. By the 1998–1999 school year, 39 of 64 elementary schools in the district had adopted NAS designs. Table A.8 lists the number of schools adopting specific designs in each year.

RAND collected data on a sample of 4th-grade teachers and their students during two school years, 1997–1998 and 1998–1999 (see Tables A.9 and A.10). Fourth grade was an advantageous selection for several reasons: most NAS designs were being implemented in elementary schools; the state administered its test to students in the 3rd grade, providing a baseline for test score analysis; and teacher questionnaire items were already developed and tested with 4th-grade teachers. In addition, the school district expressed its preference for a grade four focus.

Table A.8

Elementary Schools Adopting NAS Designs in San Antonio, by Year

	Number of Schools				
	1995–1996	1996–1997	1997–1998	1998–1999	Total
CON			3	1	4
EL	1	2			3
MRSH		5	4	1	10
RW	2	2	13	5	22
NAS Total	3	9	20	7	39

Table A.9

Target Sample of Schools Compared with Final Study Sample, by Type of Data Collection and NAS Design Team

	Number of Schools in 1997–1998 School Year				
	Requested to Participate	Returned Teacher Surveys	Returned Principal Surveys	Returned Stanford-9 Testing	Classroom Observations
CON	2	2	2	2	1
EL	2	2	1	1	1
MRSH	4	4	4	4	2
RW	8	8	8	9	1
Non-NAS	10	8	9	10	2
Total	26	24	24	26	7
	Number of Schools in 1998–1999 School Year				
	Requested to Participate	Returned Teacher Surveys	Returned Principal Surveys	Returned Stanford-9 Testing	Classroom Observations
CON	2	2	2	2	2
EL	2	2	1	2	2
MRSH	4	4	2	4	2
RW	8	8	7	8	2
Non-NAS	7	7	7	7	2
Total	23	23	19	23	10

Generally, in each school year we were able to gather teacher survey data and supplemental student test scores in reading (Stanford-9), including over 850 students in over 60 classrooms in over 20 schools. Moreover, during the course of this study, we were able to obtain information on all the teachers and students in the district to provide a benchmark for the analyses reported here. In 1997–1998, we were also able to observe and gather classroom artifacts from 12 teachers in NAS and non-NAS schools. In the following year, we gathered such data from 19 teachers. Each of these data collection efforts is described more fully in the sections that follow.

The assistant superintendent's office demonstrated its support for our study by asking principals to announce the study to their staff and to invite all 4th-grade teachers to participate in the study. Once the initial volunteers were reported, RAND attempted to balance the

Table A.10

Target Sample of Teachers Compared with Final Study Sample, by Type of Data Collection and NAS Design Team

	Number of Teachers in 1997–1998 School Year		
	Requested to Participate	Returned Surveys & Stanford-9 Testing	Observations
CON	6	6	3
EL	4	2	2
MRSH	12	10	3
RW	26	22	2
Non-NAS	26	23	2
Total	74	63	12
	Number of Teachers in 1998–1999 School Year		
	Requested to Participate	Returned Surveys & Stanford-9 Testing	Observations
CON	11	10	4
EL	8	6	5
MRSH	13	11	3
RW	32	27	4
Non-NAS	19	19	3
Total	83	73	19

representation of designs in the sample by approaching schools of underrepresented designs. While the RAND sample of NAS and non-NAS schools cannot be considered random, district staff indicated that the schools selected were typical of elementary schools in the district. Comparisons of demographic and other characteristics for students (i.e., gender, race, limited English proficiency status, special education status, average test scores, and mobility rates) and teachers (i.e., gender, race, highest degree earned, years of teaching experience) indicated no significant differences, on average, between the RAND sample and district populations. Each teacher selected was asked to administer the Stanford-9 to his or her 4th-grade students and to complete a teacher survey. Teacher focus groups were conducted in eight schools during the 1997–1998 school year. A subset of teachers agreed to provide classroom logs, and samples of student work and allowed classroom observations once in the spring of the 1997–1998 school year and three times in the 1998–1999 school year. In addition, principals in the sample schools were asked to complete a telephone interview, during which a survey was completed.

Teacher Data

In the late spring of the 1997–1998 school year, with the help of district staff, we contacted 74 teachers in 26 schools to participate in the study. Three of the schools refused to participate in our study. Of those 74 teachers initially contacted, 63 teachers in 23 schools agreed to participate, returned completed teacher surveys, and their students completed the Standford-9 reading test resulting in an 85 percent response rate for teachers and classes with student achievement scores.

In 1998–1999, we returned to the 23 schools that participated in our study the previous year. Because we wanted to increase our sample of teachers, we supplemented our teacher sample and contacted 83 teachers in these 23 schools. Of those contacted, we received completed teacher surveys and Stanford-9 tests from 73 teachers (88 percent). Between spring 1998 and spring 1999, one of our sampled schools went from having no design in place to adopting RW.

Not all teachers had complete survey data across both years, given that different teachers were included in both years. Thus, for the longitudinal descriptions of NAS and non-NAS classrooms, we tracked indicators for the 40 teachers for whom we had complete data from both the 1997–1998 and 1998–1999 school years (see Table A.11). In addition to these teacher data from RAND surveys, we also obtained information on teachers from the district, such as demographic characteristics (race-ethnicity and gender), years of experience, and highest degree obtained.

The analysis only included the sample of 40 4th-grade teachers who completed surveys in both the spring of 1998 and 1999 and re-

Table A.11

Longitudinal Sample of Teachers in NAS and Non-NAS Schools, 1997–1998 and 1998–1999 School Years

	CON	EL	MRSH	RW	Non-NAS	Totals
Number of Schools	2	2	3	6	7	20
Number of Teachers[a]	4	3	8	11	14	40

[a]Teachers who completed the survey in both spring 1998 and spring 1999 and who were in the same school, same design, and teaching 4th grade in both years.

mained in the same school/design/teaching assignment. This was because our interest lay in examining what changes, if any, occurred during the early stages of implementation in school organization, teachers' professional work lives, and their classroom instruction.

We also compiled survey results from the larger sample (66 teachers in 1998 and 83 in 1999). A comparison of average response rates found few differences between the two samples. A detailed analysis of individual teacher responses found no substantive differences between these larger samples and what we find in the longitudinal teacher sample of 40 teachers.

Because of the small size of the longitudinal sample analyzed, we did not focus much attention on testing the statistically significant differences between NAS and non-NAS teachers. Given the design, most standard statistical tests comparing the 40 NAS and non-NAS teachers in the longitudinal sample would fail to detect many real differences. However, in conjunction with the qualitative data from this study, the NAS and non-NAS comparisons shed light on a variety of factors related to implementing NAS designs in a high-poverty urban district.

Surveys. The teacher survey fielded during the spring 1998 semester and then again in spring 1999 was designed to provide a broad measure of instructional practices in NAS and non-NAS classrooms. Teachers were asked to report on a range of instructional strategies, some of which reflected a focus on basic skills and tended toward more conventional practices, and others of which reflected more reform-like methods. Given that the NAS designs emphasize changes in instructional conditions whether through building basic skills and then higher-order thinking (e.g., RW) or through theme-based projects that last for several weeks (e.g., CON or EL) (see Bodilly, 2001), we would expect the implementation of designs to result in changes in teaching strategies.

General topics covered in the survey include school and classroom characteristics, instructional strategies and materials, skills and assessments emphasized, resources, parent involvement and community relations, impact of design team and reform efforts, professional development, and perceptions and attitudes toward teaching.

Two versions of the survey were fielded in each year, one to 4th-grade teachers in a sample of schools adopting NAS designs, the other to 4th-grade teachers in non-NAS schools. The two forms of the surveys varied only slightly. For instance, three items specifically related to the implementation of NAS designs were not included in the survey received by non-NAS teachers. A few items in other sections also referred specifically to NAS designs. On the non-NAS version, these items were either omitted or had slightly different wording (e.g., whereas NAS teachers were asked about the NAS design being implemented in their school, non-NAS teachers were asked about the school reform efforts in their district). For example, an item on the NAS version that asked if an activity was "specifically oriented toward the design team program activities" was changed to "specifically oriented toward the reform efforts of San Antonio" on the non-NAS version.

These surveys were developed in conjunction with RAND's ongoing case study work (Bodilly, 1998). As part of our overall instrument development, we conducted phone interviews with design team representatives about what specific indicators and events would be observed in design-based classrooms. For the survey development, we also relied on other studies that have examined instruction with surveys (Newmann et al., 1996; Gamoran et al., 1995; Burstein et al., 1995; Porter, 1995; Porter and Smithson, 1995; Porter et al., 1993; see also Mayer, 1999).

Longitudinal Sample of 40 Teachers Compared with Elementary Teachers in District. Overall, it appears that in demographic terms, the longitudinal survey sample of 40 teachers was a fairly representative group of teachers within the school district. There were few differences when comparing teachers in our sample with all 4th-grade teachers in the San Antonio school district (Table A.12). Teachers in this sample and the district as a whole were similar with respect to gender, racial-ethnic characteristics, and average years of experience. Whereas 40 percent of teachers in the district had earned master's degrees, 45 percent of the teachers in the longitudinal sample had attained this level of education.

Table A.12

Teacher Characteristics—Districtwide Versus RAND Survey Sample, 1997–1998 School Year

	District (n = 329)	Survey Sample (n = 40)
Male	11%	8%
With master's degrees	40%	45%
Average years teaching experience	13	13
White	37%	33%
African American	15%	20%
Latino/Latina	47%	47%
Asian American	0.3%	None
Native American	0.3%	None

Observations and Logs of Instructional Activities.[18] In the spring of the 1997–1998 school year, RAND conducted classroom observations of a subsample of 12 teachers from the larger group of 64. These observations consisted of a RAND researcher shadowing a teacher for a day, writing detailed summaries of classroom activities, taking notes on the general description of the classroom and the resources in it, and informally discussing design team activities with the teacher.

School observations first began in the spring of 1998 and continued throughout the 1998–1999 school year. Observations, targeting the 4th-grade level, covered ten different schools. Data were collected in two CON, two EL, two MRSH, two RW, and two non-NAS schools. In the first year of our study, in addition to observations, we aimed to gather more-extensive classroom data through (1) teacher logs of assignments, homework, projects, quizzes/tests/exams, and papers or reports over a five-week period, and (2) illustrative teacher-selected samples of student work related to a major project assigned during the spring semester. Because we could not gain entry into these classrooms until May, right after the administration of TAAS, and because our logs were overly burdensome, the response rate for these 12 teachers was less than desirable. Five of 12 teachers (42 percent) returned completed logs.

---

[18]Each teacher who participated in this part of the study received a $200 honorarium.

Therefore in the second year, we significantly revamped our data collection methods for observations and logs of instructional activities. Teachers were not asked to submit logs of assignments. Rather, arrangements were made to observe 19 teachers across ten different schools—two CON, two EL, two MRSH, two RW, and two non-NAS schools—on three separate occasions. Moreover, a staff person on site in San Antonio interviewed them at length over the course of one school year. In addition, teachers provided work assignments, lesson plans, and even district memos when appropriate.

Interviews. In the spring of 1998, we conducted focus group interviews with 4th-grade teachers from eight different schools, including schools implementing each of the four NAS designs and some comparison schools. Our aim was to get a representation of teachers within NAS schools to provide information about what activities were undertaken across grade levels. These interviews were conducted to help us better understand design team program characteristics, the nature of instructional strategies, the variety of professional development activities, and the types of available classroom-level resources. Additional information about these schools, professional development activities, and the resources available for design implementation was provided by 45-minute structured interviews with principals.

During the 1998–1999 school year, after each observation, teachers were interviewed about what occurred during the observation as well as about other more-general issues pertaining to design implementation, instructional strategies, professional development, and other matters related to design and district initiatives.

In addition, we conducted interviews of NAS design team leaders, district staff, school instructional leaders, and principals.

Student Data

Data for individual students were obtained mainly through the cooperation of the central office staff, who provided district files on students to RAND for analysis.

Student Achievement. In this study, student achievement was measured in a variety of ways. First, we asked teachers to administer the

Stanford-9 open-ended reading test. We decided to use the Stanford-9 because, as a commercial test that could be nationally normed, it differed somewhat from conventional multiple-choice tests. The Stanford-9 requires students to use an open-ended response format. The test takes about 50 minutes to administer.

In addition, RAND obtained the TAAS mathematics and reading scores for all of the district's 3rd-, 4th-, and 5th-grade students during the time of this study. Our focus was mainly on the 1997–1998 4th-grade cohort. Not only did we track their achievement back to when they were third graders, but we also obtained their scores from the 5th grade to examine achievement growth. Specifically, we analyzed the TAAS mathematics and reading Texas Learning Indices (TLI). These data were linked to teachers and schools in our survey sample. They allowed us to examine achievement across schools and classrooms for the entire district in addition to the RAND sample that included teacher surveys and Stanford-9 tests.

Student Characteristics. Other information available for individual students from district data files included student race-ethnicity, gender, date of birth, poverty status (economically disadvantaged or not), number of weeks the student was in the school during the academic year, limited English proficiency status, and participation in Special Education or Talented and Gifted programs.

Examples of Student Work. The teachers we observed in the 1998–1999 school year were asked to provide examples of students' work. We randomly selected one-quarter of the students in each class every three months. Once a student was selected, his or her name was removed from the class roster. While no criteria were established with regard to what was submitted, we asked teachers to provide examples of typical work assignments that students produced.

We cannot claim that the submitted work was representative of all student assignments made by a given teacher. However, these examples did provide a glimpse of the types of activities assigned by each of the teachers in our sample.

REFERENCES

Ambach, G. (1991). "The essential federal role." In *Voices from the field: 30 expert opinions on America 2000, the Bush Administration strategy to "reinvent" America's schools.* Washington, DC: The William T. Grant Foundation on Work, Family, and Citizenship and the Institute for Educational Leadership, pp. 39–40.

American Association of School Administrators. (1995). *Great expectations: Understanding the new Title I.* Washington, DC: AASA.

Ball, D. L., Camburn, E., Cohen, D. K., & Rowan, B. (1998). *Instructional improvement and disadvantaged students.* Unpublished manuscript, University of Michigan.

Berends, M. (1999). *Assessing the progress of New American Schools: A status report.* Santa Monica, CA: RAND (MR-1085-EDU).

Berends, M. (2000). "Teacher-reported effects of New American School designs: Exploring the relationships to teacher background and school context." *Educational Evaluation and Policy Analysis,* 22(1), pp. 65–82.

Berends, M., & King, M. B. (1994). "A description of restructuring in nationally nominated schools: The legacy of the iron cage?" *Educational Policy,* 8(1), pp. 28–50. (Also RAND RP-458.)

Berends, M., & Kirby, S. N. (2000). *Analyzing state assessment data within the context of federal evaluations of Title I and the Comprehensive School Reform Demonstration (CSRD) programs.* Washington, DC: RAND, unpublished manuscript.

Berends, M., Bodilly, S., & Kirby, S. N. (forthcoming). "Reforming Whole Schools: Challenges and Complexities." In J. Petrovich & A. W. Wells (Eds.), *Bringing Equity Back*.

Berends, M., Chun, J., Schuyler, G., Stockly, S., & Briggs, R. J. (2002). *Conflicting school reforms: Effects of New American Schools in a high-poverty district*. Santa Monica, CA: RAND (MR-1438-EDU).

Berends, M., Grissmer, D. W., Kirby, S. N., & Williamson, S. (1999). "The changing American family and student achievement trends." *Review of Sociology of Education and Socialization*, 23, pp. 67–101.

Berends, M., Kirby, S. N., Naftel, S., & McKelvey, C. (2001). *Implementation and performance in New American Schools: Three years into scale-up*. Santa Monica, CA: RAND (MR-1145-EDU).

Berman, P., & McLaughlin, M. (1975). *Federal programs supporting educational change, vol. IV: The findings in review*. Santa Monica, CA: RAND (R-1589/4-HEW).

Bikson, T. K., & Eveland, J. D. (1992). *Integrating new tools into information work: Technology transfer as a framework for understanding success*. Santa Monica, CA: RAND (RP-106).

Bikson, T. K., & Eveland, J. D. (1998). *Groupware implementation: Reinvention in the sociotechnical frame*. Santa Monica, CA: RAND (RP-703).

Bikson, T. K., Law, S. A., Markovich, M., & Harder, B. T. (1997). *Facilitating the implementation of research findings: A summary report*. Santa Monica, CA: RAND (RP-595).

Bodilly, S. (1996). *Lessons from New American Schools Development Corporation's demonstration phase*. Santa Monica, CA: RAND (MR-729-NASDC).

Bodilly, S. J. (1998). *Lessons from New American Schools' scale–up phase: Prospects for bringing designs to multiple schools*. Santa Monica, CA: RAND (MR-1777-NAS).

Bodilly, S. (2001). *New American Schools' concept of break the mold designs: How designs evolved and why*. Santa Monica, CA: RAND (MR-1288-NAS).

Bodilly, S. J., & Berends, M. (1999). "Necessary district support for comprehensive school reform." In Orfield, G., & DeBray, E. H. (Eds.), *Hard work for good schools: Facts not fads in Title I reform.* Boston: The Civil Rights Project, Harvard University, pp. 111–119.

Bodilly, S., Purnell, S., Ramsey, K., & Smith, C. (1995). *Designing New American Schools: Baseline observations on nine design teams.* Santa Monica, CA: RAND (MR-598-NASDC).

Borman, K. M., Cookson, Jr., P. W., Sadovnik, A. R., & Spade, J. Z. (Eds.) (1996). *Implementing educational reform: Sociological perspectives on educational policy.* Norwood, NJ: Ablex Publishing Corporation.

Bratton, S. E., Horn, S. P., & Wright, S. P. (1996). *Using and interpreting Tennessee's Value-Added Assessment System: A primer for teachers and principals.* Knoxville, TN: Value-Added Research and Assessment Center, University of Tennessee.

Bryk, A. S., & Raudenbush, S. W. (1992). *Hierarchical linear models: Applications and data analysis methods.* Newbury Park, CA: Sage Publications.

Bryk, A. S., Lee, V., & Holland, P. (1993). *Catholic schools and the common good.* Cambridge, MA: Harvard University.

Bryk, A. S., Raudenbush, S. W., and Cogdan, R. T. (1996). *HLM: Hierarchical linear and nonlinear modeling with the HLM/2L and HLM/3L programs.* Chicago: Scientific Software International.

Bryk, A. S., Thum, Y., Eaton, M. J. Q., & Luppescu, S. (1998). *Academic productivity of Chicago public elementary schools.* Chicago: Consortium on Chicago School Research.

Burstein, L., McDonnell, L. M., Van Winkle, J., Ormseth, T., Mirocha, J., & Guitton, G. (1995). *Validating national curriculum indicators.* Santa Monica, CA: RAND (MR-658-NSF).

Chun, J., Gill, B., & Heilbrunn, J. (2001). *The relationship between implementation and achievement: Case studies of New American Schools.* Santa Monica, CA: RAND (DRU-2562-EDU).

Clune, W. (1998). *Toward a theory of systemic reform: The case of nine NSF statewide systemic initiatives.* Madison, WI: Wisconsin Center for Education Research, University of Wisconsin–Madison.

Coleman, J. S., Campbell, E. Q., Hobson, C. J., McPartland, J., Mood, A. M., Weinfeld, F. D., & York, R. L. (1966). *Equality of educational opportunity.* Washington, DC: U.S. Government Printing Office.

Cook, T. D., Habib, F. N., Phillips, M., Settersten, R. A., Shagle, S. C., & Degirmencioglu, S. M. (1999). "Comer's school development program in Prince George's County, Maryland: A theory-based evaluation." *American Educational Research Journal,* 36(3), pp. 543–597.

Cook, T. D., Hunt, H. D., & Murphy, R. F. (1998). *Comer's school development program in Chicago: A theory-based evaluation.* Unpublished manuscript, Northwestern University.

Cuban, L. (1984). "Transforming the frog into a prince: Effective schools research, policy, and practice at the district level." *Harvard Education Review,* 54(2).

Daft, R. (1995). "Bureaucratic versus non-bureaucratic structure and the process of innovation and change." *Research in the Sociology of Organizations,* 1, pp. 129–166.

Datnow, A., & Stringfield, S. (1997). "The Memphis restructuring initiative: Development and first year evaluation from a large scale reform effort." *School Effectiveness and School Improvement,* 8(1).

Darling-Hammond, L. (1988). "Policy and professionalism." In Lieberman, A. (Ed.), *Building a Professional Culture in Schools.* New York: Teachers College Press.

Darling-Hammond, L. (1995). "Policy for restructuring." In Lieberman, A. (Ed.), *The work of restructuring schools: Building from the ground up.* New York: Teachers College Press, pp. 157–175.

Darling-Hammond, L. (1997). *The right to learn: A blueprint for creating schools that work.* San Francisco: Jossey-Bass.

Desimone, L. (2000). *Making comprehensive school reform work.* New York: ERIC Clearinghouse on Urban Education, Teachers College.

Edmonds, R. R. (1979). "Effective schools for the urban poor." *Educational Leadership,* 37, pp. 15–27.

Elmore, R. F., & Rothman, R. (Eds.) (1999). *Testing, teaching, and learning: A guide for states and school districts.* Committee on Title I Testing and Assessment, National Research Council. Washington, DC: National Academy Press.

Eveland, J. D., & Bikson, T. R. (1989). *Work group structures and computer support: A field experiment.* Santa Monica, CA: RAND (N-2979-MF).

Fashola, O., & Slavin, R. E. (1998). "Schoolwide reform models: What works?" *Phi Delta Kappan,* 79(5), pp. 370–378.

Fordham, S., & Ogbu, J. (1986). "Black students' school success: Coping with the burden of acting white." *Urban Review,* 18(3), pp. 176–206.

Fullan, M. G. (1999). *Change forces: The sequel.* Philadelphia: Falmer Press/Taylor & Francis, Inc.

Fullan, M. G. (2001). *The new meaning of educational change, 3rd edition.* New York: Teachers College Press.

Gamoran, A. (1987). "The stratification of high school learning opportunities." *Sociology of Education,* 60, pp. 135–155.

Gamoran, A. (1992). "The variable effects of high school tracking." *American Sociological Review,* 57, pp. 812–828.

Gamoran, A., & Berends, M. (1987). "The effects of stratification in secondary schools: Synthesis of survey and ethnographic research." *Review of Educational Research,* 57, pp. 415–435.

Gamoran, A., & Dreeben, R. (1986). "Coupling and control in educational organizations." *Administrative Science Quarterly,* 31, pp. 612–632.

Gamoran, A., Nystrand, M., Berends, M., & LePore, P. C. (1995). "An organizational analysis of the effects of ability grouping." *American Educational Research Journal,* 32, pp. 687–715.

Garet, J. S., Birman, B. F., Porter, A. C., Desimone, L., Herman, R., & Yoon, K. S. (1999). *Designing effective professional development: Lessons from the Eisenhower program.* Washington, DC: U.S. Department of Education.

Gitlin, A., & Margonis, F. (1995). "The political aspect of reform: Teacher resistance as good sense." *American Journal of Education,* 103, pp. 377–405.

Glennan, T. K., Jr. (1998). *New American Schools after six years.* Santa Monica, CA: RAND (MR-945-NASDC).

Grissmer, D. W., & Flanagan, A. (1998). *Exploring rapid achievement gains in North Carolina and Texas.* Washington, DC: National Education Goals Panel.

Goggin, M. L., Bowman, A., Lester, J., & O'Toole, L. (1990). *Implementation theory and practice: Toward third generation.* New York: HarperCollins.

Hall, G. E., Hord, S., & Griffin, T. (1980). "Implementation at the school building level: The development and analysis of nine mini-case studies." Paper presented at the American Educational Research Association Annual Meeting.

Hallinan, M. T. (1994). "Tracking: From theory to practice." *Sociology of Education,* 67(2), pp. 79–83.

Herman, R., Aladjem, D., McMahon, P., Masem, E., Mulligan, I., Smith O'Malley, A., Quinones, S., Reeve, A., & Woodruff, D. (1999). *An educators' guide to schoolwide reform.* Washington, DC: American Institutes for Research.

Hess, A. G. (1995). *Restructuring urban schools: A Chicago perspective.* New York: Teachers College Press.

Hoffer, T. (1992). "Effects of community type on school experiences and student learning." Paper presented to the 1992 annual meeting of the American Educational Research Association, San Francisco.

Huberman, M., & Miles, M. (1984). "Rethinking the quest for school improvement: Some findings from the DESSI study." *Teachers College Record*, 86(1).

Jencks, C. S., Smith, M., Acland, H., Bane, M. J., Cohen, D., Gintis, H., Heyns, B., & Michelson, S. (1972). *Inequality: A reassessment of the effect of family and schooling in America.* New York: Basic Books.

Jennings, J. F. (1996). "Travels without Charley." *Phi Delta Kappan*, 78, pp. 11–16.

Jennings, J. F. (1998). *Why national standards and tests? Politics and the quest for better schools.* Thousand Oaks, CA: Sage Publications.

Keltner, B. (1998). *Resources for transforming New American Schools: First year findings.* Santa Monica, CA: RAND (IP-175).

Kirby, S. N., Berends, M., & Naftel, S. (2001). *Implementation in a longitudinal sample of New American Schools: Four years into scale-up.* Santa Monica, CA, RAND (MR-1413-EDU).

Kirby, S. N., Sloan, J. S., Naftel, S., & Berends, M. (in review). *Title I schools receiving Comprehensive School Reform Demonstration (CSRD) program funds: Recent evidence from the National Longitudinal Survey of Schools.* Washington, DC: U.S. Department of Education.

Kirst, M. (1991). "Toward a focused research agenda." In *Voices from the field: 30 expert opinions on America 2000, the Bush Administration strategy to "reinvent" America's schools.* Washington, DC: The William T. Grant Foundation on Work, Family, and Citizenship and the Institute for Educational Leadership, p. 38.

Koretz, D. M. (1996). "Using student assessments for educational accountability." In Hanushek, E. A., & Jorgenson, D.W. (Eds.), *Improving America's schools: The role of incentives.* Washington, DC: National Academy Press, pp. 171–196.

Koretz, D. M., & Barron, S. I. (1998). *The validity of gains in scores on the Kentucky Instructional Results Information System (KIRIS)*. Santa Monica, CA: RAND (MR-1014-EDU).

Kreft, I., & De Leeuw, J. (1998). *Introducing multilevel modeling.* London: Sage Publications.

Lee, V. E., & Bryk, A. S. (1989). "A multilevel model of the social distribution of high school achievement." *Sociology of Education*, 51, pp. 78–94.

Lee, V. E., Bryk, A. S., & Smith, J. B. (1993). "The organization of effective secondary schools." *Review of Research in Education*, 19, pp. 171–267.

Lee, V. E., & Smith, J. B. (1995). "Effects of high school restructuring and size on early gains in achievement and engagement." *Sociology of Education*, 68(4), pp. 241–270.

Lee, V. E., & Smith, J. B. (1997). "High school size: Which works best and for whom?" *Educational Evaluation and Policy Analysis*, 19(3), pp. 205–227.

Levin, H. M. (1991). *Learning from accelerated schools.* Pew Higher Education Research Program, Policy Perspectives. Philadelphia: Pew Charitable Trusts.

Lippman, L., Burns, S., & McArthur, E. (1996). *Urban schools: The challenge of location and poverty.* Washington, DC: National Center for Education Statistics, U.S. Department of Education.

Lortie, D. (1970). *School teacher.* Chicago: University of Chicago Press.

Louis, K. S., & Miles, M B. (1990). *Improving the urban high school: What works and why.* New York: Teachers College Press.

Mayer, D. P. (1999). "Measuring instructional practice: Can policymakers trust survey data?" *Educational Evaluation and Policy Analysis*, 21(1), pp. 29–45.

Mazmanian, D., & Sabatier, P. (1989). *Implementation and public policy.* Lanham, MD: University Press of America.

McDonnell, L. & Grubb, N. (1991). *Education and training for work: The policy instruments and the institutions.* Berkeley, CA: National Center for Research on Vocational Education, University of California.

McLaughlin, M. W. (1987). "Learning for experience: Lessons from policy implementation." *Educational Evaluation and Policy Analysis,* 9(22), pp. 171–178.

McLaughlin, M. W. (1990). "The RAND Change Agent study revisited: Macro perspectives and micro realities." *Educational Researcher,* 19(9), pp. 11–16.

Meyer, R. H. (1996). "Comments on chapters two, three, and four." In Ladd, H. (Ed.), *Holding schools accountable: Performance-based reform in education.* Washington, DC: Brookings Institution, pp. 137–145.

Mickelson, R. A., & Wadsworth, A. L. (1996). "NASDC's Odyssey in Dallas (NC): Women, class, and school reform." *Educational Policy,* 10(3), pp. 315–341.

Miller, M., Rollefson, M., Garet, M., Berends, M., Adelman, N., Anderson, L., & Yamashiro, K. (2000). *Summary and implications from a conference on student achievement and the evaluation of federal programs: A working paper.* Washington, DC: American Institutes for Research.

Mirel, J. (1994). "School reform unplugged: The Bensenville New American Schools Project, 1991–1993." *American Educational Research Journal,* 31(3), pp. 481–476.

Mitchell, K. (1996). *Reforming and conforming: NASDC principals discuss school accountability systems.* Santa Monica, CA: RAND (MR-716-NASDC).

Montjoy, R., & O'Toole, L. (1979). "Toward a theory of policy implementation: An organizational perspective." *Public Administration Review,* pp. 465–476.

Murphy, J. (1992). *Restructuring schools: Capturing and assessing the phenomena.* New York: Teachers College Press.

New American Schools Development Corporation (1991). *Designs for a new generation of American schools: Request for proposals.* Arlington, VA: NASDC.

New American Schools Development Corporation (1997). *Bringing success to scale: Sharing the vision of New American Schools.* Arlington, VA: NASDC.

Newmann, F. M., & Associates (Eds.) (1996). *Authentic achievement: Restructuring schools for intellectual quality.* San Francisco: Jossey-Bass.

Oakes, J. (1994). "More than misapplied technology: A normative and political response to Hallinan on tracking." *Sociology of Education,* 67(2), pp. 84–88.

Oakes, J., Gamoran, A., & Page, R. N. (1992). "Curriculum differentiation: Opportunities, outcomes, and meanings." In Jackson, P. W. (Ed.), *Handbook of research on curriculum.* New York: Macmillan, pp. 570–608.

Orr, M. (1998). "The challenge of school reform in Baltimore: Race, jobs, and politics." In Stone, C. N. (Ed.), *Changing Urban Education,* Lawrence, KS: University Press of Kansas, pp. 93–117.

Parsons, T. (1959). "The school class as a social system: Some of its functions in American society." *Harvard Educational Review,* 29, pp. 297–318.

Perrow, C. (1986). *Complex organizations: A critical essay, 3rd edition.* New York: Random House.

Pogrow, S. (1998). "What is an exemplary program, and why should anyone care? A reaction to Slavin and Klein." *Phi Delta Kappan,* 27, pp. 22–29.

Pogrow, S. (2000a). "Success for All does not produce success for students." *Phi Delta Kappan,* 81(2), pp. 67–80.

Pogrow, S. (2000b). "The unsubstantiated 'success' of Success for All: Implications for policy, practice, and the soul of our profession." *Phi Delta Kappan,* 81(8), pp. 596–600.

Porter, A. C. (1994). "National standards and school improvement in the 1990s: Issues and promise." *American Journal of Education*, 102(4), pp. 421–449.

Porter, A. C., & Smithson, J. L. (1995). *Enacted curriculum survey items catalogue: Middle school and high school mathematics and science.* Madison, WI: Wisconsin Center for Education Research, University of Wisconsin–Madison.

Porter, A. C., Floden, R., Freeman, D., Schmidt, W., & Schwille, J. (1988). "Content determinants in elementary school mathematics." In Grouws, D. A., & Cooney, T. J. (Eds.), *Perspectives on Research on Effective Mathematics Teaching.* Hillsdale, NJ: Erlbaum, pp. 96–113.

Porter, A. C., Kirst, M. W., Osthoff, E. J., Smithson, J. L., & Schneider, S. A. (1993). *Reform up close: An analysis of high school mathematics and science classroom.* Madison, WI: University of Wisconsin–Madison.

Powell, A. G., Farrar, E., & Cohen, D. K. (1985). *The shopping mall high school: Winners and losers in the educational marketplace.* Boston: Houghton Mifflin.

Pressman, J., & Wildavsky, A. (1973). *Implementation.* Berkeley, CA: University of California Press.

Purkey, S. C., & Smith, M. S. (1983). "Effective schools: A review." *Elementary School Journal*, 83(4), pp. 427–452.

Ralph, J. (1990). "A research agenda on effective school for disadvantaged students." In Goldberg, S. S. (Ed.), *Readings on equal education, volume 10: Critical issues for a new administration and Congress,* New York: AMS Press.

Rosenholtz, S. J. (1985). "Effective schools: Interpreting the evidence." *American Journal of Education*, 93, pp. 352–388.

Rosenholtz, S. J. (1989). *Teacher's workplace: The social organization of schools.* New York: Longman.

Ross, S., Troutman, A., Horgan, D., Maxwell, S., Laitinen, R., & Lowther, D. (1997). "The success of schools in implementing eight restructuring designs: A synthesis of first year evaluation out-comes." *School Effectiveness and School Improvement*, 8(1), pp. 95–124.

Ross, S. M., Sanders, W. L., Wright, S. P., & Stringfield, S. (1998). *The Memphis restructuring initiative: Achievement results for years 1 and 2 on the Tennessee Value-Added Assessment System* (TVAAS). Unpublished manuscript, University of Memphis.

Ross, S. M., Wang, L. W., Sanders, W. L., Wright, S. P., & Stringfield, S. (1999). *Two- and three-year achievement results for the Tennessee Value-Added Assessment System for restructuring schools in Memphis*. Unpublished manuscript, Center for Research in Educational Policy, University of Memphis.

Ross, S. M., Sanders, W. L., & Wright, S. P. (2000). *Fourth-year achievement results on the Tennessee Value-Added Assessment System for restructuring schools in Memphis*. Unpublished manuscript, University of Memphis.

Ross, S. M., Sanders, W. L., Wright, S. P., Stringfield, S., Wang, L. W., & Alberg, M. (2001). "Two- and three-year achievement results from the Memphis restructuring initiative." *School Effectiveness and School Improvement*, 12(3), pp. 265–284.

Sanders, W. L., & Horn, S. P. (1994). "The Tennessee Value-Added Assessment System (TVAAS): Mixed-model methodology in educational assessment." *Journal of Personnel Evaluation in Education*, 8, pp. 299–311.

Sanders, W. L., & Horn, S. P. (1995). "Educational assessment re-assessed: The usefulness of standardized and alternative measures of student achievement as indicators for the assessment of educational outcomes." *Educational Policy Analysis Archives*, 3(6).

Singer, J. D. (1998). "Using SAS PROC MIXED to fit multilevel models, hierarchical models, and individual growth models." *Journal of Educational and Behavioral Statistics*, 24(4), pp. 323–355.

Sizer, T. R. (1984). *Horace's compromise: The dilemma of the American high school*. Boston: Houghton Mifflin.

Sizer, T. R. (1992). *Horace's school: Redesigning the American high school.* New York: Houghton Mifflin.

Slavin, R. E. (1987). "Ability grouping and student achievement in elementary schools: A best-evidence synthesis." *Review of Educational Research,* 57, pp. 293–336.

Slavin, R. E. (1990). "Achievement effects of ability grouping in secondary schools: A best-evidence synthesis." *Review of Educational Research,* 60, pp. 471–499.

Slavin, R. E. (1997a). "Design competitions: A proposal for a new federal role in education research and development." *Educational Researcher,* 26(1), pp. 22–28.

Slavin, R. E. (1997b). "Design competitions and expert panels: Similar objectives, very different paths." *Educational Researcher,* 26(6), pp. 21–22.

Slavin, R. E. (1999). "Rejoinder: Yes, control groups are essential in program evaluation: A response to Pogrow." *Educational Researcher,* 27, pp. 36–38.

Slavin, R. E. (2000). "Research overwhelmingly supports success for all." *Phi Delta Kappan,* 81(9), p. 720.

Slavin, R. E., & Madden, N. A. (2000). "Research on achievement outcomes of Success for All: A summary and response to critics." *Phi Delta Kappan,* 82(1), pp. 38–66.

Smith, L., Ross, S., McNelis, M., Squires, M., Wasson, R., Maxwell, S., Weddle, K., Nath, L., Grehan, A., & Buggey, T. (1998). "The Memphis restructuring initiative: Analyses of activities and outcomes that impact implementation success." *Education and Urban Society,* 30(3), pp. 296–325.

Stringfield, S., & Datnow, A. (1998). "Scaling up school restructuring and improvement designs." *Education and Urban Society,* 30(3).

Stringfield, S., Millsap, M. A., & Herman, R. (1997). *Special strategies for educating disadvantaged children: Findings and policy implications of a longitudinal study.* Washington, DC: U.S. Department of Education.

Stringfield, S., Ross, S., & Smith, L. (Eds.) (1996). *Bold plans for school restructuring.* Mahwah, NJ: Lawrence Erlbaum Associates.

Sykes, G. (1990). "Fostering teacher professionalism in schools." In Elmore, R. F. (Ed.), *Restructuring schools: The next generation of educational reform.* San Francisco: Jossey-Bass.

Timpane, M. (1991). "A case of misplaced emphasis." In *Voices from the field: 30 expert opinions on America 2000, the Bush Administration strategy to "reinvent" America's schools.* Washington, DC: The William T. Grant Foundation on Work, Family, and Citizenship and the Institute for Educational Leadership, pp. 19–20.

U.S. Department of Education. (1993). *Improving America's Schools Act of 1993: The reauthorization of the Elementary and Secondary Education Act and other amendments.* Washington, DC: U.S. Department of Education.

Weatherley, R., & Lipsky, M. (1977). "Street-level bureaucrats and institutional innovation: Implementing special education reform." *Harvard Education Review*, 47(2), pp. 171–197.

Wise, A. E. (1989). "Professional teaching: A new paradigm for the management of education." In Sergiovanni, T. J., & Moore, J. H. (Eds.), *Schooling for tomorrow: Directing reforms to issues that count.* Boston: Allyn and Bacon.

Wong, K., & Meyer, S. (1998). "Title I school-wide programs: A synthesis of findings from recent evaluation." *Educational Evaluation and Policy Analysis*, 20(2), pp. 115–136.

Yin, R. (1979). *Changing bureaucracies.* Lexington, MA: Lexington Books.